I WAS BETTER LAST NIGHT

HARVEY FIERSTEIN

I WAS BETTER LAST NIGHT

a memoir

ALFRED A. KNOPF   NEW YORK   2022

THIS IS A BORZOI BOOK
PUBLISHED BY ALFRED A. KNOPF

Copyright © 2022 by Harvey Fierstein

All rights reserved. Published in the United States by Alfred A. Knopf,
a division of Penguin Random House LLC, New York, and distributed
in Canada by Penguin Random House Canada Limited, Toronto.

www.aaknopf.com

Knopf, Borzoi Books, and the colophon are registered
trademarks of Penguin Random House LLC

Library of Congress Cataloging-in-Publication Data
Names: Fierstein, Harvey, [date] author.
Title: I was better last night : a memoir / Harvey Fierstein.
Description: First edition. | New York : Alfred A. Knopf, 2022. | Includes index.
Identifiers: LCCN 2021018554 (print) | LCCN 2021018555 (ebook) | ISBN
9780593320525 (hardcover) | ISBN 9780593320532 (ebook)
Subjects: LCSH: Fierstein, Harvey, [date] | Dramatists, American—Biography.
| Gay dramatists—United States—Biography. | Actors—United
States—Biography. | Gay actors—United States—Biography.
Classification: LCC PS3556.I4213 Z46 2022 (print) | LCC PS3556.I4213
(ebook) | DDC 813/.54 [B] —dc23
LC record available at https://lccn.loc.gov/2021018554
LC ebook record available at https://lccn.loc.gov/2021018555

Although this is a work of nonfiction some of the names and identifying
details have been changed to protect my innocence. Any resulting
resemblance to persons living or in hiding is entirely coincidental
and unintentional. Still, I'm telling you, this shit happened.

Jacket photograph by Guzman
Jacket design by Chip Kidd

Manufactured in the United States of America
First Edition

To the radical fairies who flew before me

CONTENTS

LOOK BACK, BUT DON'T STARE

I was his road not taken. He was retiring from an upstate white-collar job, reassessing his life choices and seeking a path forward.

"I know I really messed things up between us. I never gave us the chance to be happy. That's all going to change now. I'm going to be the lover you always wanted and deserved. Okay, Harvey?"

"Well . . ." I stuttered. "Uh . . . How about we have dinner next time you're down here?"

"Harvey. Did you hear what I just said?"

"I think so."

"And?"

"You sound maybe a little . . . Are you okay?"

"Are you fucking kidding me? You've been begging me to do this for years!"

"Forty years ago."

"I don't believe you. What are you saying? I'm too old? You're older than I am! And I'm in a hell of a lot better shape than you ever were."

"How about I drive up there and we can talk?"

"You know what? Fuck you! You're a selfish fucking prick. You can go fuck yourself! And don't call me again."

"You called me . . . Hello? . . . Hello?"

—

Only science and mathematics offer do-overs. History may echo but never repeats. Humans struggle to get a recipe right twice in a row. I can't count the times I've had friends visit after a performance only to hear myself say, "I was better last night." Of course I was better last night. I was younger, fresher, braver, and had one less day of life clogging my brain. But most of all, it was last night. Time upgrades survival to triumph.

So, if you can't *go* back, what's the harm in *looking* back?

Twelve Step programs counsel "Look back, but don't stare." Wonder why? Because it's fucking painful! I'm sitting comfortably at this lovely computer in my homey home office and almost everything coming to mind is about what an asshole I was and am still capable of being. So many stupid mistakes. So much selfishness and ego-driven thoughtlessness to bathe in. Sure, I recall the victories and joys and laughs and lovers, but for reasons beyond me, those happier remembrances are cloudy, dimmed, and distanced. I have to reach for them. Whereas the miseries and hurt, every mistake, misfortune, and betrayal I endured or delivered remains conveniently at my fingertips. The guns are loaded, the knives still cut, and the adage "Time heals everything" makes a lovely lyric but is a fucking lie. Time heals nothing. Amnesia doesn't come in a bottle. It doesn't. Trust me. I tried that. Pain and regret are our brains' legacy residents with great views and easy access to the world outside.

In Twelve Step work we look back to identify the bad stuff we are responsible for and, if it's possible to do so without causing more harm, we make amends for our wrongdoing. I recommend this cleansing exercise of exorcising. Suddenly, glancing over your shoulder is less frightening. There are fewer shadowy figures following you. You are freer to move about unencumbered, knowing that the scary shit of the past has been peaceably entombed. Unfortunately, entombed is not destroyed. It waits quietly in the dark for someone to dig it up again. Bad shit is patient.

So, here I am with my work clothes on and my shovel in hand. If you're willing to listen, I'm willing to dig.

I WAS BETTER
LAST NIGHT

1

QUEEN FOR A DAY

1959

Philomena Marano got the role of the Evil Witch and I was cast as the King. The *King*? Who wants to be the King? Sure, he gets a crown and cape, but the Witch gets green skin, red lips, and long black fingernails. I wanted green skin, red lips, and long black nails! Second grade was not working out the way I'd hoped.

I was given the largest role in *Sleeping Beauty* because I was generally perceived as having the most theatrical flair in class 2-1 of P.S. 186 in Bensonhurst, Brooklyn. In 1959 they called it "flair." I have never understood why, but from early childhood, seeking it or not, I've stood out in a crowd. I remember years later when I was dead broke and begged director Tom O'Horgan to put me in the chorus of this new show he was doing—*Jesus Christ Superstar*. He hugged me warmly and said, "If I put you in the chorus, I have no chorus."

There's no denying I blossom whenever I'm the center of attention. My high-school painting class was invited to demonstrate life drawing in Macy's Herald Square store. Thirty of us set up easels around a platform where a live model posed. I began to sketch with brightly colored pastels on an oversized pad of newsprint paper. Before long I had attracted a crowd. The more they grinned, pointed, and nodded their approval, the faster and more wildly my hands flew. I'd never drawn like that before—or since. I was on fire. People were reaching out to catch my drawings as I tore them from the pad and tossed them aside. Others begged to pose for me. I had no idea where this energy and inspiration was coming from. I was possessed. I can still feel the rush of that explosive creativity. I'd somehow tapped into the positive attention of onlookers and rode their wave of excitement, not unlike when I connect with a theater audience. A rush of electricity shoots up my spine and every cell of my body vibrates with energy. I come *alive*. The people in the audience are attached to me. I sense my emotions molding theirs. It's an extraordinary high. Attention is nourishment.

But back in the fairy-tale play of second grade, I begrudgingly recited my lines and waved my royal scepter while never allowing my concentration to drift from Philomena awaiting her entrance in the wings. Old Lady Berlant chided me, "I can't hear you, Harvey F."

I was Harvey F. because there was also a Harvey S. in my class. There were a lot of Harveys in P.S. 186. Three greatest mistakes of the fifties: Formica, thalidomide, and naming children Harvey.

"I can't hear you," Miss Berlant said again. "Speak louder or I'll have to take the role away from you."

Take it, my inner voice spat back. *You think I'm dying to wear this stupid Reynolds Wrap crown and drag a chenille bedspread cape behind me? Fuck this goatee my mother drew on with her eyebrow pencil. I'm not in this for the art. Give me lipstick or show me the exit!*

My inner voice spoke truth. My outer voice just spoke louder.

The day of the performance I begged for color so insistently that my mother finally painted two hot-pink spheres of rouge on my cheeks. I was not mollified.

When Halloween arrived I rushed home from school and stripped off my clothing. I wrapped a bath towel around my chest, went into my parents' room, and liberated the stash of makeup from my mother's vanity. I went at my face with abandon. Eyeliner, mascara, blush, and her brightest shade of red lipstick. I stood back and admired the results in the mirror. I gawked. With this act of defiance something shifted. Something magical had happened. Staring into the mirror, squinting away the imperfections, my outsides at last matched my insides, and I heard the voice in my head ask that most frightening of questions: "Are you a girl?"

Where did that come from? Why would a child wonder such a thing? My mind was struggling with jigsaw-puzzle pieces that came in an unmarked box. I had no reference for this. I had no language. No experience. Nowhere had I heard another person ask anything like that. I was demanding explanations from my seven-year-old self, to whom this was all new but not unfamiliar.

Clichéd as it sounds, for years I'd been singing along to Original Broadway Cast albums. In the proscenium of my bedroom mirror I was always the leading lady, although I'd accept a featured role if the number was juicy enough. Let's not kid each other: no one turns down the chance to sing "I'm Just A Girl Who Can't Say No" even if it's not the starring role! Wrapped in a bath-towel dress, a T-shirt wig on my head, the curtain rose on me. Applause. Please note, there was no lip-synching. I sang full-out, leaving Celeste Holm in my dust. All familiar with the dark rasp of my adult voice may be surprised to learn that I once possessed a soaring boy soprano good enough that, for two years, I was a paid soloist in a professional liturgical men's choir.

But that Halloween's feature was a dumb show. Hidden behind this mask of makeup, I dared to pull my chubby boy tits up over the tightly tied hem of the towel, pinching the skin together to form cleavage. And when I use the word "dared," I mean "dared." My boy boobs were my enemy. They were threats to my normalcy. They were my body's betrayal of my dark, unacceptable truth. There was no hiding them. There was no shirt loose enough, no coat thick enough to camouflage this 3D scarlet letter announcing to any casual observer the gender war raging within. I was a boy with tits. During puberty I took to wrapping my chest with an elastic Ace bandage whenever leaving the house. An Ace bandage covered with a T-shirt and then a sport shirt over that. By the time I'd get home to undress, my poor skin was rubbed raw. Many times, the bandage had folded up during the day, forcing my boobs out over the top and making them twice as obvious. Who was I fooling? I'd cry while applying lotion to soothe the inflamed skin.

Boy boobs. I hated them, and truthfully, still do. But not on that day. On that day, as I squinted before my bedroom mirror, the puzzle pieces began to ease into place, revealing something I could almost put a name to. I was excited and frightened and . . .

My mother's voice: "Harvey. Come down. Your friends are here."

As quickly as I could I pulled an old housecoat of hers from the laundry hamper and covered my boyish haircut with a kerchief. Reaching up, I smeared the makeup down my face. My mysterious kohl-lined eyes became sunken cavities. The longed-for luscious red lipstick now read as blood trails. I rubbed and blended and manipulated the floral scented creamy filth until I could reasonably claim that I was not trying to be pretty. I was a monster, a zombie. A female zombie, it's true, but even so, a sociologically acceptable character for trick-or-treating. It wasn't *Sleeping Beauty*, but at last my lips were unavoidably painted ruby red. This seven-year-old gender warrior had taken the hill and planted a flag.

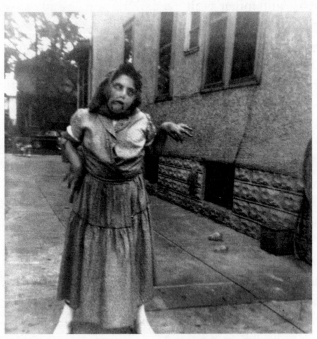

Leave it to Philomena to still have this photo of my
Halloween experiment, shot in the alley beside my home.

2

BROOKLYN BOUND

Most people know of Bensonhurst, Brooklyn, as home to the Kramdens on *The Honeymooners*, or the site of the car chase under the elevated trains in *The French Connection*. Who could forget John Travolta swinging his paint cans down those very streets in *Saturday Night Fever*, or taking up classroom space in *Welcome Back, Kotter*?

We lived in a small three-bedroom, one-and-a-half-bath semi-attached house that my folks bought from my grandparents. It stood Jew-centric with the Yeshiva of Bensonhurst down the block to the left and the Jewish Community House occupying the opposite corner. There was a time before my spiritual nullification that I wouldn't misbehave in my house simply because the rabbi passed by our front door at least six times a day coming and going from prayers. He'd know.

Anyone on the block could recite a recipe for stuffed cabbage, but no one would have heard of jicama, avocado, or chitlins. Ours was an insular world. Entire lives were lived inside a half-mile radius. When families multiplied, they stayed in as close proximity as could be managed. I have childhood friends who only saw Manhattan because our class made the four-mile journey to the Empire State Building. The signs at our subway station offered two directions: "Coney Island" and "The City." There was a social rule that people from Brooklyn could move to Queens or Staten Island.

Manhattan, the Bronx, and (heaven forbid!) New Jersey were all a bridge too far.

The men worked, the women tended to the home, and a kid who studied hard enough could grow up to be President. Jews cautiously befriended Italians, who guardedly befriended the Greeks. We all juggled our positions on the social totem pole knowing we had one thing in common: although we thought of ourselves as white, we lived on the edge of a country that did not see us that way.

The only Asian people I saw worked in the Chinese restaurant on Bay Parkway. Blacks and Hispanics traveled into the neighborhood as domestics or other manual laborers. Until high school most of the people of color I knew as a child worked at the handkerchief factory in Brooklyn's industrial park, Bush Terminal, that my father managed for the Gindi and Mizrahi brothers. (I'd lay odds he won't remember, but I first met Isaac Mizrahi at his family's holiday party in 1961. He was two months old.)

The rest of the world was glimpsed on small oval black-and-white television screens set into great big wooden cabinets or through the pages of the *Daily News* and the weekend *New York Times* that my father brought home, along with a dozen bagels, every Sunday morning. My family would rip into those newspapers in a way that would be unrecognizable today. My older brother went straight for the sports sections. It was page one for my father. And I grabbed the colorful comics from the *Daily News* along with Arts & Leisure from the *Times*, which I was under strict orders not to cut up before my mother got to read it. But before anything else, I searched for Bloomingdale's shoe ads. Not that I cared about footwear. But they were drawn by my favorite illustrator, Andy Warhol. It was years until I realized that this same Warhol was breaking into the world of fine art. Back then his pen-and-ink drawings thrilled me. They were raw and still precise. They were cartoons but completely accurate. His lines dissected defined form, using negative space in such an unconscious manner that it was almost a miracle. This little kid could not get enough of them.

This was the postwar world of my childhood. It was down these streets that I, a self-possessed three-year-old, nonchalantly wheeled my baby doll in her carriage. The neighbors chided my mother, "How could you allow such a *shonde?*"

She brushed them off: "One day he will be a terrific father."

Although she longed for more, my mother, Jacqueline, or Jackie to her friends, was a housewife. My father proudly pronounced, "No wife of mine is going to have to work," but if she could have, she would have. Her father had suffered lung damage as a result of being gassed in World War I. The older he got, the fewer hours he could manage working as an industrial electrician. Eventually homebound, he forced Jackie to drop out of school after the eighth grade and take a job to support the family. Her younger brother, Irwin, was a brilliant student who dreamed of earning a degree in engineering. All hopes for the future were placed on him. They even changed the family name from the easily identified Ginsburg to a less Semitic-sounding Gilbert to get him into the right school. It worked. With Jackie footing the bill, he became an engineer and helped develop one of the first hypersonic rockets, the X-15, for NASA.

Young, single Jackie buried her dreams in office work. My father was a salesman to, and she a receptionist for, Gordon Novelty in the Flatiron Building. They met and fell in love just as World War II broke out and my father enlisted in the Navy.

Their marriage was idyllic in many ways. As a couple they were devoted to one another. There is a line in *Torch Song Trilogy* that sums them up: "My mother once had to stay overnight in the hospital and my father would not even get into bed without her."

My father never tired of saying, "Didn't I pick the most beautiful girl in the world to be your mother?"

Jackie loved education and the arts. Every week when *Cue* magazine (the predecessor of *New York* magazine) arrived in the mail, she'd turn to the Broadway section and immediately order tickets for whatever show was opening. We always sat in the center seats of the mezzanine's first row, which cost under three dollars apiece. Can you imagine? Our family of four saw *West Side Story,*

The Sound of Music, Bye Bye Birdie, Gypsy, Oliver!, and even the
Royal Shakespeare Company for ten dollars per show. We missed
nothing.

Every Christmas morning, while all of our gentile neighbors
were opening gifts, we'd hop the subway to Manhattan and Radio
City Music Hall. Back then you not only got the world-famous
Christmas show with its real camels in a "living Nativity" tableau,
but afterwards they showed a first-run movie: Cary Grant in *Cha-
rade* or *Father Goose*—I loved Cary Grant. But it wasn't just movies and shows that we saw. Museums, botanical gardens, and trip
after trip to the 1964 New York World's Fair. My mother exposed
her "three guys" to it all.

Closer to home her interests were no less varied: she volunteered
at our schools and for charities, including Hadassah, the Jewish
Defense League, and CancerCare. I loved visiting the ladies who
gathered once a month down in our basement to roll donated
sheets into bandages for Israel. Toni Cohenan was one of those
women. Round-faced and rounder-bodied, she had closely cropped
dark hair that framed her even darker eyes, which glowed with the
wonder of a child whenever she dared to look up from her work.
But mostly she gazed down or inward like a mistreated puppy, hoping you saw that she was no threat.

I liked to sit by her and watch her work. I'd lean against her side
and study the way the numbers tattooed on her forearm twisted
and distorted with the movements of her fingers. Max was her husband's name. He was a jolly gent who covered a thick Polish accent
with an overenunciated English one. He had a silly comb-over held
in place by a jaunty beret. He, too, had the stain of inhumanity tattooed on his forearm. My father told me they'd met in a relocation
facility after the liberation of the Sobibor death camp.

More than a decade after VE Day the entire neighborhood still
lived under the shadow of World War II, whether it was Frances
DePrisco grieving her soldier husband, or someone like my father,
who survived his Navy assignment relatively unscathed, or that
sweet couple Max and Toni Cohenan, who'd witnessed the worst

of humankind and now clung to one another to fend off the night-mares. Max was so loving to my brother and me that I couldn't understand why they'd had no children of their own. As only an innocent would, I asked Max. His eyes darted protectively toward his wife before solemnly mumbling, "Bring a child into this world? No."

There is another war story that's always haunted me. My grand-mother had six older brothers for whom she cooked, cleaned, and cared. When word reached America about the Nazi roundup of Jews in Eastern Europe, Moe, Murray, Max, Herman, David, and Joseph Schatzberg took up a collection so one of them could travel overseas to seek out family members and bring them back to safety. Several months later Herman returned alone. "No one?" the others asked. "You found no relatives to save?"

He shrugged as he handed back the cash. "All I found were women."

It took years until I finally understood why women weren't worth a ship passage. A woman marries, has children, and propa-gates her husband's name. What good does that do for our family?

My mother gently lobbied my father until he allowed her to vol-unteer at our elementary school. In short order she became their librarian, a position she retained long after my brother and I moved on. Ron attended Stuyvesant, a high school for accelerated aca-demic students, and I entered the High School of Art and Design. Both schools were in Manhattan, so we were rarely home. This was Jackie's chance to push her love of learning a little farther. Return-ing to classes, she at last earned her high-school diploma and then a degree in library science. She went as far as getting her master's but stopped just short of a doctorate. "Who needs it?" she said. "I've hit the top of the Board of Ed pay scale, so why kill myself writing a thesis?"

By then she was a full-time, fully accredited teacher/librarian at Jackie Robinson Junior High, which had been built on the site of Brooklyn's famed Ebbets Field. Is there any reason to mention that she earned much better college grades than I did?

My dad, Irving, was raised in a small-town Catskill Mountain orphanage. His mother died in childbirth and his father, the town barber, could not raise a newborn alone. While relatives were willing to adopt his older sister, my father was left at the Jewish orphanage until the age of maturity—thirteen—at which time he went out on his own. His first job was driving a bakery truck in Ellenville, the town where Harry, his father, lived. Although he remained close to Harry and his sister throughout their lives, Irving had no love for the extended family that had abandoned him. Hence, I have few uncles, aunts, or cousins from the Fierstein side of the tree. Harry remarried at some point, but the new wife wanted nothing to do with children. When Harry died, the stepmother cashed in the house and the barber shop and moved to Miami. Jackie loved to tell the story of God's punishment of this selfish woman. "That *chazer* went nowhere without her diamonds and mink. A hundred degrees and that woman flounced around in fur. One day, somewhere in Biscayne Bay, she was crossing the street against the light and a delivery truck mowed her down. The people on the street all came running—but not to see if she was alive. They stripped every ring and bracelet from her arms, pulled the blood-soaked mink off her back, and left her there to rot in the gutter like the dog she was."

Jackie had a strong sense of right and wrong. Her tale of the evil stepmother taking all the money was apparently true. The only thing my father inherited was a shaving mug, most likely from his grandfather, with the name "Feuerstein" emblazoned in gold leaf.

This lack of relations made Dad a fierce defender of his own nuclear family. "Out in the world you can do no wrong," he'd tell my brother and me. "A family stands by one another no matter what."

Boy, did we test that resolve! Irving teasingly called us the *bandeets,* which is Yiddish for criminals. He was sure that no matter how hard he tried to drill a work ethic into his sons, neither of us would ever make a living.

My brother, Ron, is eighteen months my senior. Smart and logical, with a brain for learning, he excelled at schoolwork. I know you can't measure someone's insides by their outsides, but Ron always seemed able to balance his challenges with his talents to keep himself on track. He played piano and guitar, composed his own songs, and had lots of friends with whom he played every boy sport with abandon. He was a born leader, and everyone knew he would grow up to be a credit to the family. They dubbed him "the Doctor" and he got as far as pre-med before realizing that he'd been subconsciously launched in the wrong lane. He rebelled and followed his passion for music, becoming a rock-and-roll bandleader. His group, Arbuckle, even released an album with a song about the California earthquakes that hit the charts in 1972. Eventually he realized that his brain power could be put to better use on the producing side of show biz. He returned to school, earning a law degree, with which he could engage in multiple careers.

I, on the other hand, was dubbed "the Shyster"—the crooked lawyer. They figured even if I passed the bar, I would come out on the wrong side of the law. It was an accepted fact that my mouth would get me in a lot of trouble. I could not have been an easy child, presenting my parents with more than my weight in challenges. I was born with enlarged tonsils, and eating was a problem until I was of age to have them removed. The result was a great love of gorging until overfilled. I remember doing Weight Watchers with my mother at around ten years old, and I've been dieting on and off since. But tonsils and weight were the least of my challenges.

My IQ tested through the roof, and so I was always placed in advanced classes. I even skipped two grades of elementary school. The problem was that I suffered from dyslexia at a time when no one knew what the hell that was. My teachers thought I wasn't doing well in class because I was beyond the curriculum and therefor bored. The truth was that I was struggling with the most elementary reading tasks. My brain simply did not function the way others' did. I saw letters and numbers switching places. I had little ability to distinguish right from left, east from west. I could not trust my brain to decipher words. To this day I read slowly, sounding the words in my head.

The result was that I drifted into the picture-book section of the library long after I should have been cruising adult selections. And then I discovered play scripts. Here were books with all of that wordy description crap excised beyond a few necessary stage directions. Instead of my reading aloud being a distraction, it was now an added attraction. I could act out the characters and experience the full performance. The world of reading opened for me. From plays I graduated to novelizations of movies I'd seen, and from there to the original novels from which those movies had been adapted.

My first big fat look-at-me-reading book was *Of Human Bondage*. I'd seen two movie versions on TV, but the book was so much better. In school while other kids were asking why the Hardy Boys always got into trouble, I had questions about clubfeet and syphilis. From there it was on to *The Egyptian* and the Brontë sisters, all the way to *Exodus*.

Just as I was hitting my reading stride, Hebrew school was sprung on me. Hell, if I couldn't read left to right, did they really expect I'd do better backwards? For five years I struggled to speak, let alone read, this language of my people that no one I knew spoke. I could have used Yiddish classes to decipher the secrets my parents told whenever we kids were around. But Hebrew? I did my Jewish duty and remained in class until the day of my bar mitzvah and then it was adios, *yeladim*! And none too soon: I was almost expelled at least twice—once for cutting three whole weeks of classes, hiding out at my friend Joseph's house, where we'd watch *Superman* and *Soupy Sales* reruns on TV. The other time was when I took a Magic Marker and scrawled the word "fuck" in Hebrew letters down the wall of the Hebrew school's stairwell. My mother was apoplectic, but my father saw it as a sign that his son might be a real boy after all. I was just mad at Michael Greenberg for ratting me out as the before-his-time obscenity tagger. As I scrubbed the writing off the wall I wondered, "Don't I get credit for spelling it right?"

Anyone curious to know which is stronger, nurture or nature, will find compelling evidence studying my brother and me. Less than two years apart, raised in the same family with the same influences, rules, and expectations, we could not be more different. Ron had fantasy baseball teams and I had fantasy musicals. He had a gang of boys that he ran as a pack. My friends were mostly girls, and the boys I did spend time with all grew up to be gay—not everyone, but more than a few.

"What was with you boys?" Jackie once asked.

"Maybe the water?" I answered.

If my brother misbehaved, my parents sent him to his room, where he'd sit and think about what he did wrong. After a time, he'd return to the kitchen and apologize for his misdeed. Me, they never bothered punishing. They knew I'd just put on my records or take out my drawing things or watch television, never giving my misdeed another thought. I watched a lot of TV. A local station programmed old films under the banner *Million Dollar Movie*, showing the same one three times a day. It was there that I discovered my goddesses; Mae West, Marlene Dietrich, Bette Davis, Joan Crawford, Betty Hutton, Katharine Hepburn, and Maria Montez. I checked *TV Guide* every day to see what the *Million Dollar Movie* would be and if it was a favorite like *The Women* or *Stage Door, All About Eve, She Done Him Wrong,* or *A Letter to Three Wives,* I would plan on awakening with a fever so I could stay home all day to watch the same movie over and over and over again. Heaven.

I loved sitcoms, old and new, like *I Married Joan, My Little Margie, Hazel,* and *The Dick Van Dyke Show.* I was especially taken with the latter, having seen Mr. Van Dyke live on Broadway in *Bye Bye Birdie.* I adored that show but was haunted by the "Shriner's Ballet," in which Chita Rivera's innocent flirting was answered by a full-on dance attack by a group of Shriners. Or so it seemed to me. When I told Chita this story years later, she looked askance and said, "And your parents didn't know about you?"

I think I learned a lot of life's rules from television. Perhaps too many, as my own sitcom-wisecracking mouth could get me into trouble. One positive lesson came when I was around five or six. My brother was pummeling me as older brothers are apt to do. I looked up at him from my prone position on the floor and said,

"Y'know, this is *not* the way Wally treats the Beaver." Ron looked down at me, considered my assertion, and never hit me again.

In fact, that was the turning point in our relationship: we have been close ever since. Over our lifetimes he has been a collaborator, advisor, protector, defender, attorney, estate manager, and, I daresay, the person most responsible for allowing my life to be. He's also my most nitpicking, judgmental, pain-in-the-butt critic. Like I said, we couldn't be more different—or more alike.

That's me on the left with my brother and our collie, Penny, waiting for the Day Camp bus.

3

"ARTISTIC" IS ONE
WAY TO PUT IT

Whenever I had the chance, I'd put my legs together, feet flexed outward, take a deep breath, and dive into the deepest section of the swimming pool, where I'd shimmy and slither about in my finest mermaid fantasy. Yes: I wanted to be a mermaid. Underwater I floated free from the fat that weighed me down on land. I was lithe and graceful, my hands expressively guiding my way, my tail powering me soundlessly through my underwater wonderland.

My poor parents. It wasn't enough that they had to put up with my terrestrial eccentricities. Now they had to sit by the hotel swimming pool helplessly watching their little boy twirling about in full view of family and friends.

"Look, look, look!" my mother would say, feigning pride. "Like a fish in the water!"

What was to be done with me? They tried sleepaway camp, but I became incredibly homesick. It wasn't the separation from my parents. I missed my solitude. I was only truly happy shut in my room, in my own world. Even today, although I have traveled a nice piece of the globe, I still long to be left to my own devices, with my dogs, in the lair I've created for myself. My folks prayed for a sign from on high. The answer came in a phone call.

I spent hours reading comic books. Not the superhero ones; I preferred *Richie Rich* and *Casper the Friendly Ghost*. I'd even make

Mom, Dad, and me at the beach

my own strips, copying my favorite characters and inventing stories
for them. In the back of most comics, among the ads for X-ray-
vision glasses and boutonnieres that sprayed water, were advertisements that challenged *"Draw me!"* along with an illustrated face.
"Try for a FREE $280 Art Course. You've got nothing to lose and
everything to gain. Mail yours in today!"

I don't know how many times I copied those faces and tossed
them aside, but one time I did not. I carefully drew the faces, filled
out the form, and mailed it in. Why not? As the ad said, I had nothing to lose.

Just before dinner one evening the telephone rang. It was the
art school calling to say that Harvey Fierstein had won a scholarship to take their art course. My mother said that the salesperson
exploded in ecstasy when she explained that the drawing was by
her eight-year-old son. "Your son has a natural talent that cries out
to be nurtured" is how she relayed the story to family, neighbors,
and friends. At last, she had a plan for what to do with this puz-
zling child. He'll be an artist.

While I did love to draw and paint, truthfully, I never thought I
had much talent. I did have an aptitude for copying, but that makes
you a technician, not an artist. But Jackie, with her fingers crossed,
was on a mission. She sent me off to art school. And no kiddie class

for this genius: I was enrolled in an after-school program at the Brooklyn Museum. Several weeks later she assessed my less-than-stellar output and shook her head.

"Is this what you did?"

"Uh-huh."

"What does the teacher think?"

"I guess he thinks it's okay."

She did not concur. She looked for another school to support my growth. She found an adult painting class where hobbyists were taught to copy established artists' work. You'd choose a piece of art from the file drawers and the instructor would mark the outlines onto a blank canvas. You then sat down to paint in the colors. I was better at this than at creating my own masterpieces, but I had my limits. Whenever I thought I had finished the assignment, the teacher would repair my work into something almost acceptable. My family walls were soon filling with these third-rate paintings. But the *mishpuchah* was impressed, which was all the proof Jackie needed to keep me on that path. Staring at a freshly framed Parisian street scene now hung in place of pride over the living-room sofa, Jackie mumbled to herself, "So, that's what it is. He's an artist."

I was in eighth grade and just about to turn thirteen when the Board of Education decided to reorder the public school system. No longer would middle school have a ninth grade. My class would be shuffled off to high school in September. For me that meant attending the school that later would inspire *Welcome Back, Kotter.* Lafayette High had a rough reputation. I was not looking forward to spending the next four years of my life ditching gym class there. Happily, with my new identity as an artist, my mother made a push for me to get into a special school in Manhattan, the High School of Art and Design. It was a vocational school that required the presentation of an art portfolio and an interview. Somehow, in the rush of reorganizing the school system, I passed and was accepted. I moved toward eighth-grade graduation with relief and excitement. My only obstacle was surviving my bar mitzvah. Yes, it was time for that greatest moment in a Jewish boy's life, when the fistful of checks given to him by relatives and family friends are snatched away to pay for the chopped liver and cha-cha band. *L'chaim!*

My grandma, Bertie, whom I called Granny Goose, simply could not stand attending any family gathering without being the center of attention. My mother warned her to behave or there would be consequences; but as soon as I was called to the altar to sing my portion of the Torah, she threw up her arms, cried out, and fell back fainting into her pew. Without pause Jackie ordered some men to carry Granny out to the lobby while Mom used a payphone to call 911. Obviously, there is no applause in temple, but take my word, I killed it! Still, when I looked out at the assembly for any kind of recognition, there was no one even facing my way. All attention was on my mother as she returned to her seat, having sent Granny Goose off in an ambulance after telling the EMT: "And don't bring her back. We'll pick her up tomorrow."

The reception was more of an Altman movie than an Irwin Allen disaster flick. While us newly minted teens showed our prowess dancing the Monkey and the Jerk, Margie Nudleman, a zaftig woman of seventy, scandalized the room by drunkenly climbing up on top of a dining table, rubbing her hands suggestively over her sequined-emerald-green-sheathed body and performing the hootchy-kootchy. She, too, killed it. I overheard the temple president's wife say, "Nice for Harvey."

This last summer before high school I attended the JCH day camp. It was a simple summer spent with kids my age. I even had a girlfriend named Harriet. She was skinny and freckled and giggled nonstop whenever we were together. We sometimes made out on the bus on our way to outings. She even let me feel her tits. I'd put my arm around her neck and reach into her peasant blouse, pushing my way into her polyester lace training bra to find a nipple. No great thrill: mine were bigger. I was no clearer about sex at this point than I was about gender. I just rolled with the punches, hoping shit would shake out eventually.

Although I couldn't put words to it, I was unmistakably attracted to boys. Not only boys but men, too. If I watched a romantic movie I identified with the female lead; the matinee idol he-man was who

I fantasized kissing. My major crushes were on Sean Connery, the original James Bond; TV's Tarzan, Ron Ely, with his steely blue eyes and sinewy, sensuous legs that went on forever; and then there was Luke Halpin from the TV show *Flipper*. I even wrote Luke a letter carefully telling him that I was one of his "many boy fans." He sent back a photo—autographed. But most important was Dr. Kildare, Richard Chamberlain. He was more than a crush. I followed him from TV stardom to his stage performance of *Hamlet*, back to his groundbreaking TV event *The Thorn Birds*. I was devoted.

A million lifetimes later, 1983 or so, Mr. Chamberlain came to see me in *Torch Song Trilogy*. I about died when he stepped into my dressing room. I professed my love, being very careful not to use the word "childhood," and asked if he'd help me live out an innocent personal fantasy. He laughed and agreed. I asked him to go out into the hallway, close the door, count to twenty, and then reenter as if returning home from a hard day's work. As soon as he left, I turned off all the lights except for one small table lamp, threw myself across the couch, and pretended to be asleep. I heard the door open and the rustle of his clothing as he approached, and then . . . oh, then . . . I felt his warm lips on my cheek as he gave me the sweetest kiss and said, "Hi, hon, I'm home."

My heart almost exploded!

Just for the record, I still haven't met Ron Ely, but I once met Sean Connery backstage in London. When I took this opportunity to tell him how I lusted for him as a youngster, he stared at me in a way that made me think he didn't speak the language. After an awkward moment or two, his wife stepped forward, shook my hand, and said, "He wants to say thank you."

But we were talking about sex. I really didn't understand much of anything until one fateful day when a pimple popped up on my penis. Pimples I understood. I'd watched my older brother struggle with acne, and I was currently battling my own curse of adolescence. But a pimple on my penis? So I went to the bathroom, took out my brother's face scrub, applied it to the offending spot, and made sure I rubbed it in good . . . Cue the fireworks, brass orches-

And still I wait in my dressing room for
Richard Chamberlain to return.

tra, and cymbals! I'd accidentally stolen my own virginity. I experienced an earthshaking, body-quivering, mind-exploding orgasm, and in that moment of peak autoerotic pleasure my first thought was a joyous pronouncement: *I'm not sterile!*

"I'm not sterile"? Where the hell did that come from? I couldn't recall the subject of sterility ever arising anytime in my life, but those were definitely the words I heard shouted in my mind at the moment of climax . . . *I'm not sterile!*

No time to worry about how strange I was, this masturbation thing was too fantastic! As you can guess, for the rest of that summer my adventure with Phisohex was repeated over and over as I worked my way through every ointment, liniment, and lubricant in that medicine chest, many times a day, many days a week, many weeks a month, for many years to come. I was ready for high school. Nice for Harvey.

4

HIGH IN HIGH SCHOOL

The High School of Art and Design was a very *moderne* blue-and-yellow-tiled building on Second Avenue and Fifty-Seventh Street. Another world from Bensonhurst, this was the classy East Side of Manhattan. The subway stairs led directly into Bloomingdale's Department Store. From there, we walked past doorman buildings, boutiques, and as many poodles as there were taxis.

Art and Design was a vocational school that trained talented students from all across the city for careers as commercial artists. Both Philomena Marano and I applied and were accepted. You remember Philo: she was the evil Witch when I was the King. Now we were going to be art students together. Philo was the one with true talent. Still, here we both were, taking the train together from Brooklyn to Manhattan five days a week to become employable artists.

My first high-school lesson was how to smoke. Having harangued my father to give up cigarettes for years, I now found them a necessary tool for survival. I'd skipped two vital grades of elementary school, meaning I was younger, less mature, and more confused than all of my classmates. I was probably the least self-aware high-school freshman ever. I needed the prop to make me look older when we hung outside school before the bell and on the terrace during lunch period. Oh, yes, A&D had a smoking terrace for the students. Hello, 1965!

Common belief is that weaker dogs seek alphas for protection. It's actually the other way around. You can't be an alpha without a pack beneath. Michael was beautiful. Thick, dark hair, parted on the left, that bounced under its own weight. Brown, almond-shaped eyes and generous lips bracketed by deeply cut dimples. His neck was long and swanlike. He was olive skinned and painfully slim; his hips pushed forward what appeared to be a very ample groin. Michael was the strongest, most self-possessed, and surest person I'd ever met. He knew who he was inside and out. He understood his effect on people and used that power to manipulate them. Boys were seduced and girls were charmed as he strode his path with an assurance of ownership. Once he'd spotted me, it didn't take Michael long to claim me. Left on my own, I gravitated toward friendships with girls and made lots of acquaintances, some of which last to this day. But when Michael called I went running. I was clearly his project—until an unfortunate and deeply disturbing event separated us three years later. More on that to come.

Twenty-five years after our A&D graduation, our mutual friend Lisa brought Michael to my home in Connecticut. She brought him to say goodbye. AIDS had ravaged his beauty and memory but not his demeanor. Regal as ever, he sat at my dining-room table while Lisa and I reminisced, hoping that something would spark his participation. So many changes since the last time we three sat together: I had my career; Lisa was a painter who tragically had gained world attention as the daughter of Leon Klinghoffer, the wheelchair-bound tourist tossed to his death from a cruise ship by Islamic terrorists; and Michael . . . Michael was being consumed by AIDS. Lisa and I hoped that our casual chatting would bring him comfort, but it was clear that our remembering things he couldn't only made him jumpy. We were torturing him with our ease. Have you witnessed someone's mind deteriorate? AIDS provided me with more than a few front-row seats to the death of self. To watch memories fly out of grasp like escaped scraps of paper on a windy street; to feel your files of memories emptying out, to be discarded as useless; to sense a drape of darkness obscuring the ordinary until nothing is recognizable is—simply terrifying. It's the erosion of self that is irrevocable. Watching friends, lovers, acquaintances go through that process proved to me that ideas of life after death were foolish fantasies. The brain is flesh and flesh is dust. Resurrection is a tale we tell children to make them behave.

Michael was no more, long before he was no more.

Michael and me on his final visit to my home

But a lifetime before then he had his assignment: remake Harvey.

Plaid button-down shirts and black chinos were not going to cut it in our school, but I could not pull off anything he could wear. Skintight cotton turtlenecks and flannel hip huggers with go-go boots were not for Jews. More than my shape, they didn't fit my budget.

"Mom, I need money for school clothes."

"So you can slop them all up with paint?"

"The other kids go to the Army-Navy surplus store. They've got great stuff."

"Used clothing?"

My father chimed in, "No son of mine is wearing used clothing."

"Not used. Surplus. I want a Navy peacoat."

"Irving, where's yours? Can Harvey wear it?"

My father considered my corpulent frame and said, "Why do you want to wear that? Aren't you all against the war?"

My mother took me shopping and I emerged from Macy's with the makings of a new uniform. Sweatshirts with their crew necks and wrists cut off and worn inside out, blue jeans and sometimes overalls, a knockoff peacoat, and a colorful scarf that could be carefully arranged to cover my boy boobs. Unfortunately, I couldn't wear sneakers on Tuesdays or Thursdays because if I did, I'd blow the excuse that I'd forgotten them at home and that's why I couldn't go to gym class. Work boots were my solution. With them I was set.

Making my way around school, riding up and down the escalators provided for us instead of staircases, I began to notice that I was far from the strangest kid in class. Pablo carried his antique baby doll and nursed it during algebra. Karin dressed in floral-print A-line dresses with matching drawstring purses and oversized sun hats that her mother made and insisted she wear. She didn't love them; I would have killed to wear them. There were nerds and geeks and druggies and longhaired, guitar-toting cool kids. What struck me most was how many students identified as gay or lesbian. In a TV interview I once joked that I attended an all-gay school until they passed a law forcing them to bus in heterosexuals. I knew all about queers and fags and homos from the rough talk in Brooklyn, but I never attached those labels to people. Faced with this reality, even my backwater brain began piecing things together.

"I think I'm gay," I whispered to Michael as he took a light off my cigarette. He barely looked up, just grinned. *He knew? How did he know?*

I got the same reaction from all of my school girlfriends. No one was surprised. I even sprung my newly discovered truth on Mrs. Lang, our science teacher, who wore miniskirts and a Twiggy wedge hairdo. She, too, smiled and said, "Is there something I can help you with?" and moved on to current news. *What the hell? Why was I the last to get the memo?*

Telling my parents was less of a sure thing. I knew that they knew, but I didn't know *what* they knew. Sheldon was my mother's favorite cousin and Sheldon was certainly, if unspokenly, gay. My brother and I, not really sure what the word meant, nicknamed him "My Cousin the Queer." Sheldon even brought a male date to my bar mitzvah. It was quite the scandal—not that Sheldon brought a man, but that the man he brought was Black. I can still hear the yentas *mitchkering* my mother: "He's going to sit by us? You're going to feed a *schvartze*?"

My Cousin the Queer was Jackie's favorite, but there is a difference between a cousin and a son. She didn't hang the family's future on Sheldon's propagating. Now that I think of it, Jackie must have been the one from whom we learned the word "queer" to begin with, so telling my folks and expecting a festive coming-out party was probably off the table. I decided to keep it secret, along with my cigarette smoking. What was there to tell them, anyway? I had feelings. That's all. I had done more with Harriet in the back of the JCH bus than I had with any boy. Even the men in the photographs I used to beat off to were fully clothed. Were feelings something you had to share? I decided to just be. I wouldn't hide, but I wouldn't volunteer information.

My brother was interviewed about me once and when the reporter asked these specific questions he said, "Harvey was always Harvey. We just assumed he had it all worked out, so we accepted him as he was."

5

PLAYING CARDS

A&D was a vocational school, where we were sent to learn a useful trade and not become starving Greenwich Village artists. Freshmen took a rotation of classes, exposing us to all of the school's curricula: illustration, fashion design, architecture, cartooning, sculpture, stagecraft, photography, and advertising. We were taught hand-lettering, photo printing (I even set up a darkroom in my basement), mechanical drafting, and executing pasteups. Second-year students chose a major, but it was that first year's focus on technique that changed my life. Concentrating on technical tasks unbound my creativity. Shifting attention from product to procedure freed my inner vision. It's like teaching someone to cook. Give them the techniques and the flavor will follow. Learning to paint taught me to paint. I no longer needed another's ideas to copy. I was becoming an artist after all.

Most of our teachers were accomplished in their own right. Painter Al Hollingsworth, printmaker Joseph Paul Di Gemma, sculptor Benedict Tatti, and my most influential mentor, Max Ginsburg. Max was a sociopolitical painter who favored protest marches, picket lines, and homeless folks. He ran his classroom like a consciousness-raising seminar, urging us to get involved in politics as he played protest records on a portable turntable: Dylan, Donovan, Baez, and Guthrie blared as we worked.

28

There were also two English teachers who had a great effect on me. Miss Bella Rosenkranz was a little mouse who wore bottle-thick glasses that magnified her eyes into comically open orbs. She taught Dickens in a way that made me feel he wrote of my time and life. In later years dementia claimed her reason, and she reached out to me several times to warn of evildoers hunting me. In her heyday she encouraged me to write. "You, my sweet child, have the soul of a storyteller. There's nary a teacher in this building without a strong belief in your imagination. Take that to heart."

Miss Daisy Aldan was a Pulitzer Prize–nominated poet and translator. Through mascara-caked lashes and pursed lips she opened the world of poetry and metaphysics to us. What teen doesn't want to mess with the unknowable? I took to reading the works of British warlock Aleister Crowley and studied the art of reading tarot cards.

One sunny day we arrived in class to find Miss Aldan had brought a guest: the internationally renowned author Anaïs Nin. Having studied her work under Miss Aldan, we were all agog. I wish I could remember anything of her lecture, but I was so star-struck I could barely breathe, let alone listen. Honey hair arranged in a chignon; her eyes were pastel blue and moist as if she'd just been laughing or was on the verge of crying. Her skin was peaches-and-cream and her lips were thin and tinged orange. She spoke with an accent so delicate that it promised to be from an imagined land. When class ended Miss Aldan asked if I could stay behind.

Miss Nin addressed me: "Your instructor tells me that you have taken up the art of the tarot."

"Me?" I asked. "I kid around."

"Would you do me the honor of reading mine?"

The two women grinned behind some secret they shared. I dug to the bottom of my art portfolio and retrieved the cards that I always kept carefully wrapped in a silk handkerchief I had swiped from my mother's drawer. I shuffled the deck and placed the cards in a pile on the desk.

"Please cut them once with your left hand," I instructed.

Miss Nin obliged.

I laid out the cards in front of me in a pattern the books instructed. I looked them over, silently praying I'd remember the meanings I'd spent so many hours memorizing, but they were gone. The card faces were indecipherable. The words and symbols jumbled. The colors blurred and blended until I saw a red macaw hovering, in two dimensions, just above the cards. He adjusted his footing along the branch on which he perched and turned to look behind him to the left. He nodded and then turned to face right. He strained forward and was gone. What the hell was that about? The ladies stared at me. I didn't want to sound all mystical and shit, so I simply told them what I'd seen.

"Yes, of course," Miss Nin said, as naturally as commenting on the weather. "I've been making notes about my time in South America, and so a colorful parrot looking behind. I've also been considering a journey back, and there's your parrot looking forward. And since you saw it lurch in that direction, I will take that as a sign that I should go." She reached out to hold my hand. "You are a delight."

I messed around with the cards a little while longer, but what thrill could match that interaction? I dug a grave for them in Central Park, not far from Bethesda Fountain, and gave the silk-wrapped cards a final resting place.

6

YOU NEVER LOSE MORE
THAN YOU GAIN

It wasn't that Michael was loose. He was handsome and flirtatious and raging with the hormones of a sixteen-year-old whose gaydar was fine-tuned to the forbidden fruit of older men. He discovered that being a pretty boy got you lots of attention. Wherever we went, if there were gay men around, they were drawn to him. Hence, we never went anywhere that there weren't gay men around. The West Village was a favorite haunt. Like a "Homes of the Stars" tour guide, he led me on an expedition to see all of the gay hot spots.

"This is Julius'. Forget it. Nothing but old men . . . And you can eat at Mama's Chicken Rib . . . Down those stairs is *the* Bon Soir, where Barbra Streisand tries out new material . . . The Ninth Circle is over there, and just around the corner is the Stonewall."

We were too young to patronize any of the bars, but sidewalks are open to everyone.

There was a bookstore with a carpeted seating ledge under its window on Eighth Street—a perfect spot for me to people-watch and Michael to manhunt. We'd sit and chat until some nice-looking gentleman noticed Michael. They'd usually pass us by once or twice before stopping to examine some interesting book in the window behind us. Michael would lean back into the gentleman's focus and . . .

"Hi."

"Hi."

"What are you boys up to?"

"Not much."

"You're together?"

"We're friends."

"I live across the way . . ."

The first few times I sat and waited for Michael to return. He rarely did. I usually walked back to the subway alone. One day while waiting I looked up to see my idol Buffy Sainte-Marie walking hand in hand with her boyfriend. I wanted to scream. I worshipped that woman with the long black locks, distinctive vibrato, and ringing guitar. I had every one of her albums and had even seen her perform at Carnegie Hall. Before the day of the concert I drew a large portrait of her and carried it to the stage door. Shockingly, the guard let me in and I voicelessly presented my gift to her. She smiled at me before being swept into a circle of congratulating friends. And now here she was right in front of me. I didn't dare speak to her. Instead I followed the couple down the street, in and out of shops and boutiques, occasionally catching her bewildered eye, which then became an embarrassed eye, and eventually one of annoyance, at which point they took refuge in a movie theater, the Greenwich. I had no money for admittance, so I gave up the chase and floated home. However hot Michael's guy was, I highly doubt he'd remember him as vividly as I recall my almost-run-in with Buffy Sainte-Marie.

Michael made friends easily. Scott lived right down the street from school. He was a little older than us, a high-school dropout who still lived in an apartment with his divorced mother. His father had left them well off, and no way was Scott going to waste his time working when he couldn't fathom how he'd spend the funds already at his disposal. Scott's Fifty-Seventh Street apartment made a convenient place to hang out on the days we cut school and the weather kept us from wandering Central Park. I loved school and rarely cut, but there were days when I simply couldn't face a math exam or when Mr. Ginsburg was out and some saccharine substitute who loved being around artistic kids showed up and told us how lucky we were to be talented. Anyhow, Michael saw Scott much more than I did and, in my absence the two of them had devised a plan.

I had barely walked through Scott's door when Michael snatched my jacket and pointed behind him: "Joey is waiting for you in the guest room."

"Joey?"

Michael took a half-smoked joint out of Scott's mouth and shoved it into mine.

"You know Joey. My friend from Gravesend. The one we went for pizza with that time."

"Oh, right," I said, having no memory of this boy.

"It's time. And it will be good for you. You can't sit around waiting for someone to magically appear. That's not the way the world works. You want something to happen, you make it happen. And Joey volunteered."

I still had no idea what he was talking about. "Suck," he said. I realized he was referring to the reefer in my mouth. I took a long, deep toke. He snatched the joint back and ordered, "Go! He's waiting."

Finally, the fog was lifting . . .

"Have fun and make me proud" were Michael's last words as I entered the room.

Joey was lying on the bed, already naked, and grinning as he rocked his head back and forth and said, "Hello."

He was kind of adorable, I must admit. A very different type of Italian boy than I'd grown up with: his body was almost hairless, and his head was a mass of golden curls. And his penis . . . I'd seen penises all my life: in my own home, at the Sunset Park pool locker room, in the JCH swimming pool when everyone bathed naked on Men Only nights. But I'd never seen an uncircumcised one before except in statues and paintings. Even porn stars were circumcised, which made me stop to wonder if they were all Jewish.

Joey reached out and pulled me to him. It was a small bed. It was a big deal. He kissed sweetly, guiding me along, and when we were done, I bolted from the apartment as quickly as I could, making my escape back to Brooklyn by subway. As it was Friday night, my mother and father volunteered to pick me up at the station to save me the walk from the elevated train. They'd be out anyway, driving my Uncle Paul home from dinner. Uncle Paul had been coming to our weekly Sabbath dinner meals for decades. My grandfather's brother, he was a postal worker whose wife went mad soon after their honeymoon. He'd returned from work one evening to discover her under their bed screaming. Their apartment windows looked out over the elevated train tracks, and family folklore said that it was the people looking in her bedroom window as they passed by that drove her to madness. I guess that's as good a reason as any, although hundreds of thousands of others, in cities all over the world, have endured passing trains without becoming Ophelia.

Refusing to divorce her, Uncle Paul placed Cecile in a facility, where he visited her weekly for half a century. Under such care, she outlived him by a decade.

Uncle Paul was already standing outside the car waiting when I bopped down the staircase from the train. I got in back with him and faced what felt like a barrage of questions about my evening. I don't know if it was the pot or the penis, but I was way too lost fiddling with my jigsaw pieces to come up with any sensible responses. My father shook his head dismissively. My mother shifted the rearview mirror to get a better look at me. And Uncle Paul gently burped and said, "You missed a wonderful brisket."

My brain kept rushing back to Joey buried in Scott's guest room's sheets, but then I'd suddenly catch myself grinning or breathing hard and quickly looked up to be sure my parents hadn't caught me. I tried disguising any inexplicable sighs I might have unwittingly emitted by humming softly to myself. I pulled the collar of my coat around my face to check my breath. The taste of Joey lingered on my tongue. Could they smell it? I rode home in all the silence I could manage and spent the night expelling memories into gym socks until I fell asleep to dream.

This was 1967 and I was fourteen.

I saw Joey only once more. It must have been the early eighties. I recognized him right away, although the club was dark and he was in full drag. We barely chatted. We were both with friends. Not long after I heard he'd passed with AIDS.

As for Scott, his mother became involved with a very high-profile politician, who proposed marriage with one condition: she had to do something about her layabout fag son. So she did. Scott was committed to an asylum to undergo conversion therapy. Neither Michael nor I was allowed to visit for months, and when we finally made the trip uptown, we found that Scott was no longer the carefree youth we'd known. Bloated by medications, his skin yellow and blotchy and covered with scratch marks, he chattered and giggled mostly to himself, like a character out of a medieval morality play, and asked us to join in his happiness; he'd at last found love and planned to wed. We were then introduced to the object of his affection—a very large and most unattractive nurse who was nevertheless very understanding of Scott's condition. She was able to gently deflect his physical advances as he tried time and again to kiss her. Michael and I did not stay long, and I have no idea what became of the boy.

For the record, as of this writing, conversion therapy is still legal in many of the United States and throughout most of the world.

7

FUNNY THINGS HAPPEN WHEN YOU SAY YES

1967

Jill Bray dropped out of A&D to pursue a bohemian lifestyle of drugs and free lesbian love. Arriving at school a year later, her younger sister, Lauren, had a lot to live up to. Their father was a professional painter, and their mother had artistic longings of her own. One day Lauren asked if anyone wanted to help make posters for a play her mother, Joan, was putting on. Michael heard the word "play" and immediately volunteered us. He, too, had longings. A group of us toiled in the basement kitchen of a Unitarian church in Flatbush, Brooklyn, hand-lettering posters for the premiere production of a brand-new community theater, the Gallery Players. I must have been high on Magic Marker fumes when Lauren's mother asked if any of us would like to work backstage, because I said yes. This time Michael followed my lead. We worked on lights, pulled the curtain, painted sets—that grunt kind of stuff. My parents didn't mind the late nights as long as I kept my grades up, but as Jackie tells it, she spent many nights sitting on our front stoop until she spotted me safely bouncing down the street toward home.

Michael got very excited when Thornton Wilder's *Our Town* was announced as the second production. "There's a role for a young boy," he told me.

"You going to do it?"

"Of course. But first I have to audition."

"Oh, you'll get it," I said.

"*You* have to audition, too."

"No. Why?"

"We are the only two boys around here and I don't want to get the role because there was no one else. We'll both audition, I'll get the role, and you can do the curtain stuff."

As it turned out, there were two roles for boys. Brothers.

Obviously, I got the bigger role, or I wouldn't be telling this story.

The next production was *Dark of the Moon*, and I got the role of the lead's annoying little brother. Michael was a townsfolk. After that production he left the Gallery Players.

Joan imported Bruce Wyatt from the Gallery Players in New Orleans to be resident director. Bruce was a very tall and slender gentleman with a jaw so angular he could have been a Dick Tracy cartoon. Under a mass of neatly coiffed silver hair, his manner defined elegance. Whether smoking a cigarette or directing an actor, he was forceful, clear, and unequivocal. He and his partner, Bud, had been together for almost thirty years. Bud was a banker and amateur actor. When the theater job was offered, they relocated to Staten Island, where they quickly gathered a community of gay men around them. Bruce and Bud were what I expected to one day be: a happily married gay man.

As my gay identity was evolving, it never occurred to me that I wouldn't meet someone, fall in love, settle down in a home (not on Staten Island), and maybe even adopt some kids. Well, why wouldn't I? Isn't that what people do, besides pursue careers and fiddle with hobbies? No one would have been surprised if my straight brother wanted to fall in love, get married, and have children. Why the shock that I'd envision my life similarly? We grew up in the same house, with the same parents, who taught us the same values, no?

Meeting and spending time with Bruce and Bud proved it was possible. It was only my gradual exposure to the wider world that showed me gays as sad, lonely, self-loathing victims. I was not happy reading plays like *Suddenly Last Summer*, *A Taste of Honey*, *Fortune and Men's Eyes*, *The Boys in the Band*, *The Children's Hour*, and *Staircase*. Real life seemed, to my young self, a breeze compared to our lives expressed in literature. The gays I knew at school and in theater were nothing like that. I now excuse that expression of pain by Williams and Crowley et al. as a cry for acceptance; but as a teen, I saw this vision only as an unhappy existence that I wanted no part of. I wondered where all of that pain was coming from in the first place and struggled to piece it together. I knew that being gay was something that I had to hide from my parents. But these others I was looking at were adults. Why were they hiding? I wasn't a complete idiot. I knew that homosexuality was against the law. I knew people who'd been arrested. I'd heard that you could lose your job if they found out you were gay. But none of that answered my question why. Was it because gay is not the norm? What the fuck *was* the norm? The norm, I began to realize, meant nothing but the majority. This was starting to make sense. I understood prejudice. The majority looks down on minorities. I'd seen it and felt it and to some extent was taught it. So here was just another kind of prejudice, having nothing to do with skin color or country of origin. In this instance the heterosexual majority was looking down upon and judging the gay minority as lesser. The judgment of the majority then defines the minority as wanting. If the majority is right, then the minority must be wrong. And if all of my reasoning was true, then heterosexuals were my oppressors. No? Yes. I began to eschew straight people.

I wandered the streets of the gay ghetto, Greenwich Village, with and without Michael. I watched gay men—well, the ones my gaydar could discern—as they socialized and shopped and enjoyed life. These were the days of protest marches and sit-ins for civil rights, peace, and free love. I joined in a few antiwar marches, but these were straight events and I wasn't really sure where I fit in. And then, one June night in 1969, our time arrived. I was not at the Stonewall, but I came running as soon as I saw the images on television the next morning. The streets were litter-ridden from the moment I rose out of the West Fourth Street subway station. Walking down Washington Place, still blocks from the bar, I heard voices. Turning the corner, there they were: men and reporters and police and women and neighbors and street folks, everyone hollering and waving in grand gestures, and what struck me most was that this wasn't nighttime. It wasn't dancing, drinking, or cruising time. These weren't gay people covertly sneaking away from their day jobs for drinks and sex. No one was hiding from the police or cameras. No one covered their faces or panted in fright because they might be identified as homosexual. Here was the community standing purposefully in the light of day demanding their place in the world. Hiding was over. Being second-class citizens was done. Intimidating us back into the closet was not going to work anymore. The revolution had been engaged, and even naive little me knew that retreat was unacceptable. The bandages covering our wounds of shame were discarded. We'd now heal in the light of day or bleed out. I had just turned seventeen.

I joined the movement as best I could, attending Gay Activists Alliance meetings at the Wooster Street Firehouse and those of the Gay Liberation Front and even of the Street Transvestite Action Revolutionaries (STAR). Being underage did not exclude me from political meetings, but most of the older members shied away. Having witnessed a veritable platoon of pederasts pursue my underage friend Michael, I appreciated the reverence for youth these men displayed.

Back at the Gallery Players, my friends were not happy with the protests. They had spent their lives fitting in, or at the very least, keeping their heads down and out of trouble. What good could come from riots? Liberation was not an aim they embraced. Equality was an impossible goal. They flourished in the safest place they could find. They never saw it as a prison.

But me? Newly awakening me? I was a taxpaying American citizen and, as such, had the right to anything a heterosexual did. If straights could hold hands on the street, then I could as well. If they had the right to marry, then why shouldn't I? The American dream, as it was taught to me, included the freedom to guide your own destiny, make your own choices, live your dreams. Since when was the pursuit of happiness defined by gender or race or sexual preference? Our nation's inventors specified no qualifications. Jeez, but it was fun to be a teenager dropped into the middle of a revolution!

My high school gang—Linda, Lisa Klinghoffer, Margaret, me, and Michael at the entrance to the 59th Street Bridge

8

EVEN HIGHER EDUCATION

1969

The last thing I wanted was to sit in a classroom for another four years.

"Well, you're not sitting around here," my mother made clear. "What's the best job you've had so far?"

"Besides the Gallery Players?"

"The Gallery Players don't pay enough to cover your carfare."

"I had that job delivering dry cleaning. The tips were phenomenal."

Even a great Jewish mother couldn't disguise the disgust she felt hearing that. "You want to work with your father at the factory?"

My eyes and mouth shot open in dissent.

"Don't look at me that way. Theater is what you do when you don't have a job or when you have such a great job you can afford to take time off."

"Maybe I'll travel," I volunteered.

"You don't leave the house to go to the movies."

"I don't know what I want to do."

With a flip of her hand she pronounced, "That's what college is for. You'll get your degree, and then, if you still don't know what to do with your life, you'll teach."

At Pratt Institute I could study art and also get a teaching degree. It was a private college, and since I had no scholarship, and my parents couldn't afford tuition, I ended up in deep debt earning a degree that only my mother wanted. At least it was in Brooklyn, so I could live at home.

Philomena went to Pratt, too, but had the good sense to drop out. I think she was in love or something; I'll have to ask her. But here's the thing about Pratt: they accepted any graduate of Art and Design with open arms—and then tortured us. We'd been trained to be employable craftsmen. Pratt wanted us to be struggling artists. My professors were mostly failed artists supporting themselves as teachers. Apparently, everyone had a mother. Unluckily, my color-theory teacher was one such loser. He'd look over our assignments and grunt his disapproval while pronouncing "No work is precious!" and tossing the work back to us or onto the floor. Boys mostly got theirs on the floor; girls mostly got it on the desk, if you know what I mean. Charming pig, may he grow like an onion with his head underground! (That's an old Yiddish curse Estelle Getty taught me.) All the progress Mr. Ginsburg had made in unleashing my artistic fancies was undone in one semester under the tutelage of that piece of crap. I switched majors to ceramics. There, in that dust-covered world, I met three of the most wonderful artisans that it's ever been my pleasure to know. David and Edmee were teaching interns who teased and encouraged my creativity. Byron Temple was a world-famous potter who, besides being a brilliant vessel maker, was adorable and just coming out of the closet. The ceramics room became my fortress against Pratt. Working in a very gritty clay I began to hand-build exaggerated vessels with animal, Martian, insect, and even human characteristics. I made teeth for them from porcelain. I forced clay through a tea strainer to create hair. David brought me a child's Play-Doh set that had tools for making other textures. I fashioned teapots and vases and bowls, mugs, planters, and pots. As individual as each of these creatures was, they had one thing in common: they all sported genitals. Penises formed handles, vaginas provided pouring spouts; and sometimes, as in life, the genitalia only served as decoration. I called my progeny Bad Boy Jugs. The hardest part of creating these pieces was keeping them from disappearing. As soon as they were pulled, still warm, from the glazing kiln, they began to disappear. The teachers had to lock them in their office for safety. Only a few students are rewarded with an exhibition of their work in the Pratt Gallery at the end of term. That showing was often a stepping stone to finding representation and a commercial gallery to launch an artist's career. My professors nominated my Bad Boy Jugs for this honor, but after a spirited discussion with the deans and boards of directors, I was rejected. My work was deemed obscene and not the aesthetic they wished to showcase when hitting up alumni for donations during the exhibition.

I'm relating this whole story because despite the fact that my career path to theater seems predetermined now, had the Pratt governors shown my work, and had it received the kind of attention that my professors predicted it could, my entire life might have gone in another direction. In that artistic infancy I was guided by approval. Like a puppy in training, if you gave me a treat, I would happily repeat that trick. Hey, why am I hiding behind youth? Isn't applause the same payment? I'm still working for approval. But the rejection of my work at that moment changed the trajectory of my life. I never touched clay again.

Marijuana made me hungry, and I had enough problems with my weight, so during college I switched to pills. Seconal and Tuinal were both downers that revved me up in a very mellow way. Drugs were different then—nothing like the potent locoweed people get these days. When we scored pot, it was a blend of twigs, stems, and seeds. The sixties happened mostly in the imagination.

One morning, I ran into some friends on the quad as I was rushing to my history of art class. I had the bullshit job of operating the slide projector. It didn't pay anything, but since I could read the captions on each slide, I got an automatic pass on exams. Score! The gig was to fetch that day's carousel of slides from the office, load them into the projector, and wait for the professor to click his clicker. One click directed me to advance the slide, and two clicks alerted me to adjust the focus. This professor was a piss—a fussy old queen perennially in three-piece suits and spouting the most wonderful stories: "We adventurers disembarked the bus in Athens and followed our guide. As our feet were only protected by the native sandals purchased that morning at the bazaar, we stepped carefully along the stone-strewn street. Geoffrey stopped suddenly and, with a masterful magician's wave, bade us look forth. 'Gaze now upon the Parthenon, the world's most famous white marble edifice.' I'd barely lifted mine eyes when my traveling companion shrieked, 'Oh, dear God, it's beige!'"

Well, that morning I was relieved to run into this particular group of friends, as they were never without a stash of pills and I needed something to keep me amused through that day's lecture on Raphael. I swallowed my meds and was off.

Not twenty minutes into the lecture my stomach began to turn. I never had bad reactions to pills, but, then again, who really knew what the hell we were taking?

I heard the sound of the professor's clicker and, despite my deteriorating condition, managed to change the slide to Raphael's *Coronation of the Virgin*.

Now I was getting dizzy . . .

Click, and we were viewing *Marriage of the Virgin*.

I broke out in a cold sweat, began to breathe heavily . . .

Click, and the class was entranced by *Madonna of the Meadow*.

Just then my guts dropped to my pit and boomeranged back up . . . I had to vomit . . .

Click, where was I going to throw up?

Click, where was there a bag or trashcan?

Click, I couldn't hold back any longer and let loose my breakfast into the carousel of slides.

Click click click!!!!—"Mr. Fierstein, are you with us?"

"Yes, sir. Sorry," and I advanced the slide to *Madonna of the Pinks*, but there was nothing pink about her. The image was slimy and spotty, out of focus, covered with vomit.

Click click—*click click*—*click click*—"The focus, Mr. Fierstein! Please! Focus!"

I reversed the order of the slides, pulled that one from the projector, wiped the spew on my shirt and put it up on the screen. It was streaky, but it was there. The professor regarded the image with disdain. "Madonna's looking a little blue today, wouldn't you say?"

I had to repeat this cleaning of every slide for the rest of the lecture. I survived, but I never took another pill to get high. Not one. EVER. Which is not to say I didn't dabble in a bit of coke and speed and heroin and poppers and hash along with a dash of LSD, but pills and I were through. Oh, and alcohol. Let's not forget alcohol.

But first Warhol . . .

9

SUPERSTAR

1971

The Gallery Players moved twice while I was with them. Our new facility, a church gymnasium in Flatbush, had a real stage and lighting equipment, allowing our presentations to grow in ambition. We staged productions of *The Lion in Winter*, *A View from the Bridge*, and *A Shot in the Dark*. I hadn't acted in many productions, although I was assigned to understudy the two younger men in *The Lion in Winter*. One night our King Philip came down with the flu and I squeezed myself into his costume, but fifteen minutes before curtain he appeared to bravely go on. Fuck him! The maxim declares that the *show* must go on, not the actor.

When Neil Simon's *Barefoot in the Park*, was announced, the director assigned the role of the Telephone Repairman to me. I think he felt sorry that, although I was designing scenery and running shows, I had not had a role all season. This character appears only twice in the play, but it's a great comic turn, arriving onstage out of breath after climbing five flights of stairs to the apartment. That was the running gag of the show: all of the characters arrived onstage in various degrees of collapse. I was eighteen at the time and barely shaving. They costumed me with a hunting hat to cover my long hair, painted beard stubble on my peach-fuzz chin, and on I went. And I was funny! Well, Neil Simon was funny, but I took the bows. My parents were always very supportive of the Gallery

Players and my work there. Jackie organized theater parties of her Hadassah friends when it was a fun show. She must have seen this one four times. Even my father stayed awake for both acts. We were a hit.

The Gallery Players had a strong reputation, and reviews in the neighborhood newspapers were always supportive, so I never paid attention when dressing-room whispers announced, "The critics are here."

There were three trade publications that covered New York theater: *Backstage*, *Show Business*, and of course *Variety*. We always placed casting notices in those papers, so I shouldn't have been surprised that one of them, *Show Business*, finally sent a critic to cover us. The only local newsstand that carried those papers was under the elevated train on Kings Highway. I stood openmouthed on the sidewalk while reading the review of our show. *What the . . . ?* I was practically Sally Field at the Oscars: *They liked me, they really liked me!* My first-ever review, and it was a rave! I bought a second copy. If I had had the money, I would have bought a third. I read the damn thing cover to cover, over and over, each time pretending to be surprised to come upon my good notice.

But there was something else in that edition—something that would change my life. There was a casting notice for a play by Andy Warhol.

Warhol was putting on a play and seeking actors. *Hey, I'm an actor—sort of.* Fully inflated with self-confidence, I figured I could at least get in for the audition, and even if they tossed me out, I still might get to meet the man himself.

The ad asked for a prepared audition piece. The Gallery Players had a wonderful older woman, Madame Barbara Bulgakova, who claimed to have immigrated from Russia with legendary Hollywood actress Maria Ouspenskaya. Do you remember Ouspenskaya? She played the Romani fortuneteller in the Lon Chaney Jr. version of *The Wolf Man*, who warned him, "Beware the fool moon, my son." Madame said the two had been members of Stanislavsky's Moscow Art Theater together.

On Saturday afternoons, down in the lunchroom of the church, Madame gave acting lessons, which as a working member of the company I was allowed to attend for free. Madame told me that I was a natural character actor who wouldn't start working until my forties. In the meantime, she thought stock boy roles were not emotionally challenging enough for me, so she had me work on lead female characters in plays like *Member of the Wedding*, *Romeo and Juliet*, and *This Property Is Condemned*. Who cared why she actually gave them to me? I loved playing all of those great girl roles. I got to be the witch after all.

Madame's teaching style was singular. While you performed, she would busy herself unwrapping candies from her purse or adjusting the veil on her hat, seemingly paying no attention to you—*but*—if she caught your eye glancing over toward her or sensed any break in your attention, she would rise from her seat and unceremoniously smack you in the head with her purse: "Concentrate!"

Casting notice, résumé, and home-printed eight-by-ten photo in hand, I walked down East Fourth Street in search of something called La MaMa ETC. I saw a marquee for the Truck and Warehouse Theater, and another for the 82 Club (New York's last drag nightclub), but no La MaMa. A woman was sweeping the street, cursing under her breath at the debris. She looked up at me checking addresses, "This is it, baby," she said, in a distinct French accent.

"Sorry?"

She was not pleased that I made her repeat herself. "What you're looking for. La MaMa, *oui*? Zees ees eet."

She indicated a set of plain wooden doors with tiny transom windows, a small bronze plaque above reading "La MaMa etc."

"Thank you," I said. "Do you work here?"

"*Bébé*, I *am* here."

The woman with the short dreadlocks, mid-length Indian skirt, puffy white blouse, her arms weighed down with a ton of amber bracelets that jangled as she swept the sidewalk, was La MaMa herself. This was my first encounter with Ellen Stewart, founder of

La MaMa Experimental Theater Club and mother of the Off-Off-Broadway theater movement. "Go, *bébé*. Get on in."

There was a sign-up sheet and a bevy of hopefuls waiting in the lobby. I really don't remember much until a wildly energetic young man with long stripped platinum hair opened the red metal fire door, checked his list, and announced in a Carolinian drawl, "Harvey Feer-a-stan?"

I pushed my way through the others like a bargain hunter on Black Friday. I handed him my photo and résumé as we climbed the industrial staircase.

"I'm Leee, three *e*'s, and I'll be stage managing."

"Is he here?"

"Andy? No. Everyone asks."

Well, why wouldn't they? Why do you think we're here? Then I realized that most of these people actually wanted to be in a play, the one I was about to audition for, and I had never before auditioned for a real play, and now I was standing in a small black-box theater facing actual professional theater people, and . . . What the hell did I think I was doing here?

The room was dark. It had bleacher seating filled with black-padded office chairs sparsely peopled with all sorts of characters whom I really couldn't make out . . . I took my place, alone, center stage and squinted into the darkness . . .

A large, jovial man with a mass of curly black hair, oversized thick-rimmed glasses, and a scraggly beard jumped up to greet me. Tony Ingrassia was the director and creator of this piece. Unkempt and in perpetual motion, he laughed more than spoke.

"What have you got?" he asked.

"Shakespeare's *Romeo and Juliet*? The balcony scene."

The people in the dark laughed. Were they laughing at me or my choice of material? Oh, shit. Tony shrugged and waved me on.

"Thou know'st the mask of night is on my face,
Else would a maiden blush bepaint my cheek
For that which thou hast heard me speak to-night

Fain would I dwell on form, fain, fain deny
What I have spoke: but farewell compliment!
Dost thou love me? . . ."

They howled. Howled! I pushed on.

". . . I'll prove more true
Than those who have the cunning to be strange.
I should have been more strange. I must confess . . ."

. . . And I got a role in the show. Only two of us were cast from the
open call. All the other actors were friends of the director. Floating
out of the building, I ran into Ellen again. She read my face.
    "You got it?"
    "Yeah."
    "Good for you, *bébé*."

Here's Mama and me celebrating the *Safe
Sex* opening on Broadway in April 1987.

I felt so special when she called me *baby*. I didn't know that she
called everyone baby because she couldn't possibly remember all
the names of the people dependent on her, and I never cared. She
called me Baby and I called her Mama. This was the woman who

would support, encourage, and employ me and shape my career as a theater artist. Even my real mother would come to accept Ellen as my Mama.

Warhol was an observer. Leave a movie camera running for a while and you had a film. Click away at things with a Polaroid and you had photography. Turn a tape recorder on while people gossiped and you had . . . What did you have?

Brigid Berlin was an artist, an employee, and friend of Andy's. Nicknamed Brigid Polk because she frequently injected herself, and any willing victim, with speed (Polk = poke). She was a constant dieter thanks to her mother's disapproval. Amphetamines helped control her appetite. She loved relating stories about her mother to Andy and the other denizens of his large art studio known as the Factory. Warhol captured them all on tape as was his way. One day he handed those Polk tapes to Ingrassia, asking, "What can you do with these?"

Tony listened to the hundreds of hours of rantings and phone calls and chatter, and, whenever there was a bit he thought funny or juicy he'd stop the machine, cut out that section, and stick it to the wall with a piece of Scotch tape. Once he'd been through all of the material, he spliced the pieces together into a "highlights reel" and handed it off to a typist. The result was the script we were about to stage: *Andy Warhol's Pork*.

First-day-of-school jitters had my legs shaking when I arrived at the rehearsal loft on Great Jones Street. Everyone there knew one another but I had only spoken to Leee Black Childers, the stage manager, and Tony, the director. I was definitely not in a room full of Gallery Player actors. Wayne County, now Jayne County, was a wild punk rocker. Gerri Miller was a hugely endowed Metropol stripper whom I'd seen in *The Magic Garden of Stanley Sweetheart* when I was an usher at the Paris Cinema. Cyrinda Foxe came to New York and worked for a while for Greta Garbo. She went on to marry David Johansen and then Aerosmith's Steven Tyler. There were fifteen people in the cast, each as individual as they were unforgettable. I was handed my purple-leatherette-bound script with the word *"Pork"* engraved in gold, and we were off.

I was to play Pork's mother's maid. She had no lines, but as Tony worked to shape a show from the chaos, I got lines and bits and eventually we developed a character. I became Amelia, an asthmatic lesbian maid with a penchant for porn mags and plate jobs. If you don't know what a plate job is, you can go look it up or just accept my general note that *Pork* displayed more than a passing fascination with excrement. It's not every day you get offered the role of a coprophiliac.

Tony suggested I come to rehearsal in drag. Good idea—except I didn't own a dress. I had never done drag—not really. I remembered that a women's clothing chain called Lane Bryant was where my mother shopped whenever she hit a generous weight. There was a branch on Fourteenth Street.

"I'm looking for a dress . . . for my mother."

"All right," said the saleswoman. "Do you know her size?"

"No. Maybe she's about my size."

"Uh-huh. And height?"

"About my height. All right—it's for me. I'm doing a play and I need a dress."

The saleswoman took out her order pad. "Here's the address of a used-costume shop. I'm sure they can take care of you."

I followed directions to an East Village storefront jam packed with costumes and masks. Pushing through the racks of clothing, I discovered a whole bunch of red-and-gold cancan outfits in larger sizes. I tried one on and it fit. Taking it to the cashier, I noticed there was a name tag: Joe Namath. *Joe Namath?* The famous football player Joe Namath? The saleswoman explained that the New York Jets had put on a show where the team wore these cancan dresses. I brought it back to rehearsal, where everyone was too nice to laugh right in my face. I wore it that day but didn't dare take it home with me, so I hid it in the loft. It was gone the next day. A few months later I attended a performance of Jackie Curtis's show *Vain Victory: Vicissitudes of the Damned,* and there was Agosto Machado wearing my cancan dress. I replaced it with a bright tangerine housecoat bought at another store on Fourteenth Street. Tony said this was probably a better choice in any case. I added a sassy short red wig and some pink lipstick, and Amelia, the asthmatic lesbian maid, came to life. Actually, Jayne, the southern punk rocker, helped me with the makeup. I had no idea what I was doing, so she'd paint me up while chattering on in her honey-dripping drawl about rock music, bad boys, and how she'd love to be a woman except she could never stand the sight of a vagina.

Ingrassia was an outrageously inventive director. He was a bad boy, a troublemaker, poking at the social and sexual norms of his time. Restrained on the visual side but exuberant on the conceptual, this production would play as modern now as it was then. The set was an all-white box furnished with all-white beds and chairs and props. The back wall of the stage consisted of revolving panels. The opening of the show found us leaning against the panels, one on each side, and revolving as we chanted:

"Watch out
Watch out

Here's Warhol and the cast of *Pork*. If you look
really hard you can spot me fourth from the right,
my head peeping out between two big hairdos.

Watch out for Amanda Pork.
In one hand she carries a needle.
In the other hand a fork."

I had my brother come to see the show before inviting my parents. It was the beginning of a tradition that lasted several years. Ron would come and judge whether or not it was suitable for parental attendance. My culture-loving mother didn't need details to follow his direction. She knew. My father didn't need any explanation at all to stay home. Ron also used my projects as a measure of how open-minded his dates were. If a young lady could watch his brother run around in a dress, then maybe she'd be fun to hang out with.

Pork enjoyed a two-week run at La MaMa, during which time we were the toast of the downtown glitterati. We were photographed and interviewed and invited by everyone to everything. I'd arrive via subway and ride home in a limo provided by a Rothschild. Each night, if there was no better party, we'd travel en masse to Max's Kansas City, where we'd occupy a giant table in back, eat dry chickpeas and drink, all of it on Warhol's tab. I asked Tony Zanetta, the actor who played Warhol in our show, "Doesn't all of this cost him a fortune?"

Tony laughed, "Max's sends a bill up to the Factory and the Factory sends a painting back to cover it. It all works out."

I was loving my time at La MaMa, getting to know the staff and office people. I once ran into Ellen in the stairwell. "Ah, *baby*. Come upstairs and have a talk."

Like all hard workers, Mama lived above the store, on the top floor of the building that was once a hot-dog factory. It was furnished in golden oak antique pieces. The brick walls had memories of shows and travels. Every surface was covered with bowls and cups and strands of beads which she'd string into jewelry. "You're still living at home?" she asked incredulously.

"I go to college full-time, so . . ."

"Good for you."

Mama spoke with a French Creole accent she'd developed for public consumption, but if she trusted you, she was plain-talking Ellen from Chicago. The accent, I think, besides lending an air of exoticism, allowed her the pretense of translating her thoughts from French to English, thereby giving her time to consider what she wanted to say.

"I'm an art student."

"You know what that means? I am expecting something from you."

"You don't have a lot of free wall space," I joked.

"I'll find room," she said, not joking.

I laughed. "I'm not very good."

She studied me. "What is it you want?"

"I don't know."

"That's all right. We'll find out and then see if we can make it happen."

I floated out of Mama's apartment.

Ellen did guide me in a way all her own. One lesson she taught still amuses me today. "If someone asks for something and you're not sure, tell them no. If you say you want to think about it, they will torture you until they get an answer. If that answer turns out to be no, they will accuse you of breaking your word. If the answer is eventually yes, they will hail you a hero. Always say no and you will do well."

I subscribe to an alternate and more direct philosophy: nothing changes when you say no, so say yes and let the world know you're open to possibility.

But did I ever get to know Warhol? That answer is yes and no. Andy came to see the show a couple of times but mostly paid attention to the director and the stars. I once was placed next to him for a photo and he said, "Oh, you were very funny," but that was as good as I got. He gave each of us a large piece of his cow wallpaper, which he autographed and personally inscribed with our names in ballpoint pen. A decade later I hung mine in my friend Jay's East Village bar, the Last Resort. When the police raided and closed the place for serving food without a license, we put it in another friend's closet for safekeeping, and it's never been seen again. Somewhere out there in the world there's a blue-and-brown Warhol cow inscribed in ballpoint pen, "From Andy Warhol to Harvey Fierstein," and I hope it's making someone happy.

When Andy came to see *Torch Song* I reminded him that I'd been in *Pork*. He nodded and smiled in that blank way he had, as if saying "Of course" but meaning "I have no idea what you're talking about." His diaries were later published and he mentioned this meeting, saying he still didn't remember me.

In many ways I had already moved on from admiring Andy from afar and was becoming more enamored with the world of performance art. I met Candy Darling and Jackie Curtis and Holly Woodlawn, the three most famous of the Warhol drag superstars. I met Viva and Ultra Violet, both of whom were portrayed in *Pork*.

This is my woodblock portrait
of Viva and Ultra Violet.

I proudly shared a woodblock portrait I'd done of them, adapted from a *New York Times Magazine* cover photo. I was definitely feeling like part of the Factory.

There were rumors backstage as to what would happen to *Pork* once the run was over; Off-Broadway, a movie, Broadway . . . And then we were called to a meeting. Warhol's European gallery dealer was taking the show to London and we were all invited to go. I was just finishing my sophomore year at Pratt, so my mother was dead set against my leaving school, but my father argued that this was the chance of a lifetime, so they agreed to let me go.

The publicity department arranged a photo op for us all to have our passport pictures taken together at the post office. When I handed in my ID, the producer realized that I was barely nineteen. "The authorities will never allow someone underage to perform a scene with a nude woman using a vibrator."

"But I brought a permission slip from my father."

I don't know why he singled out the vibrator. The scene where Geri douched center stage while I watched seemed much more daring to me.

That summer the cast of *Pork* went off to London and I got a job as a drama counselor at a Jewish sleepaway camp.

10

THE PRIVATE LIFE
OF JESUS WHO?

1971

I wanted to *be* camping, not *go* camping, but here I was at a summer camp for overweight kids. How do you follow the adventure of a lifetime with a production of *You're a Good Man, Charlie Brown* performed by ten-year-olds? After an unhappy week I apologized to my bosses and hopped the bus back to the city.

Now what? Do I try to get a job in the art field? Was *Pork* a door opening in a new direction? If I don't make the best of that opportunity, will it be wasted? I asked my college friend Irene Stein to take some photos of me, went down to my basement darkroom, and printed up a bunch of headshots. I xeroxed an equal number of résumés at the library, bought a copy of a trade paper, circled all of the auditions that were open to non–union members, and I hit the streets.

I was standing on the altar of a Chelsea church when the director of the theater company housed there called out to me, "Be a freshly ironed shirt."

"Be a *what*?"

"Can you or can you not be a freshly ironed shirt?"

I stood straight up, my arms held stiffly at an angle.

"Are you on a hanger or in a box?" she asked.

"A hanger. See? My arms are flopping out."

"What color are you? Are you plain or striped? Button-down or flat collar?"

58

A portrait of a serious actor by
college friend Irene Stein

"I'm . . ."

"Don't tell me. Show me."

"Show?"

"Don't show. Be."

Walking back to the subway, reassessing this acting idea, I heard a voice calling my name. It was that director chasing after me.

"I'm glad I caught you. I've never done this before, but I feel it's my duty. Auditioning is difficult. Sometimes bad actors do well, or great actors bomb. I know that you are at the beginning of your career, just starting out, putting all of your energy into this. So, I hope you can digest these words in the spirit of generosity with which they are spoken. You need to stop. I'm sorry to be so blunt, but you simply don't have what it takes. I've been teaching acting for many years. If your problem was a lack of technique or experience, I would encourage you to study, but it's not that. You have no talent. I'm sorry, but it's better to know now instead of wasting years of your life banging your head against doors that cannot and will not ever open for you. I'm sorry." She put a hand on my shoulder. "Are you okay?"

"I guess. But how do you be a striped shirt?"

She shot me a pitying smile, adjusted the crocheted shawl around her shoulders, and walked soundlessly away on her ballet flats. For the record, I knew she was right. I'd never land a role as a freshly ironed shirt.

I got hired for a developmental workshop of a musical called *The Screaming Tangerine*. The producer/director/author had the bright idea to rip off the Beatles' *Yellow Submarine*. He had no script or score, only someone else's idea. We met every day at a YMCA rehearsal studio, where we'd improvise and rehearse and even write numbers. After weeks of work our producer/director/author vanished, leaving us with the rental bill.

Next up was a casting call that looked more encouraging. It was for replacements, which meant the show had been running long enough for someone to leave. It was called *Xircus: The Private Life of Jesus Christ*. I sought out the SoHo address, fingers crossed that this wouldn't be a trick to get actors to join a Jesus cult. My Granny Goose once went looking for a bathroom at the 1965 New York World's Fair, walked through a wrong door at the Billy Graham Pavilion, and by the time we found her was second in line for a baptism. This was not that—oh, boy, was it not!

The Performing Garage was a big open performance space on Wooster Street. Three stories high, with a system of platforms and ladders erected against all four walls. Depending on the show, the actors or the audience could occupy the platforms or the floor. It was home to the revered Performance Group, birthplace of Spalding Gray, Richard Schechner, and Elizabeth LeCompte. While they were on tour it was up for rent.

I was greeted at the door by the director/author/designer of the play, Donald L. Brooks. He insisted on using the L. so as not to be confused with the dress designer. This Mr. Brooks was compact and wiry. He wore his thinning ginger hair in a long ponytail and stomped about the open space in army boots as he ranted about the importance of art while studying my résumé.

"You don't have to make things up," he said.

"I didn't."

"Andy Warhol?"

"It was a show I did at La MaMa."

"Neil Simon? Shakespeare?"

"Community theater in Brooklyn."

"And these movies?"

"Student films. I go to Pratt."

He didn't buy it, and the funny part is that decades later, he still accused me of faking my résumé. I asked what kind of role he was looking to fill. He told me to come back that evening and watch the performance. We'd speak afterwards.

Xircus was an explosive assault on the senses. Flashing lights in saturated colors mixed with movie footage and slides projected around the room. Actors hollered over a sound collage of blaring music and old movie soundtracks. Every now and then I was able to discern a scene from *The Ten Commandments* or *Land of the Pharaohs*. The plot appeared to tell the story of Jesus returning to earth and landing in Times Square, which was a huge carnal carnival. Innocent and carrying the word of God, he was trans-formed into a clown, used and abused by whores, hustlers, and drug addicts, eventually succumbing to a second crucifixion that culminated in an apocalyptic vision of war and chaos. Jesus once again appears, now as a mad homeless woman, Our Lady of Forty-Second Street, crown of thorns on her head, crying a warning to anyone who will listen.

This was beyond anything I thought a play could be. It was less a show and more an environmental experience. Bad or good, to me it was art—immersive, invasive, aggressive, living art. The political and social commentary stood as front and center as the pain and emotional damage of its creator. Donald offered me the role of the bag lady at the end of the show. He told me it paid a hundred dol-lars a week, which was double what I made at La MaMa. I was in. He took me around the upstairs dressing room and introduced me to the cast—and to my amazement, I recognized someone. Without her wig and makeup, I realized that the woman I'd be replacing was the very same woman who had followed me out of that audition to tell me that I was talentless. She showed no sign of remember-ing me, and I didn't want to make a scene. But several years later we were seated together at an awards show. Relaxed and in a spirit of fun, I related the incident, about which she swore she had no memory. Funny how that is. The jockey never recalls using a whip. The horse never forgets.

I had four days to rehearse before going on. Donald assigned the lead actor to coach me. Russel was very striking. His body was long and lean; his eyes were deeply set. Dark, wavy, shoulder-length hair flew wildly to the bop rhythm of his walk. Russel was experienced in this world where I was completely at sea. He told me who everyone was, where everything was, and exactly what was expected of me. I thought I'd just been cast in some Off-Off-Broadway show, but I quickly realized that I had landed smack dab in the middle of an entire universe. Donald L. Brooks, he informed me, was an original member of the Caffe Cino crowd. The Cino was the birthplace of this experimental theater movement, and Joe Cino, its founder, had hacked himself to death with a butcher's knife on the stage of his club some months after his lover had died tragically. Grieving his friend, Donald wrote a play about the incident in which he blamed the community for not taking better care of Joe. When *Superfreak* was produced, the entire Off-Off-Broadway family turned on Donald and split apart. Ellen Stewart banned Donald and any of his troupe from working at La MaMa. Others followed her lead. What had I fallen into?

I rehearsed my monologue over and over with Donald and Russel until they deemed me ready. Donald fashioned my costume by ripping and burning layers of old clothing. I wore tights with oozing sores painted on them, stockings rolled down, and shredded slippers on my feet. I painted my face with clown white, with red lips and blackened eyes which I then smeared. They gave me a ratty wig which approximated Russel's own locks but grayed and filthy. A crown of thorns held it in place. I carried overstuffed shopping bags, guarding them as dearly as jewels. I was a sight.

Standing in the shadow of a platform and watching the performance, I readied myself during the crucifixion scene, and when it was done I entered, accompanied by a soundtrack that included Kate Smith singing "God Bless America," along with an endless

This makeup was more than a little reminiscent
of my childhood Halloween disguise.

cacophony of bomb explosions and trumpet wails. Over that din I screamed my warning of the world's coming destruction. As proof of the prophecy, I offered evidence of what society's selfishness had done to me. I violently lifted up my tattered skirts to reveal a bloody gash where my genitals had been, crying out, "But I've got it. I've got it. I've got it!"

I rummaged through my bags until I found a mason jar, which I held up for all to see. Inside the jar, floating in an unhealthy chartreuse brine, were my male genitals.

Now *that* was theater.

11

THE VILLAGE'S VOICE

1972

Donald had a patron, a producer, who used his day-job salary to finance his projects. Richard Briggs was the production stage manager of *The David Frost Show*, a TV gabber that was filmed at the Little Theatre on Forty-Fourth Street. Many nights, after *Xircus,* we'd walk from SoHo to swarm his West Village garden apartment, where we'd smoke and party while he cooked spaghetti for us.

Dick was a gay Santa Claus, white beard, jolly belly, and all, but garbed in a floor-length caftan, topped off by a straw hat that hid his bare head. He giggled when he spoke, a joint perpetually hanging from his lower lip while he nursed a glass of red wine and stirred the pasta. He was quick to accept me into the family but almost immediately recognized that I wasn't prepared for the job. Never planning to be an actor, I had no voice training. Screaming my role over the prerecorded soundtrack caused immediate wear to my vocal cords. I sprayed a constant stream of over-the-counter meds to numb the pain. There isn't a voice teacher, doctor, singer, actor, or idiot who would have thought this a good idea, but it's what I did. Dick gently suggested I seek help, but I did not, and so by the end of the run of *Xircus* I had done permanent damage to my vocal cords.

That's not the complete story of my unique sound. My father had a voice very much like mine, which I assure you he didn't get by screaming monologues over Kate Smith. He had, and I inherited, overdeveloped false cords. We all have two sets, but some have enlarged secondary cords that result in a double voicing, like a violinist playing two strings at once. Harry Belafonte, Louis Armstrong, and Jimmy Durante are examples of others with that sound, which is no excuse for abusing my instrument, but it wasn't all my fault.

Some nights Russel and I hung out with other gay men and street queens on Christopher Street. There was Gilly Glass, the stained glass artist whose studio storefront stood just before the highway. Paul Bellardo, cousin to Kaye Ballard, who at his shop sold his ceramic hippo sculptures to decorators. Albert Fine made avant-garde music, and Ray Johnson was the founding mind behind a movement known as mail art. He'd fashion collages on postcards using ads and photos and then he'd mail them to friends, who were expected to affix their own embellishments before mailing them back. Christian Soldier was a beautiful Puerto Rican prince who tutored me in street lingo, and Miss Marsha P. Johnson, who has become a legend for her life and death, always stopped by to chat on her way to or from her highway post, where she entertained gentlemen from the boroughs in their vehicles. Marsha was one of the first queens to throw a bottle at the police igniting the Stonewall riots. Her death was far less valorous than she deserved. Her body was found floating in the Hudson River right off the piers where she plied her trade. The cops labeled it suicide, but no one believed that. Marsha had turned living into an art. She was wild and adventurous and loved by all. She'd never abandon life for a cold, dark, wet grave. Even a block away I could always hear her call, "Miss Harvey, you got any pennies for a lady today?"

It was around this time that I discovered the Trucks, a loading dock of a warehouse on Washington Street where empty trailers, parked neatly against the platforms, were left overnight. In the warmer months, men gathered to partake of anonymous sex on the platform and in the spaces between the trailers. During cold months, some never-identified employee would leave at least one of the trailers unlocked so that the men could gather inside. Unlike

On a Gay Pride march with friends Jon Jon
and Marsha P. Johnson

the bathhouses or backroom bars, the Trucks were free, fast, and impersonal. Romance aside, that's how boys like it. As long as there's a dark corner and a zipper, boys will get theirs. The only rule was No Talking. Talking killed the fantasy. Some used the glow of a cigarette or a lighter to see who or what they were doing. Most preferred the blind sensuality of it all. With my schedule of school, home, and shows, the Trucks were a lifesaver. Looking back through the veil of AIDS, I realize that the last thing a sensible person would call the Trucks is a lifesaver, but it's no fair judging from the future. I loved the Trucks and I loved anonymous sex, as a good line in *Torch Song* attests: "I never enjoy sex with someone I know."

Not completely true, but good lines don't have to be. Great lines do. I got to know some really wonderful people after we had sex. But let me not over-romanticize the situation. The Trucks were the Wild West Side. The police respectfully kept their distance, which allowed pickpockets, muggers, and straight guys who eased their guilt by slugging the fag that got them off, to find plenty of unprotected victims. One late night this lowlife hid behind a bus, jumping out to rob guys by brandishing a twelve-inch kitchen knife. A few of us flagged down a police cruiser and rode around until we caught him. We then sat in night court to make sure he was arraigned. His legal aid lawyer claimed the butcher's knife was not a weapon but the judge, in a wonderful New York accent, quipped, "And suddenly this *shlemiel's* a *boo-chah*?"

WITH CREATURES
MAKE MY WAY

Mine was more than a double life. I was pulling triple duty at least. By day I carried a full course load at Pratt as I worked my way toward a BFA with teaching credentials. This kept my parents hopeful, if not happy. They watched me with cautious optimism, the way you watch a spinning quarter dropped on a table: you want it to spin forever but you know it's eventually going to fall flat or spin itself right over the edge. When the sun went down, my paint-splattered art-student overalls were replaced with bras and evening gowns. Performing or rehearsing, I lived and worked almost exclusively in drag. I was becoming an integral part of the art community. By day my professors lectured my class about this raw new art movement. At night I hung out with the very people creating it. Late nights were for exploring the gay ghetto, looking for love, finding sex, and struggling to figure out my place in the world before catching a subway back to Brooklyn, where this nice Jewish boychick rested his head before starting all over again.

H. M. (Harry) Koutoukas was a Christopher Street legend—actor, playwright, and poet who embraced the Susan Sontag definition of the term "camp" for his work. "You can't camp about something you don't take seriously. You're not making fun of it. You're making fun out of it."

Pulling inspiration from the same catalog of Technicolor movies as filmmaker Jack Smith while adding a level of the Oscar Wilde aesthete, Harry created ebullient scripts that always began, "As the curtain rises . . . and this play MUST be performed in a theater with a curtain . . ." Sadly none of the Off-Off-Broadway venues producing his stuff ever had a curtain.

His play titles reveal a lot about the work itself: *With Creatures Make My Way, Turtles Don't Dream,* and *Awful People Are Coming Over So We Must Be Pretending to Be Hard at Work and Hope That They Will Go Away.* He was an original member of Caffe Cino as well as La MaMa and even claimed to have his own theater group, the School for Gargoyles.

One morning Russel grabbed my hand and led me off to visit Harry, who'd been confined to the psych ward at St. Vincent's Hospital. Again. Harry was overly fond of shooting speed, which, along with the sought-after energy and elation delivered a less desirable punch of paranoia, often landing him in the wacky ward.

"Did you bring the jewels?" he called from the far end of the dayroom. Harry slunk over to us, clutching the collar of his hospital robe, pulling it tight to his neck in Garbo fashion, while swiveling his head to stare over his shoulder, making sure we were not alone.

"Let them watch. Let them learn," he teased. His performance was as much for the nurses as for us. "Grab a catcher's mitt and meet me under the laundry chute at midnight. Tell everyone or they'll be suspicious."

Finally done with the theatrics, he proposed a deal.

"They're observing me for another forty-eight hours. Take the keys to my apartment. Clean it and I will pay you with a play all your own."

Russel had the keys and was halfway out the door before Harry finished.

"Let no one in. Let nothing out. Tell no one what you've seen."

We brought garbage bags, a roll of paper towels, a bottle of Windex, and a feather duster, but we needed so much more. A sign on the apartment door read: "Do not knock unless entering with dramatic material." Russel unlocked the top lock, then the second, and turned the handle. The door wouldn't open.

"Maybe there's a trick to it," I suggested.

Russel stepped back and charged, hard as he could, until the door finally gave way a few inches. Peeking inside, we realized that there was stuff, shin high, filling the room and jammed against the door. We managed to push our way inside. Russel clicked on the overhead light and we stood in overwhelmed silence. We assumed that under the layers of garbage, papers, and cardboard boxes was a studio apartment, kitchen and bath at the rear, a bank of windows facing the street. Sheer fabric shawls draped from the ceiling. The walls were collaged with photos and magazine pictures. Every surface was covered in rainbows of velvets and brocades. Journeying out across the room, I reached the windows and pulled back the curtains to reveal Halloween masks staring sightlessly out at the world, meant to frighten away intruders. Now, with daylight struggling in through the security gates and the nicotine-stained glass, we spied Day-Glo green, yellow, and pink polka dots like sprinkles scattered over everything. Closer examination revealed that the dots had been painted on the backs of cockroaches, thousands of cockroaches, mostly expired, but not all. We went to work sorting the chaff from the wheat. Poems were put in these boxes, plays over here; scribblings had their own receptacles and cockroaches theirs. We filled every garbage bag we'd brought that first day and another supply the next.

I can't claim we cleaned the apartment, but one sling chair was now available for sitting, the bed could possibly be slept on, and the kitchen table was exposed enough to hold the typewriter. The boxes of Harry's writings were piled and labeled, if not organized. We'd done our best.

As I recall, it was the final week of *Xircus* when Harry showed up with the script of *Christopher at Sheridan Squared*. We had the Performing Garage for another month. Donald said that if we all pitched in, we could open the show and run for two weeks. Dick Briggs would produce, Donald would design and direct, Russel would play the statue of General Sheridan that stood in the square, and I was to play a Harry-like figure called Noel Swann. Donald reached out to some of Harry's friends and they came running. Choreographer James Waring staged a ballet to the music of

Albert Fine. Gerry Ragni, coauthor of *Hair*, volunteered a friend, Kevin Geer, to join our merry band of players.

Donald insisted that Harry at last have a curtain. We muscled an abandoned backdrop from the Metropolitan Opera House into position and somehow rigged it to open and close across the three-storied expanse. We spent many hours, sometimes struggling overnight, creating that production, while Donald regaled Russel and me with tales of his adventures. This was one of my favorites:

Donald was a brilliant touch typist who could easily earn a living picking up temp work, but he hated the hours and preferred to earn his rent employing other talents. He stripped at a gay club, the Tom Kat, on Forty-Second Street. Although protected by the Mafia, now and then the vice squad raided male clubs to give the women dancers a break. Hey, what's more fun than handcuffing fags while they plead, "I came with a friend—I had no idea what kind of place it was!"?

Donald was once nabbed and tossed into a holding cell with a great big, tough, musclebound hoodlum who, realizing that Donald was gay, began to move in on him threateningly: "I am going to fuck you to death."

Standing toe to toe with the guy, Donald replied, "You're going to have to kiss me first."

In a remembrance that Donald posted on his website after Harry's death in 2010, he recalled that *Christopher at Sheridan Squared* played to a packed house on opening night and then empty audiences for the rest of the run. He went on to say that I was a "demanding diva." That could have been. Donald and I collaborated on another six or seven productions together, a few of which he conceived just for me, so I guess he liked demanding divas. He slept with nearly everyone in our circle—men, women—but never me. He never even kissed me. I don't think he ever hugged me. I would not have minded.

Two men showed up at the opening-night after-party for *Christopher at Sheridan Squared*. I elbowed Russel: "Clock that pair."

"That pair," he said, as if speaking to the dumbest person alive, "are the Tavel brothers. I thought you worshipped Warhol." Indi-

Backstage at the Performing Garage with
Christian Soldier (left) and Russel Krum (right)

cating the taller, slimmer, and more affected of the two, he said,
"Ron wrote Warhol's early movies—*Chelsea Girls, The Life of
Juanita Castro, Hedy, Horse* . . ."

I studied them more carefully.

"And his brother appears in lots of them."

They both had long, dark, curly hair strategically held in place
with braided leather headbands to disguise receding hairlines. Ron
was a nervous type, constantly plucking tobacco leaves from unfil-
tered Pall Malls off his lip. The brother was much more carefree,
laughing and chatting up everyone.

"And the brother's name is Harvey," Russel said.

"Wait. Not Harvey and Ronald."

"Yes. Harvey and Ronald Tavel."

"My brother's name is Ronald."

"Did your brother create the Theater of the Ridiculous? Because
that Ronald did."

The Ridiculous movement was born when John Vaccaro staged
some of Ron's screenplays. At that time people were mounting

everything from *Wonder Woman* comics to magazine articles. Ron's plays were politically savvy attacks on current events, whether adapting a magazine interview with Fidel Castro's sister, Juanita, or imagining a radio station that spread propaganda to American troops in Vietnam. When asked by a reporter if theirs was an off-shoot of theater of the absurd, Ronald famously quipped, "We have gone far beyond the absurd. Our position now is absolutely preposterous."

Ron began to write more and more elaborate and difficult pieces, like *Indira Gandhi's Daring Device* and a beyond-bawdy comedy called *The Life of Lady Godiva*. His trademarks were the use of literary references and an unending onslaught of puns. It didn't take long for theatrical egos to flare and split the group apart. Lead actor Charles Ludlam went off to create the Ridiculous Theatrical Company, whose work veered to the low camp side of the road, drawing inspiration from classic movies. Vaccaro, almost in defiance of Ron's academically challenging scripts, dragged his kegs of glitter over to La MaMa to establish the Playhouse of the Ridiculous, specializing in visual and aural chaos. Ronald stuck with the elements of classic playwriting to create brilliant concoctions of wordplay, social disarray, overt sexuality, and political satire. One of his musicals, *Gorilla Queen,* taking its cue from vintage *Tarzan, King Kong,* and other jungle movies, found commercial success in an Off-Broadway move. Now, in 1973, he and his brother were opening their own theater to produce Ron's plays themselves. They'd come to our show to entice Donald into designing their first production, *Boy on the Straight-Back Chair.* Donald said yes and we were all off to the Theatre of the Lost Continent.

The Jane West Hotel was a large flophouse on the corner of Jane Street and the West Side Highway in the Village. Harvey Tavel used his New York City high-school-French-teacher salary to finance the transformation of the hotel's ballroom. *Boy* opened but closed quickly, leaving the Tavels with an empty theater. We stayed on to produce a variety of projects. Harvey directed a production of two of Ron's early scripts, *Kitchenette,* starring Mary Woronov of *Chelsea Girls* and me, coupled with *The Life of Juanita Castro,*

That's Mary Woronov, Nancy McCormick, Fred Savage,
with me on the potty in Ron Tavel's *Kitchenette*.

starring Warhol's Ondine. Next up was Donald's all-male production of *The Trojan Women*, starring more Warhol personalities like
Jackie Curtis, who'd make her entrance as Hera riding on a motor-
cycle; Mario Montez as the only Cassandra you'll ever hear with
a thick Puerto Rican accent; again Ondine, this time as Menelaus
and Poseidon; and me as Andromache.

Ondine and I were hanging out in the auditorium during a technical rehearsal one day when Harvey played a recording of Maria
Callas singing *Tosca* over the house system. Ondine began to
scream with excitement. When I told him that I really didn't know
much, or care much, about opera, he gasped, "Say goodbye to the
world as you know it."

For two hours he translated *Tosca* line by line, opening the world
of opera to me and introducing me to the genius of Maria Callas.
She and opera have been part of my inner soundtrack ever since.

The Trojan Women was a hit, saving the theater for that season.
I relished my role as Andromache. How often do you get to fling
your child toward an enemy soldier while screaming, "Take him.
Cast him down if so you will. Feast on his flesh! God has destroyed
me, and I cannot save my son." Neil Simon doesn't give you that
kind of shit to say.

Here I am getting all dramatical
in *The Trojan Women.*

I still didn't think of myself as an actor. When the Tavels insisted that I appear in their next production, *Vinyl Visits an FM Station,* I was uneasy. This called for an actor who did plays. I did shows, but I agreed. Set in a Vietnamese radio studio during the war, it was a brutal satire on political propaganda. I played a POW strapped to a parrot perch, blinders over my eyes, a gag shoved down my throat and perpetually tortured to speak. Leggy legend Mary Woronov once again took the lead, but also in the cast were two unknowns a breath away from stardom: Danny DeVito and Rhea Perlman played evil henchmen. The production was a zero and the theater steadily slid back into its flophouse roots. A lifetime later I heard DeVito regale a late-night talk show host with a story about a door that connected our balcony to the hotel. Quite often, homeless gents snuck in to sleep up there, and when nature required, they'd relieve themselves over the railing onto theatergoers below. That production closed the Theater of the Lost Continent. The following season Danny was cast in an Off-Broadway revival of *One Flew Over the Cuckoo's Nest* at the Mercer Arts Center, and Hollywood took it from there.

Thirty years later, he cast me in two movies he directed. *Duplex* was uneventful, but I was positive that *Death to Smoochy* would be a huge hit, which proves how little I know. It was a satirical comedy with a cast led by Robin Williams and Edward Norton, both big draws at the time. The script was dark, dumb, fun, allotting plenty of opportunities for both leads to go wild. Also featured was Jon Stewart in a rare acting gig. I was most impressed with the movie's lighting design. Shooting in shadowy locations, the designer used saturated color in complementary hues to transform the world of children's television from rainbow happiness to the unnervingly conflicted. Being on set was visually exciting. But then, when I saw the movie, the colors had been diluted and dulled. Maybe it was all too much when they viewed the footage.

I remember filming in Times Square, right outside what was then the Toys "R" Us megastore. It was an all-night shoot, which costs plenty, so there's no cancelling even if you get hit with a blizzard. We got hit with a blizzard. We needed to shoot a scene in which I, a tough gangster type, threaten the life of Edward Norton, a wimp, in the back of my stretch limo. They put it off as long as they could, hoping the snowfall would let up so you could see something beyond the car windows, but it was not to be. The sun was about to rise and the snow showed no sign of stopping. Danny soldiered on and shot the scene, and then my close-ups, but by the time he turned around for Edward's singles, everyone was exhausted. Danny took me aside and said, "Poor Edward's in the back of the car, practically dead. All I need is a close-up of a truly frightened look on his face and we can wrap for the night. I'm counting on you. Get in there and say something really scary so I can grab the shot and we can get the fuck out of here."

"I'll try," I said, racking my brain for something that would frighten an actor who'd played opposite Marlon Brando, Robert De Niro, and Frances McDormand. Danny put me in place, almost on top of Edward, squeezing him into the corner of the car's back-seat. I brought my face inches from his, as close as I could without getting in the frame, and as soon as Danny called "Action," I began to darkly hiss into his mouth:

"You so pretty. I wish't I had a doll of you. I wish't I had a doll of you and I would fuck it." Edward's face turned white. Danny hollered "Cut!"

Edward sprang out from under me and bolted from the car, off into the blinding snowstorm. Not that we run in the same circles, but I don't think he's ever spoken to me again.

Danny does like the look of danger. In another scene, which I think was excised from the movie, he had me threaten Jon Stewart by standing on his privates. He laid poor Jon on the ground and had me tower over him, the heel of my shoe dangerously close to his genitalia. Of course, they placed rails for me to lean on so I wouldn't accidentally slip and destroy his future lineage, but it was still a scary prospect for Jon, and, just as soon as Danny called "Cut!" Mr. Stewart sprang out from under me. Although we don't run in the same circles, I don't believe he's ever spoken to me again.

13

LEAVING HOME

1973

I told Ron Tavel a dream I'd had. I was lying on my bed reading when the closet door swung open and my clothing, still on hangers, began to sway from side to side. Shirts and pants and jackets and shoes suddenly danced their way out of the closet, through the bedroom door, down the stairs and out of my house. I floated after them. Ron smiled at me and said, "I guess it's time to leave home."

The Tavels and I became very close during those years. Ron suffered from agoraphobia, limiting his wanderings within a mile from his SoHo digs. I, who was his eager student in all cultural subjects from Carmen Miranda to Shakespeare, was a willing service pet. I provided safe passage wherever he wanted to go, from a visit to his mother in Brighton Beach to a guest stint as playwright-in-residence at the Actors Studio where, after the final performance of the piece Ron created for me, *Gypsy*'s original Miss Mazeppa, Faith Dane, and other students, Lee Strasberg himself asked me, "What were you supposed to be playing?"

To which I answered, "A freshly ironed shirt."

By now, fully immersed in the Off-Off-Broadway community, I was being offered roles at every theater, accepting as many as I could juggle. I remember a holiday season when I rehearsed a show at Theatre Genesis during the day, performed in an eight o'clock play at La MaMa and a ten p.m. show at NYTE, and then sang a song in WPA's midnight Christmas revue.

78

I loved performing in the Ridiculous ensemble. We encrusted our faces with glitter, after which we mostly ran amok, annoying the hell out of the principal actors. Vaccaro breathed pandemonium, disorder, and outrage. He asked me to be in his production of *Satyricon*. Because I was crafty, he had me construct the glow-in-the-dark phalluses and vaginas for the chorus to wear during the huge orgy scene. We'd all pile into a pit created in the center of the theater, where, lit with black light, we indulged in an orgy. Because of the black light neither the audience nor Vaccaro ever caught us slipping off our glow-in-the-dark genitalia, waving them around overhead while actually having sex right there onstage. Ellen Stewart came to our dress rehearsal and seeing the phalluses insisted on knowing who made them.

"I did," I confessed.

"Mr. Fierstein, I don't know who you are trying to impress, but you will cut down every one of those things by two inches. Two inches off the top or this show don't open."

One day Ellen ordered me to follow her up the three flights to her apartment. She plopped down onto a pressed-back oak dining chair and pronounced, "My *baby* ain't wearing bloomers no more."

She grunted, shook her head, and scratched the skull under her wig. Smoking had taken its toll and, as with the accent, she used her panting to stall her speech while forming her thoughts. "Look at them, Mr. Fierstein. You look at my children in their lipstick and bloomers. You know I let them do all that because that's all they can do. And if they didn't do it here, they'd just go off and do it somewheres else. Not you. You can do more. I don't know how much more, but we'll never find out until we get them bloomers off you. So, no more of that. It's done. Okay?"

Where was all of this going?

"Members of the Negro Ensemble Company are doing a show here and they want you to be in it."

"Are you kidding?" I said excitedly.

"All right, then. I'll tell them yes."

What they didn't tell Ellen was that the gig involved playing one of two "white devils" who'd appear in clown-and-glitter makeup—

Irene Stein took this shot of
me in the East Village.

not quite the new leaf she wanted me to turn. The play was written by *Saturday Night Live* original-cast member Garrett Morris. My memory's low on details, but I recall the comradery of working with director Bill Duke and a cast that included Obba Babatundé and his brother, Akinwole, and Frank Adu. We shared a dressing room filled with the sensual scents of incense, candles, body oils, inciting an intoxicating joy. I had to sing a song I'd never heard before, "If You Don't Know Me by Now." I can still feel the warmth of being surrounded by the cast as they taught it to me:

If you don't know me by now
You will never, never, never know me . . .

At this point in my development, I no longer worried about sexuality. I had eased into a groove that allowed me to be whatever the hell whenever the hell. I was comfortable with my gay identity and at ease in a world of gay and lesbian artists. Heterosexuals were outsiders. Even the vast majority of gays, whether in or out of the closet, were only distant cousins. We were the underground, the elite forces of civilization, creators and keepers of art and culture. We were full of ourselves, and the last thing we wanted were apologists diluting the bloodline. In other words, I thought we were hot shit!

Gender felt similarly handled for now. Performing in drag allowed more than enough opportunity to express the female within. Drag was a lot of work! The hair, the makeup, the padding, the styling were exhausting. Being a girl was a full-time job. Being a girl inside a boy's body was a breeze. All I seemed to need was a place to express my female identity and I was sorted. Theater gave me that.

Because I couldn't have cared less about it, college life had also taken a stressless position in my consciousness. The professors I liked were invited to my shows, so they cut me some slack, and I was taking enough credits that I could afford to blow off the ones I didn't like and still graduate. Actually, I missed graduation, thanks to a nasty bout of syphilis which taught me never to let a family doctor dose you for a gay strain of a disease. They don't teach you that in health ed.

That summer, right after my college graduation, Harvey Tavel bought a half-dead VW bus, into which he, Ronald, and I loaded our stuff and took off for a cross-continental tour of Canada. Sometimes the only way to get the damn thing started was to let it roll downhill until the engine caught. Note: the Rockies are only half downhill, which meant that for half of our journey we'd have to push the car to turn it around and let it coast downhill until the motor caught, at which point Harvey would hook a U-turn and return to pick Ron and me up. Harvey did all the driving, Ron did all the talking, and I sent all of the postcards home journaling our adventures.

Ron had planned the trip to research the world of his new play, *Gazelle Boy*, about a feral child raised by nuns in the Northwest. Harvey, desperate for any life-changing moment, was along for the ride. And I was there as royal jester and buffer between the two. It was the summer of the Watergate hearings, and the last thing anyone who loved his country wanted to be was American. With my long hair and East Village wardrobe I thought I'd try to pass as a member of an indigenous tribe, only to learn that some of the gentle, loving people of Canada were not all that gentle or loving to the people whose land they'd stolen. Just on my looks I was barred from quite a few watering holes and restaurants along the way. I fell in love in and with Vancouver. He was an ex-minister of indecipherable denomination who boasted the best weed connection in town. Ron questioned him endlessly for details of religious life he could use in his play. Harvey appreciated his taste in marijuana and invited him along with us everywhere. I was simply lovestruck with this mad, curly-maned stallion who treated me like a beloved possession. If Vancouver had had a rocking theater scene, I might never have returned. It didn't, so I did, but left a piece of my heart on English Bay.

Finally sick of chauffeuring his brother and me around the continent, Harvey ordered us to shut up, pack up, and get our asses into the bus: we were heading home.

Unsatisfied with that adventure as a change of life, Harvey abandoned his roach-infested East Village apartment and bought a brownstone in Park Slope, Brooklyn. His best friend/ex-lover, Norman Glick, occupied the top floor. Harvey had the library and bedroom on the second, and he offered me the unfinished basement, rent free, if I would fix it up into something habitable. I never got it to the level of a legit garden apartment, but by the time I was done it was homey. The walls were whitewashed cinderblock, the exposed overhead pipes served as an expressway for the occasional mouse, and my boiler-room closet housed the asbestos-clad furnace. Which would you rather die of—cold or lung cancer? But I collaged the tiny bathroom with photos from *After Dark* magazine, I constructed walls out of discarded doors salvaged from dumpsters, and I found that a gallon of hot-pink paint could brighten the dingiest concrete floors. Earning the tiny stipends experimental theater paid, I could never have afforded more than a room elsewhere. Harvey allowed me to have a home. My parents, wanting to encourage my independence, did what they could to help me on my way without looking like they were still supporting me. Jackie sometimes dropped by with a loaf of bread or random leftovers or even canned goods that she bought in "error" and would never use. My father miraculously ran across furniture that this or that friend was tossing out. His greatest find was a pair of art nouveau wrought-iron garden gates lying around in someone's garage. Heavily ornamented with flowering foliage, nude male hunters aimed their arrows at deer that leapt above the ivy-filled arches. I nearly fainted when he pulled them from his car trunk. I hung them as a headboard, and they became my most treasured possession. That almost garden apartment was coming along. Eventually it would be the love nest of a few of my greatest heartbreaks.

14

IN SEARCH OF THE
COBRA JEWELS
1973

Harvey was directing Jackie Curtis's new play, *Amerika Cleopatra*, at the WPA Theater on the Bowery. Jackie wrote a hysterically funny role for me—Incredible, mother of Cleopatra, who barges in on her Las Vegas honeymoon demanding Caesar pay for her underage daughter's virginity. Ron Tavel and I were hanging around on a break when he casually said, "You should write a play."

I looked at him incredulously.

"You act in all of these shows, most of which aren't very good. I'm sure, if you tried, you could do as well. You're smart. You're funny . . ."

"You're nuts."

"Why?"

"I can't spell. I can barely type. I get the letters backwards . . ."

With great sincerity he said, "There are people who make two dollars an hour who'll fix your typing. You go ahead and write."

Much like the art teachers who freed me, Ron unlocked a cage into which I'd put myself. Neither of us knew if I could write, but without his permission I never would have tried. I don't remember much about my first attempt other than showing it to Ron, Harvey, and Donald. Donald spared the other two from having to tell me it sucked. He tore it up and said, "Did you ever hear the expression 'Write what you know'? Do that."

What the fuck did I know? I knew . . . I know! I typed:
Act 1, scene 1. The Trucks. Midnight.
I wrote lyrics for an opening song about having sex in the Trucks.

Okay. So what else did I know? Harry's apartment! Yes. I began
to fashion a fantasy with a chorus of Day-Glo-painted cockroaches
and a Harry-like character ruling over them in his secret lair. Like
my first attempts at painting, not knowing what I was doing, I
mimicked and filched from those around me. I was not a natural.
My goal was to please Ron, Harry, and Donald. Nothing more.
There was a poem Harry had given me to recite:

Death has embraced me more warmly,
More formally on more occasions
Than most lovers.

Why not bring that character of Death onstage for Harry to battle? I wrote that role for Harvey. And then I did my best Ron imita-
tion, creating a leather-daddy character based on him. I brought
out that old Technicolor-movie stalwart Maria Montez as guard-
ian of the Cobra Jewels. And just like that, *In Search of the Cobra
Jewels: An Archeohistorical Poeseurie in Two Short Acts* was now
typed out on onion skin, with two carbon copies that I gave to Ron
and Donald to read.

Donald looked at the pastiche I'd cobbled and found something
he could stage. "But you can't be in it," he declared. "You have to
watch the show, watch the audience, and figure out how what you
say affects them. You can run the lights."

He took the play to Bastiano's, the last surviving of the coffee-
house theaters, where, with Dick Briggs's generosity, he put it on.
Harry was more than willing to play himself, Harvey Tavel signed
on as Death, and Ron played the sadist. Mario Montez didn't have
to be asked twice to play Maria Montez, and whenever anyone
else said they wanted to be in it, I wrote them a role. Alexis Del
Lago, dressed in her best Dietrich tuxedo, performed the prologue;
Agosto Machado played me; and Flash Storm played Russel. The
ensemble was made up of street friends and adventurers, includ-

ing Wilhelmina Ross, who would find immortality as a model in Warhol's drag-queen-portrait series, *Ladies and Gentlemen,* before passing with AIDS.

Donald designed a spiderweb setting that encompassed the three-quarter-round theater, and a friend, Jon Heward, composed the music. Using the skills I'd learned back at A&D, I created the poster, spelling each word out with press type, letter by letter, and swiped illustrations from a copy of Dante's *Inferno* to hype the text.

Sorry I wasn't better with a camera, but hopefully you can make out Mario Montez fleeing on the right, Harry Koutoukas in his striped robe center, and Harvey Tavel draped in black as Death toward the left. Agosto Machado and Flash Storm are down left during this rehearsal.

The opening-night audience was packed with underground celebs. It was such an event that we drew the attention of the police. Arthur Bell, culture writer for *The Village Voice,* was arrested for holding another man's hand as they crossed the street. You read that correctly. It was 1973, and you could still be arrested for holding another man's hand in public. Michael Smith, theater critic for the *Voice,* showed up to review. This was a highly unusual move, given I was a first-time writer having his first performance anywhere, but the spotlight had nothing to do with me. Michael worshipped Ron's writing and intellect. His opinion of Donald, ever since *Superfreak*, was less than embracive. Whatever Michael thought of Harry paled beside the need Harry attached to attention from Michael. The ego-feeding frenzy among the denizens of Off-Off-Broadway was a melodrama all its own.

Act 1 of the play ended with Harry delivering a monologue entreating Death. In an unscripted move Harry pulled a razor blade from his pocket and sliced open his wrists. BLACKOUT. INTERMISSION. Having practiced this move before, Harry only scratched his skin deep enough to draw a bit of blood; still, Donald chased him to the dressing room screaming, "If you do that at every performance, by the end of the run you will be nothing but chopped meat!" Harry returned to the stage for act 2 and completed his performance as directed.

Mr. Smith took to his typewriter. "Once again Donald L. Brooks has done a production that gets to me so personally that I can hardly talk about it coherently. Once again he has concocted an indecipherable mixture of brilliance, ineptitude, and nearly pathological acting-out . . . First I was entertained, then I was frightened, then I didn't know where I was and my mind was left burning with contradictions. What kind of theater is that?"

Mr. Smith then accused me of ripping off Harry's style. Duh. What about Ron's, Jack Smith's, and Vaccaro's? And hadn't I self-identified as a poseur in the title?

I said to Ron, "Well, I don't have to do that again."

"You absolutely do," he answered. "Whether you realize it or not you've done something new. It's their job to catch up. Yours is to keep going."

What did I think of writing? Even at this infantile stage I found something titillating about typing a bunch of words, handing them to someone, and having them brought to life. I still feel that kick at first readings of scripts. Often, I am so excited to hear the words out loud that I can't judge what's good or bad.

15

FREAKY PUSSY

1974

A career in underground theater guaranteed I'd stay penniless. Most people around me supplemented their incomes with food stamps or welfare. Once a harmless way to pay the rent, dealing pot was made treacherous in May 1973 when Governor Rockefeller passed a set of statutes with mandatory sentences for minor drug offenses. A member of the Playhouse of the Ridiculous, caught in a sting selling two ounces of pot, found himself in prison for the next fifteen years.

Although I worked hard, without Harvey's generosity I would have been homeless. I took whatever employment I could find. I sold encyclopedias door-to-door, waited tables at a retirement home, hung coats at the Metropolitan Opera, and painted 3D flowers in a lamp factory. Needlepoint was a current craze and, specializing in movie-star portraits, I painted original canvases to be sewn for a store called Pandemonium. Mr. Bruce of Serendipity Two hired me to embroider folky designs on denim clothing. I created wardrobe pieces for *The Tonight Show*'s Doc Severinsen, and Jackie O, and my brother commissioned an embroidered shirt as a gift to John Denver. My brother helped me out quite often. He even hired me to strip paint from the windows of his brownstone.

I wasn't taking very good care of myself. Since childhood I'd had troublesome teeth. Living Cheetos-to-cheek, I now had several bad cavities that caused almost unbearable pain. I OD'd on over-the-counter numbing gels and swallowed aspirin like mints. Booze, I found, could quell the pain enough for me to fall asleep, so I got into the habit of soaking my mouth with Harvey's scotch just before bed. Eventually my next-door neighbor, Maureen, insisted that I see her dentist. A kind man with offices in the Empire State Building, he understood starving young'uns and graciously let me pay my bill over time. I was finally pain free. Becoming alcohol free was so much trickier.

Now it was time to see if I had a second play in me. NYU's gentrification was devouring Village real estate, and its students lurked around every corner with telescopic lenses shooting the locals as if on photo safari. I once heard a French chef say that American food sucks because we scrub the flavor from our pots and pans. New York City was getting that kind of cleansing. Subway men's rooms were their own subculture. Much like the Trucks, T-Rooms, as they were known, were frequented by gents living on the down low, looking for quick relief. Transit cops were a constant danger (unless they were horny), so regulars carried empty shopping bags that they'd open inside the stall and stand within, so that anyone spying under the closed door saw only one pair of feet. In the name of redevelopment, Mayor Abe Beame had all of the New York subway system's T-Rooms padlocked, and I had the idea for my next play.

A straight couple leases a subway bathroom with plans of turning it into the new hot underground restaurant. However, that particular T-Room is home base for a group of transvestite prostitutes. Unable to fight the tide of gentrification, and having nowhere else to go, the girls commit suicide, one by one, in protest: an IRT Masada. Layered with the usual camp references, Stella and Stanley were the names of the restaurateurs, and I was Stella's long-lost sister, Blanche Does Boys, the leader of the hookers. Did I mention it was a musical? My big brother provided the score, which was much more memorable than my lyrics.

Freaky Pussy: A T-Room Musical was booked into the small Fortune Theatre on East Fourth Street. Harvey Tavel directed on a set Donald L. Brooks created almost entirely of cardboard and duct

French photographer Gilles Larrain invited a mess of
us to his studio to be photographed for a book called
Idols. He shot my original concept for *Freaky Pussy*.

tape. I made my first entrance struggling through a seven-foot-tall
vagina to the strains of Richard Strauss's "Dance of the Seven Veils"
as if being birthed. Once free, I spoke my first line: "That, I repeat,
that was my complete and final statement to the press. Get out!"

With the play described thusly you might think it a socially or
politically worthy endeavor. It wasn't. It was mostly very crass,
obscene, and raw. The lyrics to the final song were:

I don't get it
I just don't get it
I don't see the point at all.

But my favorite line was spoken right before that. As my character was being dragged off to the Tombs (NYC's legendary jail), my

sister stopped me to ask, "There's just one thing I've got to know. How did you become a star?"

With a wry look over my shoulder I answered, "I work for nothing."

Sue me, but I still love that double entendre.

Freaky Pussy was my sophomore effort, and like any adolescent, I was acting out, but at least attempting to be original. I'd scored points for placing a scene at the Trucks in *Cobra Jewels*, and although sweet Terrence McNally was developing *The Ritz*, a farce set in a gay bathhouse, sex in the Off-Off movement was playful, naughty fun. No one swallowed. Writing a musical set in a subway bathroom where libidinous acts were more than implied would certainly nudge the political discussion in an adult direction. There was nothing polite, no excuses were offered, no rules were obeyed in *Freaky Pussy*. The in-your-face sexuality was as much my declaration of independence from the accepted as it was

The cast of *Freaky Pussy*. Notable are Donald L. Brooks as the cop, Clio Young as the toothless hooker, and Luis Macia in the T-shirt. I'm the hooker in the feathered collar.

an exposé of an unseen world. The show was an immediate hit, but something puzzled me. Although there were plenty of gay men in the house, the audience contained a majority of straight folks, mostly women in groups. I certainly appreciated their attention, but I thought I was addressing an entirely different demographic. I wondered: was my personal revolution somehow supporting or echoing the struggle of women out to claim their sexuality? I recall several of my lesbian friends telling me that they only got off on gay male porn. Convinced as they were that they were all being abused, seeing women onscreen made them feel uncomfortable. Far more enjoyable to watch men exploited.

Donald cobbled together an electric sign, the center of which had my face spinning around and around inside of a green glowing vagina. It hung in a place of pride in Phebe's restaurant until enough complaints brought it down.

Censorship was also enacted by my brother. Although he wrote the score, he once again declared this show unsuitable for parental attendance. He made the right call.

16

FLATBUSH TOSCA

1975

I don't remember how it came about, but Harvey Tavel was asked to direct the American premiere of Shakespeare's *The Two Noble Kinsmen*, suspected to have actually been written by John Fletcher. We graced this dud of a play with a dud of a production. I delivered the prologue, played the dance teacher, and finished it up by reciting the epilogue, which began:

I would now ask ye how ye like the play,
But as it is with schoolboys, cannot say.
I am cruel fearful . . .

The show was so awful that some nights the audience—not *most* of the audience, *all* of the audience—deserted well before the curtain. Rewriting the epilogue was irresistible:

I would now ask ye how ye like the play,
But cannot since you have all gone away!

I then skipped merrily offstage.

The Mercer Arts Center had several performing spaces besides ours. Genet's *Our Lady of the Flowers* was playing in one and the New York Dolls gave concerts in another when one night, after the building was shuttered, the roof collapsed, destroying the complex. Michael Feingold, another theater critic at the *Voice*, credited Shakespeare's ire toward my performance for the disaster. I thought it was a ridiculous assertion. Why would Shakespeare care what I did to Fletcher?

Megan Terry gave us two wonderful plays to perform as an evening. Harvey once again directed, and we put them on at Theatre Genesis. In *The Pioneer* I was the wealthy mother of a young woman being primed to land a successful husband. In *Pro Game* I played a very different mother. With three football-loving sons, I was a Boston ballbuster who'd do anything for her boys, including performing a full-bodied striptease as the halftime show. The best parts of that evening were the three brilliant performers playing my sons: Agosto Machado, Jayne Haynes, and the awe-inspiring Kathleen Chalfant as my eldest.

Movie types invaded our world. *The Godfather Part II* was being filmed on the Lower East Side. The Fortune Theatre, where we had done *Freaky Pussy*, housed a small, abandoned opera house on its upper floor. Built to entertain the newly arrived Italian immigrants, it had fallen into disrepair. The movie magic makers from Paramount descended like Cinderella's fairy godmothers and restored the derelict little gem with frescoed walls and velvet-curtained stage. Filming complete, the theater's owners approached me to write something suitable to reopen the space. I wasn't surprised they came to me, I was flabbergasted! I was about to answer "But I'm no playwright" when I realized that claiming to be an innocent who only dabbled in theater was getting old. It was time to commit or get gone.

How about an adaptation of Puccini's *Tosca*? Instead of her being an opera diva performing at the royal residence, my Tosca would be a drag queen performing at a club called the Queen's Palace. Her lover, Cavaradossi, would be a small-time drug dealer, and I'd transform Scarpia, the chief of police, into a vice detective with a yen for Tosca.

And so *Flatbush Tosca: Fear the Painted Devil* was born. The music was a blend of Puccini and that of an opera-loving friend, Don Crusor. Ned Levy played the score live on a piano in the pit.

We even performed Puccini's act 2 finale complete, and in Italian. In my best Callas style, after stabbing Scarpia to death, I placed a candle on either side of his body and intoned, *"E avanti a lui tremava tutta Flatbush!"*—And before him all of Flatbush trembled!

Flo Tosca (me) makes a deal with vice detective Scarpia (Norman Jacob) in this scene from *Flatbush Tosca.*

It was a bomb. Not an atomic bomb, but the only people who really enjoyed it were opera queens. It yearned to be the kind of camp adaptation that Charles Ludlam, employing his arsenal of wit and travesty, did so superbly. Great clowns touch you even as they make you laugh. They are human, maybe too human, and it's seeing our own absurdities that both amuses and moves us. I realized that's what was missing from my work. I was taking myself too seriously. I demanded the audience see things my way. I forgot what I had learned going to the theater as a child: this was a conversation, not a lecture. Without inviting the audience to be in on the joke, *Flatbush Tosca* stood its ground flaccidly.

That was no way to change the world. What d'ya know? I was becoming someone who aimed to change the world. My brother gave this one another parental thumbs-down; we played our few weeks and moved on.

17

THE HAUNTED HOST

1975

Neil Flanagan was a stalwart of the Off-Off-Broadway scene. A marvelous actor and director, he'd been around since Cino. He was directing two plays in rep to be produced in Provincetown's Town Hall. The first was an early work by Lanford Wilson, *The Madness of Lady Bright*, in which I'd play, of all things, a queen going mad. Neil starred in the original production to great acclaim, hence his affection for the piece, but I never felt it held up as anything more than a relic of those early days.

The Haunted Host was another story altogether. Written in 1964 by Robert Patrick, it also debuted at Caffe Cino, but this play celebrated, even lauded, being gay. A brilliantly witty gay playwright is struggling to get over the suicide of his lover when a young straight man, sent over by a mutual friend, knocks at his door seeking career advice. It just so happens the boy is a dead ringer for the lost love. The two then spend a night wit-wrestling in an apartment as filled with detritus as the lead character's brain.

This was a play ahead of its time. Nowhere to be found is the guilt-ridden, tragic, apologetic, second-class homosexual we've all come to know from that period. Robert Patrick gave us a character whose problem isn't being gay, it's being human.

The play was a riotous joy to perform, and thankfully, the audiences were delighted to watch. After our summer run in P-Town our producer arranged a move to the Charles Playhouse in Boston.

I had to shake my head to let this new reality settle in. I was going to be in a real show at a real theater and even get my Equity card! I was going to be a professional actor and actually earn a living wage.

A few weeks before I left for Boston I met a guy. An absolute doll. And I met him in the front room of a bar—Keller's, the oldest gay bar in New York City. He stared at me from across the room and did the one thing gay men are not supposed to do when cruising—he smiled. And oh, what a smile he had. It made me blush. He crossed the room and over the din of the jukebox said, "My name is Charlie."

His voice sounded raspy, so I asked if he had a cold. "No," he answered. "I'm deaf."

"If you're deaf, how did you hear me ask if you had a cold?"

"Do you want to get out of here?" he asked.

Charlie was six foot six with a tidy goatee and a gentle manner that could charm the bloomers off a clothesline. Thankfully he was a marvelous lip reader, allowing us to chat the entire walk from west to east. He was a marriage counselor for deaf couples. Recently divorced, he'd only just come out. He shared an apartment with two roommates, a dancer and an actor, living over what had been the Fillmore East on Second Avenue. I don't remember what it was called at that time, but it was still a rock venue and it was loud, which made it both affordable and the perfect apartment for a trio of hearing-impaired gents. They slept like babies. I never closed my eyes before four, but Charlie made up for it. I sucked at sign language thanks to my dyslexia. The signs representing whole words were okay, but the finger spelling was always too fast for me. By the time I could put together a few letters, the signer was on to the next word. Charlie was proud that I tried so hard to learn, but when we'd go out with his friends it was obvious that they disapproved of this mixed marriage. If you think racial jokes are cruel, have a deaf person relay the gags they tell about hearing people. Charlie showed me how to combine the signs for the letters I, L, and Y into a single gesture meaning I Love You. When writing to me or leaving a note he always sketched a little hand in that position next to his name. I adopted my own version of the ILY sign into my signature, where it's been ever since. Over the years, some have mistaken it for a bunny and others as a cock and balls. It's one of those situations that says more about the reader than the writer.

Charlie and I had a lovely time right up to my Boston departure. There were no computers in those days, so when apart we communicated through the kindness of familiars. Dr. Barbara Starrett—later one of the leading specialists working with AIDS patients—was a dear friend who lived with her deaf lover, Anne, an illustrator and artist. I could call on her to relay a message via TTY, a telephone with a screen and keyboard, to Charlie. Clumsy and less than intimate, we managed to stay connected. My departure was a teary one. I was Charlie's first boyfriend. He was not happy about my leaving.

The stage manager, my costar, and I shared a Beacon Hill tenement apartment through a winter so bitter that we all came down with flu. We struggled on together to survive the Boston weather until one Friday evening, just before half-hour call to curtain, when I was summoned to the production office. Charlie was due to arrive the next morning. He was driving up to spend the week with me. Rushing to the office, I assumed there was a problem with his arrangements. I was wrong. It was my Uncle Irwin on the phone. My father had died that afternoon.

Your brain goes funny when you get that kind of news. My eye caught sight of the wall calendar, Friday the thirteenth, a day my superstitious father always avoided. It was also the day before my parents' wedding anniversary. As it happened, I had gone home for a visit that past Monday on my day off. I brought a cake from a Boston bakery. My brother, having the same idea, bought a Carvel ice cream cake, and the four of us celebrated together, never imagining it would be the last time.

My aunt and uncle lived in a Boston suburb. They told me to wait at the theater and they'd come pick me up. Together we'd drive to Brooklyn. I have a vague memory of dialing and speaking briefly to my mom while still in the office. After that, not knowing what else to do, I went onstage and performed the show. I could not shake that lyric from "There's No Business Like Show Business" out of my head. You know the one:

> You get word before the show has started
> That your favorite uncle died at dawn.
> Top of that your pa and ma have parted,
> You're broken-hearted, but you go on.

Uncle Irwin opened the back door of his car for me while my roommates promised to take good care of Charlie. I hurried into the car and Irwin handed me a bottle of Chivas, which I nursed all the way home. He told me what he knew: that dad was at work arguing with someone over the phone and his blood pressure got the best of him. My father's temper could soar from zero to a hundred in a heartbeat, but then it was over and he'd let it go. Those explosions fascinated me even when I was the cause. My brother and I are both capable of exploding in that way. We are our father's sons.

When I got home, I'd never seen my mother as angry as she was. Tight-faced and focused, she busied herself pulling papers from a file drawer, tossing them to my brother to deal with.

I came up behind her and gently asked, "Did you see him?"

"Of course I saw him! What kind of a question is that?"

"At the hospital?"

"No. At the dance."

She left the file cabinet and walked into the living room. She looked around, nodding to herself, taking inventory, mentally listing what more needed to be done. Finally she settled, lighting by a wing chair for support.

"He was on a gurney. They cut his clothes off. He was so cold. I tried to warm him up. 'Irving, I'm here. Your radiator is here.' I rubbed his hands. I kissed him. I wanted to climb . . ."

The silence that followed was excruciatingly painful. Trying to breathe air back into the room, I said, "I went ahead and did my show tonight. Before Irwin and Gail got there, I didn't know what else to do, so. . . . I did my show. At one point, I don't know, I looked out in the house and I could swear Daddy was there . . ."

She cut me down with surgical precision, "Stop. If your father was going to appear to anyone, do you really think it would be you and not me?"

"I was only—"

"Go inside with the others. Go."

Then she stopped me. Her voice softened. "What am I going to do at the funeral? You know how I am. How will I . . . ?"

Ever since the death of her father, whenever Jackie was anywhere near a funeral, her nervous system hijacked her motor skills and she began to involuntarily bounce on her feet. Up and down, her head and arms jerked and shook. It didn't affect her speech or reason, only her body. She stopped attending funerals.

"What's the difference?" she answered, obviously not counting on my advice. "So I'll shake."

That she did. Ron and I walked her down the aisle of the funeral home. She hung onto us as she shook and smiled, assuring everyone, "This is just me. Nothing to worry about. I'm fine."

Years later, at my mother's gravesite, it came my turn to ceremoniously toss soil onto her coffin. The moment the shovel touched my hand I felt my legs go and I began to bounce as she did. I summoned every bit of control trying not to let anyone see. But Uncle Irwin did; he put his hands on top of mine, helping me spread the dirt onto the grave. Hiding behind the bending and rocking movements traditional to Jewish prayer, I was able to finish the service and climb into the limousine for the ride back to her apartment. I now avoid funerals as well.

My roommates were wonderful with Charlie, and he was in fine spirits when he picked me up at the airport on my return to Boston. We'd still have a few days together before he was due back in New York. He was so sweet, loving and open, while I was such a mess. No matter how hard I tried, I could not express what I was feeling to him, and he was equally frustrated trying to comfort and care for me. Our relationship was simply too new, our communication too tenuous to survive those extraordinary circumstances. Maybe if we'd been in the same city, or were able to speak on the phone . . . ? But I needed someone to whom I could pour my heart out, and the language barrier was too great. I drifted away from Charlie. I gave up. I was not strong enough to deal with our differences. After a while we lost touch. I'd get news from time to time. He and his roommate Al-B put a comedy act together and performed at schools and conventions. In 1998 word reached me that he had died due to a chronic condition lingering from early childhood. As I understood, it was the same disease that took his hearing. But then I ran into his other roommate, Sam, who said it was AIDS. He told me that Charlie never engaged with another boyfriend. Our failure had been too painful for him. I wrote about Charlie in the opening monologue of *Torch Song Trilogy* and hoped that he would know about it and understand how much I cared for him. When Michael Urie was performing the revival, someone sent him a photo of Charlie with his roommate Al-B. Michael gave it to me. It's the only photo of Charlie that I own.

For the next months after my father's death, I split my time between Boston and Brooklyn. Grief was changing Jackie. Her retirement plans were gone. She, who had always been so resolute, softened. She tried to keep her opinions to herself. She told me that she couldn't afford to lose anyone else.

"Do you cry a lot?" I asked.

"Laugh and the world laughs with you, cry and . . ."

I nodded my understanding.

"I have to be a better person," she said. "If I want to see your father again, I have to be a better person."

She considered that and then added, "Maybe I'll get a dog."

Back in Boston I spent more and more time in the bar of the cabaret below the Charles Playhouse. Although I'd depended on the pain-numbing qualities of alcohol during my time in dental distress and used booze liberally to dull the emotional sting of losing my dad, I mostly nursed cans of beer in bars or at parties. Besides the expense of bar drinks, I never liked the taste of booze, and wine gave me *agita*. I was a lousy candidate for alcoholism. I was once in London meeting the director John Schlesinger at his gentlemen's club when a waiter asked what I'd have. Not being a gentlemen's club drinker, I mumbled, "I guess I'll have a beer."

The waiter looked down upon me even more than he had before and said, "Beer drinkers are generally discouraged at the door."

The theater bartender created a cocktail for me that he dubbed Harvey's Lemonade. It was a silly, girly drink, but it did the trick. "What gives it the kick?" I asked.

The bartender fetched a glass and a bottle. "Southern Comfort," he said, pouring me a straight shot.

That was the beginning of my longest love affair. It was sweet as soda but warmed my insides like a campfire. From then on it was nothing but Southern Comfort for me, one hundred proof, on the rocks—"And don't be stingy, baby," as Garbo once famously purred.

When *Host* closed, it was back to Brooklyn, back to my basement, back on unemployment. One beautiful spring day I took a different walking route home and happened upon the city animal shelter, where I adopted a little white mutt, and having recently enjoyed the life of Chopin as told in the movie *A Song to Remember*, I named her George Sand.

18

FUCKING AS A SOLO SPORT

1976

I entered another of my dreidel-spinning periods; two performances at night, rehearsing a third by day. Ellen grabbed me in
the hallway and said I needed to attend a business meeting the
next morning at nine. I just looked at her. I wasn't going to get to
bed until four, and then I'd have to be back at nine? I decided to go
another route. I'd step out to the bars after my shows, hopefully
hook up with someone local, and spare myself the *schlep* back and
forth from Brooklyn.

After the last show I showered, slung my book bag over my shoulder, and started my journey barhopping east to west. I stopped at
all the usual spots: Boots & Saddle was dead; the Ninth Circle was
full of too-young men who probably still lived at home; Julius' was
full of too-old men who probably lived in a home; I knew everyone
at the Ramrod and Keller's was empty. My options were dwindling.
The International was a bar located a bit north of the gay cluster.
Nicknamed the Stud it had one feature other bars lacked—a back
room. At some point the management thought it would be fun to
offer movies a few nights a week in this useless, windowless black
space to draw in customers. Well, you know how boys are. As soon
as the lights went out the zippers came down and renting movies
was a waste of money. The International Stud became a popular
indoor alternative to the Trucks. I hiked over there but didn't like

anyone in the back room so I pulled a stool up to the front room bar and had a nightcap with Chickie, the bartender, before renewing my search over at the Trucks. Ah, the Trucks, where hope lingered until sunrise! I'd barely entered the alley when I was grabbed from behind by a pair of strong arms. The stranger pulled me toward him, as close as two bodies can get in a standing position, and before I could regain my balance, he was inside of me. Pleasurable or not, it ran contrary to my plan. This was not going to score me a local bed for the night. *Maybe if I talked to him . . . ?* Adjusting my position, I tried to engage him in conversation. I was repaid with a slap to the shoulder. I tried again and again was rebuked. I know, I know: fucking, yes; talking, no. He hadn't dragged his ass over here at four in the morning to chat. He needed to get off. He sought release. Impersonal, commitment-free, giddyap-let's-go, express-lane, boy-on-boy, hot-time, orgasm-achieving, tension-relieving, good old sex! When all was done and nothing said, the stranger zipped up and faded into the smoky lavender mist of sunrise, leaving me alone and out of options with four hours yet to kill. I set a sauntering pace back across the island.

Thinking about what had just happened made me sad. Don't get me wrong, I loved the Trucks and the no-nonsense service provided, but still . . . *He could have at least answered me, no? Would it have killed him to admit, just for one moment, that we were two human beings connecting on some level, even if that level was the most animalistic?* Not even a pat on the back for services rendered. Continuing to think about it only made me angrier. *What am I, an object? A convenience?* My outrage then turned again to sadness. *Is impersonal sex all I'm good for? Are my expectations of a relationship unrealistic?*

Before I reached a bench on Sheridan Square my notebook and pen were out, and my thoughts were finding words. They took the form of a monologue in which my character was trying to make a human connection during a less-than-romantic encounter. The thing practically wrote itself. I barely breathed before it was done. Across the top of the first page I scribbled "*The International Stud.*"

What a great feeling of satisfaction, to have written this indictment of sex's dehumanization! This was important stuff. I even imagined a triumphant reception for this as a feminist awakening.

I continued to La MaMa, where a friend had likewise arrived early. I asked if she wanted to hear this thing I'd just written. "Sure," she said.

I began to read, and she began to laugh. I continued to read, and she continued laughing. *What is she laughing at?* The more painful the encounter, the more raucous her laughter. Reciting the last line, I closed my notebook.

"Harvey, that's the funniest thing I've heard in, like, forever. It's great."

I was completely unnerved until it hit me: my exhausted earnestness had achieved the very thing I'd been searching for. Here was the sweet spot of human frailty, the balancing point where the man slipping on a banana peel inspires you to both laugh and offer a helping hand. My friend hadn't missed the pain. She recognized it, or it never would have made her laugh.

Not long afterward I got a call from Crystal Field, head of Theater for the New City. She asked if I had anything to perform in a festival of short plays they were producing to celebrate the Bicentennial. Did I dare try this? Miming being fucked up the ass as a tribute to America's Bicentennial might be questionable, but what the hell? They asked for something and this was what I had. I performed it and was the hit of the whole shebang. So many folks talked about *The International Stud* that I was brought back later in the week to perform an encore.

19

THE INTERNATIONAL STUD

1977

)

The following spring I was back in Boston with Neil Flanagan for an unremarkable revival of Tom Eyen's *The Dirtiest Show in Town*. A shocking entertainment of its time, it labeled pollution, war, and homophobia as obscenities while extolling sex. Its climax was an onstage orgy featuring the entire cast nude but for me. I repeat, unremarkable. Our producer leased an entire building of studio apartments on Beacon Hill and the New York–based cast moved in for the short run. Unpacking, I found a 1950s pressboard lamb, the kind used to decorate a baby's room, on a closet shelf. I tacked it to my front door, announcing, "Welcome to the Nursery. BYOB to suckle."

Eric Concklin was our production stage manager. I'd known him tangentially as a dancer with the original Trockadero Gloxinia Ballet company, a troupe of drag ballerinas who, without comment, performed classic choreography. We shared a sense of humor, a love of theater, a collection of Depression glass, and a passion for crochet. Nations have joined forces on less, but we were both hopeless romantics and in love; he with a boy he'd met and brought back from Paris, me with a member of our company, neither one a bright idea, neither having any future. We made mixtapes for each other, featuring the suicidal love songs of Ruth Etting, Billie Holiday, Judy Garland, Emmylou Harris, anyone with a broken-heart tale to tell. We shared our music, our rants, our bottles, and a ton of laughs.

Repeating a familiar pattern, the show closed soon after receiving lukewarm notices and I was back in New York, back on unemployment, back embroidering clothing, and back to writing. I called my new play *Cannibals Just Don't Know No Better*. In a far-off land lived a homosexual society. The men and women kept segregated homosexual villages, only mingling for procreation. Any resulting offspring was raised within the gender-appropriate village. Tragically, a young boy and girl fall in love and decide to elope. They are quickly recaptured, put on trial, and found guilty of heterosexuality. There is nothing to be done but cook a satisfying dinner and enjoy. I never did get that one produced.

Harvey and I, housemates again, fell into a harmless routine. After work he'd nap, cook himself supper, and then needlepoint on a canvas I'd painted especially for him as he smoked dope in front of the TV until bedtime. Every now and then, bored of the sameness, he'd call down to the basement, "Cover yourself, Tondelayo, we're going to town," and we'd share a shot before heading into Manhattan for a bit of cruising. We'd usually part ways after a beer or two. Duly buzzed, he'd go back to Brooklyn and the comforts of male companionship to be found among the bushes of Prospect Park. I'd stay in the city and go off to the Stud or the Trucks.

I remember going into the back room of the Stud one particular February night less for the intimacy and more for the warmth. It was freezing outside. Drink in one hand, cigarette in the other, I felt my way through the crowd. There was a man, tall—six foot three, I guessed. He stood alone against a wall. I made the first move and felt a cashmere sweater and woolen knit pants. Classy. I took him for a professional, still dressed from work or a dinner that left him wanting more before bed. Fine with me. Have I ever mentioned that I like men? And the taller, the better. We began to kiss. We folded into one another's arms so easily that it felt like two forms manufactured to fit together. This was no "wham, bam, thank you, ma'am—see you later when my jones is coming down." He felt it as well.

"Have you got a place?" he whispered.

"Brooklyn."

"I've got a car."

My bedroom window was no more than four feet from my friend Maureen's window in the brownstone next door. She phoned first thing in the morning.

"What the hell was going on in there?"

"Were we loud?"

"The walls are cinder block, and you woke me."

That was the beginning of my affair with Paul, the man who'd inspire *Torch Song Trilogy*. Paul was my fantasy husband. A tenured teacher who owned a co-op on the Upper West Side and a house in the country, had his own car, wasn't noticeably addicted to drugs or alcohol, and wasn't an actor. A stand-up guy who'd even done a stint teaching in Africa. This was the kind of man I could take home to mother, invite to family gatherings, count on to pick up the dry cleaning, and plan a life with. And he was phenomenal in bed. We'd been on two dates and I was choosing china patterns and ordering wedding announcements.

For his part, Paul told me that he knew he was getting into trouble from the moment he accepted that second date. As much as Paul was my fantasy, I was never his. I was an unemployed actor/writer/drag performer and a guy. Paul has always held that the guy part didn't matter, but as soon as we settled into dating, he began seeing a lovely woman whom he'd eventually bring home to mother and marry.

Back at the ranch, I did everything I could to meld us together as a couple. I even started accepting substitute-teaching gigs, hoping that if we were on the same schedule and in the same field, he would see what a perfect married couple we'd be. Actually, that teaching gambit should have been enough to show me I was chasing the wrong dream. I registered to fill in at Art and Design, and they began calling me immediately. I taught quite a few classes before the day when, instead of being sent off to a classroom, I was summoned to the principal's office. He looked up from his desk and said, "Mr. Delaney has been admitted into the hospital. He needs immediate surgery. Most likely he will not return this semester, and just between us, I can say with some certainty that this absence will be followed by his retirement."

"Poor Mr. Delaney," I offered.

"Poor him and lucky you."

He stood and smiled. "The paperwork from the board of ed will take a few weeks to complete, but I'm offering you a full-time position teaching here at your alma mater."

Applause suddenly exploded from the office door behind me. A few teachers had gathered there to witness this moment, and they were excited. Miss Aldan lunged forward to hug me. "Ask anyone, I always believed that you would be one who'd succeed. Congratulations."

Succeed? I thought to my panicked self. *Is this success?*

My life flashed before my eyes. Well, not my entire life, but the life of Mr. Fierstein, high-school art teacher. This office, this building, these people would be the next forty years of his existence. Forget theater. Forget art. He would be a New York City schoolteacher with tests to grade and lessons to plan. Sure, I wanted my life with Paul, but . . . I finished out that week subbing and never returned to teaching. There had to be other ways to convince Paul we belonged together. I made raviolis from scratch!

By now it was evident that Paul was moving on. He stopped phoning. He didn't answer my calls. I'm going to claim the naiveté card for not giving up. I was in love. I can't swear I was in love with *him*, but I know I was in love with *us*. My tender heart reached back to wrest a thought from Carson McCullers's *Member of the Wedding*, "He is the we of me."

Paul's withdrawal left me open-mouthed, open armed, open-hearted. I hung suspended, as exposed and endangered as a piñata at a kid's party. What all of those Susan Hayward melodramas don't tell you is that heartache is real. The pain is paralyzing. All that shit they sing about in torch songs is no exaggeration. It hurts! I was fucked. Recognizing my state, Harvey phoned an old college friend who'd become a shrink.

"I know, I know, I know," she said to comfort me. "I'd say you have two choices: Slit your wrists or write a play."

The surprised look on my face cued her response. "Writers hang out in dive bars hoping for heartbreak to give them something to write about. Sounds like you hit the jackpot. Get busy."

I loved her idea, but not as a constructive way to work through the heartbreak. I believed if I wrote a good enough play, Paul would see the error of his ways and come back to me. The big breakup phone call was the first thing I wrote, and like it or not, it was therapeutic. Not only could I say everything I would have said if I had time to think it over, but I could even go back, rewriting again and again until every word out of my mouth was perfect. The only bad part was having to make Paul/Ed someone the audience would fall in love with, or there'd be no play. I did my best. The rest would be up to casting.

Next, I wrote a monologue where Ed picks up Arnold (me) in the Stud. Again, fun to write, and I was able to make him funny and sexy and a lying son of a bitch. And now an opening monologue to introduce Arnold to the audience as a love-seeking drag queen with a heart of rubber. Another fun assignment.

So where was I in the process? We meet Arnold. We meet Ed. We hear about their relationship as they break up . . . What next? Hey! How about the thing that started it all? Why not use the *Stud* play? It's a perfect scene for after the breakup. Arnold returns to the single life only to find himself demoted from person to object. Into the script it went.

All that remained was the final resolve of our lovers. That scene was the most difficult. These were two really nice people and I wanted them to be happy. It killed me to admit that they probably didn't belong together—at least not at this stage of their lives. For the romantics in the house, I left the ending as ambiguous as I could, but I trusted them to do the math.

I loved the form the play had taken, showing the characters alone onstage until the last scene: only then, after it's over, can they finally come together. This was the right way to tell the story.

Blasting Billie Holiday's "Gloomy Sunday" to celebrate, it hit me; torch songs should be sung between each scene by Lady Blues, a cabaret singer, whom Arnold imagines himself to be. *The International Stud* was born.

I took the script upstairs to Harvey. We sat together reading some of it aloud. He kept nodding his approval. "I like it, but it's not for me."

I got it. My earlier plays were direct descendants or even rip-offs of his brother Ron's work. This was something different and, like it or not, he didn't relate to it theatrically. Besides, he'd just played himself in a production of Ron's play *Bigfoot*, so exhaustion gave him the perfect excuse to bow out.

I called Eric Concklin and told him to meet me at La MaMa the next morning. Ellen had me working administration on her government grant program. I hated every minute of this mostly clerical job, but it paid. Eric was still reading while I paced impatiently. "I don't care if Ellen likes it or not, she's got to put it on. She owes me for doing this crap."

Eric closed the script.

"And?" I demanded.

"Let's do it. Bring it to Ellen but tell her it's a trilogy."

"What?"

"You know how she makes everyone fight for a slot. Right now she owes you. So tell her this is part one of a trilogy and then you'll have a guaranteed spot for the next two years."

"You are an evil genius," I said. Ellen had enjoyed great success producing Andrei Serban's *Greek Trilogy* at La MaMa before touring it all over the world. Telling her she had another trilogy on her hands was brilliant.

Ellen only wanted to know one thing: "Are you wearing bloomers?"

"Only in the first scene."

"Mr. Fierstein, we have talked about this."

"I know, I know. But I need that scene to set up the character, and then no more."

She stared me down. "One scene."

"You can look at the script," I offered.

"*Baby*, I don't read scripts. I listen to my beeps."

"And what are your beeps saying?"

With a quick flip through the scrawling on her Bowery Savings Bank calendar: "February. Second-floor theater. All right?"

She shook her head and laughed as I did a little victory dance around the room. I stopped at the door. 'Oh, I forgot to tell you, it's a trilogy."

Just hanging out on MacDougal Street,
dressed and ready to start the show

When I'd performed the back-room monologue I had no set and found an honesty in that presentation. I wanted this entire play to have that same nothing-up-my-sleeve openness.

I sketched out the simplest of designs; a small platform for Ed's apartment, another for Arnold's, a tall pedestal to represent the bar and back room, a vanity and chair for the backstage, and a baby grand piano on which Lady Blues would sit.

We cast the very handsome Steve Spiegel as Ed and Diane Tarleton, a woman whose face was as open and reflective as the moon, to play Lady Blues; and Ned Levy, who'd provided the accompaniment for *Flatbush Tosca*, was back at the piano.

The simplicity worked. The audience laughed where I'd hoped

they'd laugh, and as I delivered the final monologue to them, I could see tears being wiped away. Here was the connection between play and audience I was hoping to achieve. We were in conversation.

Paul saw *The International Stud* numerous times, attended every opening night and party, always proudly introducing himself around the room, nuzzling up to the actors to tell them his side of the story. Despite objecting to some fictionalization, he bathed in the attention. I even introduced him to my mother. Oh, yes: *Stud* got my brother's parental seal of approval. After the performance her first remark was, "I wondered where those earrings disappeared." Actually, with my father gone I saw no reason to edit my life any longer. As it turned out, he was the one I didn't want to disappoint. Jackie was now free to see all of my shows, meet my beaus, hang out with my friends, and take part in my social life. The choice was hers. Anyway, it was lovely seeing Paul now that things had settled in between us. I almost wrote "now that we were friends," but exes can't be friends. There is a red line of intimacy that's been crossed. Exes know things about each other that friends never could. You've altered each other's emotional DNA. You can be friendly with an ex, but exes cannot be friends.

The International Stud was a success from its first performance. Word got out and tickets were unavailable for the run. People sat in the aisles and even stood in the hallway to listen. Ellen asked if we'd like to extend, which we did. Twice. We then were offered an Off-Broadway run at the Players Theatre, but success did not follow. Bad producing, hideous advertising, wrong venue, who knows? We just never caught on, so I returned to the typewriter to write part 2 of this supposed trilogy.

20

FUGUE IN A NURSERY

1978

Part 2 had to be a projection or fantasy. There was no more to the actual story. The characters in my play had already strayed well beyond the pasture of truth. So what the hell was I going to write? When gay playwrights are interviewed, they are always asked about their sexuality, but I've never read an interview with Arthur Miller where he had to explain how he came to be heterosexual and what it was like. And believe me, if I was going to read up on that subject, he's the guy whose opinions I would seek. Meanwhile, in interviews I'd endlessly blabber on about there being no difference between same-sex relationships and that other kind. Was that the truth? I had toyed with those ideas in *Cannibals*, arguing, in fact, that same-sex pairings were naturally superior. It could be fun to write a comedy of manners exploring the subject. What if Ed and his fiancée invited Arnold and his new boyfriend up to their country home for a weekend? The opening line wrote itself: "Isn't this civilized?"

My mind was already fiddling with ideas when Ellen called me into her apartment. "Can you use musicians? I've got to find a show for some of these government people."

Cue the proverbial light bulb.

"Four," I said. "Four musicians and a composer."

I could already picture the finished production. The musicians would enter and take their places at raised music stands. The conductor enters next, and on the downbeat, the first movement of a fugue for four instruments begins. As the music plays the stage revolves and the audience realizes that the musicians make up the headboard of a huge bed that fills the stage. All of the play's action takes place in this bed. The text would be a fugue of four characters, each represented by an instrument. They will couple, uncouple, argue, and tease one another, aching to behave as sophisticated adults although they are nothing but children. Hence the giant bed. Adopting the identity of my Boston apartment, I decided to call it *Fugue in a Nursery*.

Arnold and Ed were already established characters, leaving me to invent their partners.

I modeled Arnold's boyfriend very loosely around the young man on whom I'd had a crush during *Dirtiest Show*, and I based the young woman on an actress friend who perpetually became involved with unavailable men. Ada Janik, a brilliant composer, was part of the La MaMa program. She jumped in to create and conduct the score.

Rehearsals were a blast. This surrealistic format called on us to be sexy and silly and angry and hurt, switching emotions as quickly as a toddler turns on and off its tears. This script was fun to play. Still, I could not shake my fear of the sophomore curse, even though I had already faced it when I wrote *Freaky Pussy*. I guess I was just scared of failing. *Fugue* was nothing like *Stud*. It was funny, but it had none of the raw, naked passion of the first play. I worried it would be a letdown.

Opening night proved otherwise. Just as soon as the bed, brilliantly realized by designer Bill Stabile, came into view, the audience jumped on board for the ride. The marriage of music and text worked marvelously well. Everyone was happy. Ellen was glad that I was able to employ some of her government-program musicians and that I didn't appear in drag. My brother and mother both enjoyed this one, and she actually recommended it to her friends. She told me she liked it. But she told Jay, this nice Jewish boy I was courting, that she loved it. The audience who had embraced the characters from *Stud* were thrilled to be back with them again. And ticket sales were brisk. Again Ellen asked us to extend, and we did.

Christopher Marcantel, me, Maria Cellario, and
Will Jeffries fooled around in a giant bed.

Twice. I licensed the show to a producer who not only wanted to move *Fugue* Off-Broadway but insisted on an option for whatever the final play would be. While he went about raising money for the transfer, I went home to write Act 3.

Glamorous as this sounds, I was still barely surviving on unemployment. And something else unpleasant was happening. Where I'd usually be fielding offers from other writers and directors to act, suddenly no one called me. There may have been a tinge of jealousy at play. If you didn't see my empty pockets, it might have appeared that I was a success. Jay Harnick, cofounder of Theaterworks, relayed an old nugget to me: "Ours is the only business where not only do you have to succeed, but all of your friends must fail." I was doing them one better by achieving both at the same time. I was starving in success. Jackie wasn't back to dropping off care packages yet, but I was getting close to tapping out.

There might have been another reason for the silent phone. Speaking to fellow actor/writers, I heard the same complaint: once you start writing, people think you only want to perform your own material. That's just not true. Most of us love performing other writers' work. I did my best to remain in my own skin and in my own lane, but I was feeling isolated.

The Tavels and I were still close. I hadn't been performing in his plays but I'd designed and executed the sets and the poster for Ron's children's show *The Clown's Tail*, which Harvey directed at the Cherry Lane Theatre. But now Ronald told me he was writing a campy new play about Anita Bryant's war against gays, so I asked if there was anything in it for me. I understood him not using me in his more serious work like *Bigfoot*, which examined the relationship of the biblical brothers Esau and Jacob to the legends surrounding sasquatch, and *Gazelle Boy*, the play he'd researched on our trip across Canada, but I would have loved doing another of his shows. Ron was rethinking the direction of his work. Feeling attention waning from his last few pieces, Ronald burrowed deeper, exploring more philosophical terrain, employing denser language and more oblique references. Where once he employed outrageous humor to titillate, he now aimed obscure barbs at the audience as if to say, "I challenge you to judge me."

This new project, *The Ovens of Anita Orange Juice*, felt as if he was returning to the old mold of in-your-face politics. He asked me to design the set. At least he still wanted me around.

21

WIDOWS AND CHILDREN FIRST!

1979

'd gotten away with inconclusive endings for the first two plays, but unless I wanted to announce *Torch Song Quartet*, I needed to wrap this shit up and send everyone home satisfied. I briefly considered slapping *Cannibals Just Don't Know No Better* on to the end of the trilogy but I quickly nixed the idea. Audiences were actually following the adventures of Arnold and Ed. They wanted to know how it all ended. Here was my thinking: *The International Stud* employed characters alone onstage; the self-possessed state of childhood. In *Fugue in a Nursery*, they were adolescents acting out in a giant playpen, pretending to be adults. Now, whatever else, these folks had to grow up. Likewise, their world, abstract in the first, symbolic in the second, had to be realistic in the end. In this play the real world could no longer be ignored.

Mrs. Gettleman had been a fan of mine since *Pork*. A housewife and bookkeeper whose husband sold car windshields in Bayside, Queens, she fancied herself an actress, even auditioning to be in *Flatbush Tosca*. A delightfully annoying little dynamo, who stood no higher than my tits and who, because she'd worn heels at all times during her adult life to appear taller, could no longer press her feet to the ground, which forced her to prance about on tiptoes. After every one of my shows she'd pester me, "When are you going to write a role for your mother? C'mon, get on the ball! You write it and I'll play it."

The idea of Arnold having this little pipsqueak for a mother was amusing. Funnily enough, Estelle Gettleman was only a few inches shorter than Jackie, and if the goal of this play was to have the real world pour cold water onto Arnold and Ed's dreams, what better water bearer than a Jewish mother?

I began to write.

Alan and Arnold are a happy couple in the process of adopting a teenaged boy who'd been bounced around facilities because he was vehemently and unapologetically gay. Meanwhile, Ed has left his wife, Laurel, and seeks temporary asylum on Arnold's couch. My idea was to put three political generations of gays into one apartment and then bring the mother in to sort them all out. This sitcom structure could have the audience laughing and relaxed before I lowered the boom with whatever the play was actually about. So . . . what *was* the play actually about?

I was awakened by a rapping on my front door. It was two in the morning. The iron-barred window was level with the sidewalk, and I saw a figure crumpled against the building. I opened the gate to find Harvey, bleeding from his head and hands, crying, "Help me inside."

"I'll call 911."

"No, just get me inside."

I eased him down the few steps and into an armchair. Turning a standing lamp on, I could see that his eyes were already discoloring and practically swollen shut. I ran to the kitchen for ice and towels.

"I gotta call an ambulance."

"No."

"Just to be sure . . ."

"I begged them not to hit me in the eyes. I told them I was wearing hard contact lenses. Please, I said, please, hit me anywhere, but not in the eyes."

I held his face to the light. The contacts were not visible but broken blood vessels were.

I washed him up best I could, then made him a drink and a cup of tea. He was slowly coming back to himself. There had been a group of five gays in the Prospect Park bushes when three punks jumped up over the retaining wall, one of them swinging a bat. They began screaming obscenities and threats. He ran with the others but tripped and fell to his knees. The bastards surrounded him, leers on their faces. That's when he asked them not to hit him in the eyes, so that was the first thing they did.

He refused to let me call the police or an ambulance. I got him up the two flights of stairs to his bedroom. He didn't want to bathe. He didn't even want to undress. I stood over him wondering if he had any idea how close he'd come to being killed. He asked to be alone. I sat on the stairs outside his room until his sobbing stopped.

My entire body was shaking with rage; I couldn't stand still. I fantasized about putting a posse of gays together, going back to the park, and beating these pricks to death, but that was never going to happen. At five in the morning there was no one to call for support. I didn't even know where our third housemate, Norman, was. But there was my typewriter. There was a blank page. And there was my anger focused on the keyboard, strike, strike, strike, I rewrote the opening of the play. Ed was still hiding out at Arnold's, David was still a boy that Arnold was in the process of adopting, Ma was still coming to visit, but Alan was dead. Alan had been beaten to death by kids with baseball bats. Alan was dead. Arnold's father was dead. I was writing a play about two widows who don't know who to blame for their loss: *Widows and Children First!*

The producer of *Fugue* let me know that they'd finished the budget for the Off-Broadway move and there was no way a small theater could support live musicians. We'd have to perform to a recorded track.

"Fuck. But does that mean we actually have a theater?"

"Yes . . . No. We have our theater, but we have to wait until the current occupant closes."

That probably meant another six months until we could get going. And no live musicians. I was losing heart. Maybe it was the excitement of finishing the writing of *Widows,* but I could now envision *Torch Song Trilogy* as a whole. I wanted to see all three plays together, but I didn't know how, and I was under contract, and I still needed to test this third play. So while we waited for

Fugue to set production dates, Eric and I went to Ellen and booked *Widows*.

Estelle nearly *plotzed* when she got the news about the mother. She arrived at the first rehearsal with her own props and costumes; a suitcase, a turquoise suit, a streaked wig, and a cookie tin. We never changed a thing. Actresses playing Ma over the years were all pressed into the mold of Estelle Gettleman. Mrs. Beckoff and Mrs. Gettleman were a perfect match of character and actress. There was nothing for her to do in rehearsals but learn the lines. We ran into only one roadblock. In the final scene of the play, after Arnold and his mother have battled, she is about to walk out the door but stops herself, knowing that leaving this way could be the end of their relationship. Instead, already at the door, she forces herself to ask how he's feeling about the loss of Alan.

"Mama, I miss him," Arnold says.

She answers, "Give yourself time, Arnold. It gets better."

What follows is her final speech about what it's like to mourn someone you love. We'd almost reached the end of a pretty good dress rehearsal on the afternoon of our first performance when Estelle stopped in the middle of that final speech. "I can't say this. I'm sorry, Harvey, but I can't."

"Why not?" I dared ask.

"It's not true. I want to respect your vision as the playwright, so I've been going along with what you wrote, but tonight we'll have an audience and I just can't say this."

Again I asked, "Why not?"

"Because my sister lost her husband several years ago and this is not how she felt."

"The play is not about your sister."

"Truth is truth." Estelle shook her head. "If you want to touch an audience you have to do it with truth. You have me saying that he will get used to it."

"No. I have you telling him that it never goes away," I argued back, quoting the speech.

Eric rushed down to the stage. "Darling, we have an audience tonight. Now is not the time to ask Harvey to rewrite. Please, for me, do the speech as written and tomorrow afternoon the three of us can sit down and hash this out. Okay?"

"I don't know how to do something I don't believe in," she harrumphed.

"This is how." Eric took her place on the stage. He lifted the suitcase and said, "Harvey, give me the cue."

I did: "Mama, I miss him."

"And now, Estelle, you give him the easy answer. Go on and say it."

Estelle dutifully recited her next line, "Give yourself time, Arnold. It gets better."

Eric continued. "Wonderful. Now I want you to take a moment to think about what you might say to a friend in this position but don't want to say to your son. Force yourself to look at him but don't put down the bag. Don't come back into the room. Don't soften. Don't act. Just recite the speech exactly as written."

He motioned her over to take his place. She grabbed the suitcase from him and stood, unhappily reciting the speech as if every word burned the lining of her mouth.

"But Arnold, it won't ever go away. You can work longer hours, adopt a son, fight with me . . . Whatever. It'll still be there. But that's all right. It becomes a part of you, like wearing a ring or a pair of glasses. You get used to it. And it's good. It's good because it makes sure you don't forget. You don't want to forget him, do you? No. So, it's good."

"Perfect!" Eric said. "Now, can you do that for me just that way tonight?"

She begrudgingly agreed.

That night Estelle executed Eric's moves exactly as ordered. She delivered the disputed speech with icy detachment, strong and unyielding, letting the audience know that she wanted no part of these words.

The play ended. The lights came down. We were met with silence from the packed house. Offstage, Estelle wagged her finger at me. "I told you. I could hear them shuffling in their seats all through that speech. You have to fix it."

The silence gave way to an eruption from the audience. It did not begin with applause. They were screaming "Bravo!" and whistling and stomping their feet. Eric later explained that the shuffling we heard was the sound of people fetching tissues from their purses and pockets as they wept uncontrollably. *Widows and Children First!* was a triumph.

Estelle predictably claimed she knew that speech was a killer from the moment she read the script. She never again asked me to rewrite a word. I'd hear her pontificate, "Brilliant, isn't it? These two can't come together as mother and son but finally find each other as two widows in mourning. I told Harvey, genius."

This was Eric's favorite story to relate right up until his death.

Mrs. Beckoff was so identifiable that I listened to a constant chorus of people saying, "That was me and my mother." No one, not even mothers of gay sons, ever said, "That was my son and me." It was always "That's me and my mother." Estelle played Ma for the next six years and was always brilliant and singular and irreplaceable, but never did she come close to that first disarmed performance. I was better last night, indeed.

My own mother loved Estelle's performance. She gloried in bringing her friends to see the show in all of its iterations. If anyone asked, she'd laugh off the notion that she was the model for the character, and I'd jump in to save her: "The character is actually based on my grandmother. Growing up, I witnessed some really colorful fights between the two of them."

"She wasn't that bad," Jackie would add, laughing.

Jackie had a lot of competition in the mother department. There was Estelle onstage and Ellen Stewart claiming her status as Mama in interviews and at public events. But it was Jackie who bore the burden of Mrs. Beckoff. Mothers of gay children asked her advice. Interviewers wanted her insight into raising an LGBTQ child. She brushed off most requests saying, "I'm no expert."

Over time, she took on the responsibility as best she could. Realizing that LGBTQ children may have special needs adjusting to society at large, she recommended several to the Harvey Milk High School and the Hetrick-Martin Institute. I've heard from parents and children whom she comforted and counseled toward acceptance. Woody Allen even auditioned her to play his mother in a movie. But the action that made me proudest was her dedication to people with AIDS. She gathered her friends Shirley, Bea, and Esther and together they drove around Brooklyn delivering meals to shut-ins for God's Love We Deliver. She did that well into her eighties.

I may have had to deal with Jackie, but Jackie had to deal with her own mother, Granny Goose. Jackie moved Granny in with her until dementia made that impossible. Several times she was awakened by her mother caning her, insisting that she was an intruder. Granny Goose was moved into a facility where Jackie could visit almost daily. As my public profile rose, Granny insisted on knowing why the nurses and attendants at her facility were always talking about me. By the time *Torch Song* arrived on Broadway, she'd had enough. "Why are they asking about Harvey? That young man over there said he'd give me money for his autograph."

One evening Jackie got her all dolled up, put her in the car, and took her to see *Torch Song Trilogy.* Hoping to avoid explaining the drag scene or the back-room monologue, she timed their arrival for the first intermission. Even that didn't solve her problem. In the middle of *Fugue,* Granny Goose turned to my mom and loudly asked, "Is Harvey a homosexual?"

Jackie, nonplussed, answered, "How should I know? Do I sleep with him?"

People make up all sorts of stories as to why the set of *Widows* was covered with rabbit objects. Many assume my identity with rabbits has something to do with *Harvey,* the play about the invisible rabbit. Not so. Here's the skinny. Playing a magician in a Donald L. Brooks show called, *Infinity,* I pulled a live rabbit out of my hat. I was made caretaker of the stupid thing. I named him Arnold and carried him around in a shoulder bag. I even brought him up to Warhol's Factory once, where Andy posed him with his mini dachshund, Archie, for a few Polaroids. I named my *Torch Song* character Arnold in his honor and then tossed in a few rabbit gags, like Ma and Arnold wearing matching rabbit slippers. Eric got right into the spirit and went to town personally crocheting them.

Our designer, Bill Stabile, joined in as well, incorporating bunny props and *tchotchkes,* including rabbit stencils on the wall.

Bunnies abounded on Bill Stabile's set. Estelle was really
very patient about letting the rabbits get their laughs.

As long as I'm at it, I might as well explain the surname Beckoff. I had a childhood friend named Bennet Beckoff. His mom once gave us cookies she made from a box mix. My silly brain nicknamed her Betty Crocker Beckoff. Realizing that the script never mentioned Ma's first name, I dubbed her thus, because it always made me laugh.

22

FUGUE ON

1980

We'd been promised Second Avenue's Orpheum Theatre for the Off-Broadway production of *Fugue,* but Ann Corio's strip show *Big Bad Burlesque* was still limping along in the space. *Widows* was such a hit that when *BBB* finally closed and we were at last free to begin rehearsals for *Fugue, Widows* was still running at La MaMa. That meant doing double duty for Will Jeffries, who was playing Ed in both shows, and me. We rehearsed *Fugue* during the day and performed *Widows* at night.

It was sadly evident from first rehearsals that without the live musicians, *Fugue* lost focus, energy, and life essence. Instead of a conversation between the instruments and the voices, the pre-recorded music became something we used to keep time. We were slaves to the unwavering tempos. The tail was wagging the dog. Ron Tavel tried to cheer me on during a rehearsal: "They say you can get away with anything if you've got a great opening, closing, and don't bore them in the middle."

I added a new final scene that took place outside of the bed to beef up the evening. It added nothing but length. Almost Christmas and it was seventy degrees on opening night, so the cast weren't the only ones sweating out the middling notices. As with *Stud,* our audience did not follow us from La MaMa. Imminent failure made life hard enough, but then, one lovely night, the cab taking me home was T-boned coming off the Manhattan Bridge. My nose

and four ribs were broken. With no understudy I either performed
or we closed the show. I performed. With broken ribs, standing and
walking would have been so much easier than rolling around in a
bed. My fellow actors had to pull or push me into position for each
scene. We were mercifully gone with the new year.

The Gay Presses of New York licensed the plays for publication.
Torch Song Trilogy would be released as a book in a few months.
Still, 1980 was difficult. After the excitement surrounding *Widows,*
I felt as if my phone had rung and the voice on the other end said,
"Harvey, I've got the greatest news for you"—and then put me on
hold for a year.

Even after his losses on *Fugue* Mitchell Maxwell, our producer, believed so strongly in *Widows* that he proposed taking it to
Broadway—but he insisted on an all-new production. That meant
a new director, new designers, and new actors. His argument: I'd
already moved two shows in productions I oversaw, and they both
failed. Wasn't it time to try a different approach? Stunned, I had
to think this through. Was my ego to blame? Would the plays have
done better with a real actor in the lead? Was it a mistake for Eric
to slavishly deliver my vision? Would another director challenge
me instead? The two commercial failures deflated any argument
against Mitchell's wishes. This man had just lost a ton of money.
Didn't I owe him the chance to try things his way?

Breaking this news to Eric was easier than telling Estelle, who by
that time was readying herself for stardom by quitting her day job
and changing her legal name to Estelle Getty.

"I've waited my whole life for this role. You can't do this to me!"

"I wrote it for you. Don't you think I want you to play it?"

"Then put your foot down," she ordered. "So who does he want
for my role? Some shiksa, I'm sure. They'll do to you like they do
to Neil Simon: take a Jewish play, put a bunch of goys in it . . ."

"And make a fortune!"

"Not funny, Harvey."

"I won't let that happen."

"You won't? You already have!"

"Listen to me, Estelle. This production will never materialize. Believe me."

We repeated that conversation every week for months.

By the way, you can identify a first edition of the Gay Presses of New York publication of *Torch Song Trilogy* by looking at the cast list for *Widows*. Estelle shortened her name just as the book went to print. They were able to reset but not realign the type, so "Getty" does not line up with the rest of the cast.

As I'd predicted, this Broadway production never came to be. Meanwhile I signed with an agent at William Morris who was straight out of the mailroom. George Lane did his best contacting every theater he could think of about a production of the entire trilogy.

There were no takers for a five-hour play about the lives and loves of a Jewish drag queen.

23

WHAT THE FUCK
IS A GLINES?

1981

John Glines named his theater company after himself hoping that someday a gay theater would not have to identify as such. In addition to individual productions, John sponsored a Gay American Arts Festival around the Stonewall celebrations each year. In 1979 I put a group of actors together and we read scenes from a bunch of my plays. In 1980 I assembled a cast, including Estelle, to read selections from and tell the story of *Torch Song Trilogy*.

Lawrence Lane was the Glines's line producer. If John dreamt it, Lawrence made it happen. They were also lovers. A week after our presentation Lawrence called and asked if I'd meet him for lunch. Sitting at an outdoor café in the Village, he told me that they'd been blown away by our reading and wanted to produce the trilogy. The relief was greater than the excitement.

"We can discuss the details later. John just wants to know that this is something you'd let us do."

"Yes. Yes! Of course, yes. I'd be thrilled."

We toasted with our Diet Cokes and, getting up to leave, I must have turned a bright shade of fuchsia when I asked Lawrence if he could loan me a dollar for the subway back to Brooklyn. I came to the meeting fully prepared to walk home across the bridge. No shit, I was that broke.

Eric had a day job as a dresser on the Broadway revival of *The*

Pirates of Penzance. After work he usually stopped for drinks before heading home, so it was almost one in the morning by the time I got him on the phone.

"You're drunk!" I said.

"I'm not drunk," he assured me.

"You have to be drunk or you wouldn't say no."

"I've spent three years on those plays and what do I have to show for it? I didn't mind, because I love you and I love working at La MaMa, but what the fuck is a Glines?"

"They said we could do it however we wanted."

"For pennies. And you know that you're not going to get your live musicians."

"But we'll finally get to see the whole story put together . . ."

"I'm not giving up this job and that's it."

Harvey Tavel was not an option, either. He was away with Ronald in Thailand for the summer and planned to reward himself with a Mexican vacation in the winter. My next call was to Richard Jakiel, who'd stage managed our last few productions. He was very excited when I reached him, but an hour later he phoned back to decline. Eric had convinced him not to waste his time.

Lawrence said, "You already know how you want the plays done. You know what you want from the actors. Why not do it yourself?"

"I need someone to watch from out front."

Lawrence brightened up. "The young man we were going to use as stage manager has been studying directing. How about him?"

"Sounds like a plan."

Diane Tarleton, who played Lady Blues in the original productions of *Stud,* returned to play the girlfriend in *Fugue* as well. Estelle and I were both set, and Ned was back on piano. That left three roles to cast: Ed, the older lover; Alan, the young lover; and David, the adopted son. Auditions were held on the set of Jane Chambers's *Last Summer at Bluefish Cove,* another Glines production. One actor from that show came in to audition for us. Lonnie was much too young for Ed, but not for me. We began dating. But that's not what auditions are for, so don't do that. Ever!

Estelle read opposite the applicants, allowing me to watch from out front. We saw Eds first. A lot of handsome men, a lot of bad acting, and not a lot of hope until an eight-by-ten photo was put in front of me that took my breath away. It was Joel Crothers, an actor I'd had a crush on for years. He was on a soap opera with my friend Mary Woronov. Distinguished and poised, strikingly handsome and funny, doing soaps had trained him to bounce from emotion to emotion without straining for context. The trilogy, especially *Fugue*, required that skill. When Estelle and he were done reading their scene, she smirked at him. "Y'know, being gorgeous and talented isn't everything. You could still get hit by a bus."

John, Lawrence, and I nodded to one another, so I went up onto the stage and read a scene with him just to be sure. He was perfect. Handing his script back to the casting director, he whispered, "That kid I read with is really good. They should think about casting him."

The character of David is fifteen, but we wanted someone older to avoid union restrictions on a minor. We'd lucked out, casting someone wonderful in the original production. Most kid actors come off as if they are playing kids. We needed someone more special. The side door opened and in walked this adorable boy with his bicycle. The casting director introduced him as Matthew Broderick. Shaggy hair, a wide-eyed expression, and a runny nose made him irresistible. His audition was enigmatic. He read with such ease you'd never know he was using a script. You just believed him. At the end of the scene Estelle voiced her approval, saying, "Don't grow up, kid."

Who would have thought finding an Alan would be the challenge? He had to be gay and gorgeous. How hard is that to find in NYC? But we also needed someone who would bring an inner turmoil to the stage. Alan is a frightened child who wants to be loved but always ends up lusted instead. A parade of pretty boys pranced before us, and I thought not one of them right. Lawrence and John disagreed. There was one young man, Paul Joynt, who swept both of my producers off their feet. Gorgeous? Absolutely. Talented? Enough. I didn't see the troubled soul, but they certainly did. I caved, we hired him; and Paul became the most cherished

Joel Crothers, Matthew Broderick, and me in
the bench scene that was Sondheim's favorite

member of our company. Sadly, our producers turned out to be
dead-on about his being a troubled soul. Paul suffered from dis-
sociative identity disorder, aka split personality. There were early
signs of cutting, memory loss, and depression during our run. In
2001, after a failed job interview, his most abusive personality took
charge, climbed out onto a fire escape, and hung him by his necktie.

Paul Joynt played one of Matthew's rude friends
in the movie. Here we are rehearsing his attack.

24

FROM THE BASEMENT TO THE FIFTH FLOOR AND BACK AGAIN

Nineteen eighty was the year that *Nicholas Nickleby* introduced audiences to long shows. It ran eight and a half
hours plus a dinner break. But it was the Royal Shakespeare
Company presenting a Dickens classic. They could get away with
anything.

I opened my manuscript of *Torch Song Trilogy*, took a deep
breath, and attacked it with the thickest, reddest Magic Marker I
could find. I had to get that sucker under control. I soothed myself
with the knowledge that the plays were published and available to
read uncut, and so nothing I was chopping out would ever actually
be lost. Accepting that *Fugue* would always suffer by never again
having a live musical quartet, I transformed it into a classic second act. It would introduce the new love interests, raise the stakes,
deepen the relationships, and expose conflicts, but any resolutions
would have to wait for *Widows*. Hoping to avoid arguments with
actors, I did as much cutting as I could before rehearsals began.
Actors really do count how many lines they have. We birthed these
plays, first rehearsing them, in La MaMa's basement space, so I
called and asked if we could rehearse again there. Ellen understood
and invited us in.

The Glines leased the Richard Allen Center, which was located
on the fifth floor of an office building across from Lincoln Center. Although it had an elevator, most of our audience avoided the

lobby line and hiked up the four flights of stairs to what was basically a very big empty room, painted black, with seats lining three
walls. Our dressing rooms were a black flannel panel away from the
audience, and everyone shared a communal bathroom, which led to
very long intermissions.

It's easy for me to romanticize those ramen-noodle beginnings
because, with all of the limitations of that bare bones production,
I was experiencing the play the way I'd imagined it, and believe it or
not, even at four and a half hours the darn thing worked like gang-
busters. *Fugue* built on *Stud*, and *Widows* concluded with every
audience member cheering and weeping. Family and friends who
had seen the plays separately were ecstatic with the production.
Eric predictably found fault in minute detail but still conceded to
loving the evening.

Stephen Sondheim, an intimate of Joel's, sat contentedly in the
house and chatted after the performance. He asked if I wanted to
know what his favorite line in the show was. "It was after the boy
sets you straight. He asks if you want him to stay. You nodded and
he said, 'Now we're dancing.' Killed me."

The whole production was a mess of a magical experience. It
was live theater true to the ideals set by my tutors. Sure, there were
nights we had to place buckets around the stage to catch the melt-
ing snow that dripped relentlessly through the ceiling. One performance had Estelle open her tin of home-baked cookies to reveal
the biggest water bug you have ever seen taking his bow atop the
chocolate chips. Every now and then an audience member would
flush the toilet during an inopportune silence. Only one drawback
was inescapable—there was almost no one in the seats. We played
our hearts out to mostly empty houses.

Lawrence called me late one Friday morning, "John and I could
not be prouder. Everyone who has seen it raves. Unfortunately, we'll
need to close two weeks earlier than planned. We hoped that the
word of mouth would begin to turn things around. It just doesn't
seem to be happening. We are truly sorry."

Failure to capture an audience outside of La MaMa felt baked
into the trilogy's DNA. Lawrence told me that they would still do

what they could to get audiences and critics in to see the show, but as of now we were closing next Sunday. I understood.

That night we informed the cast. They were bummed but not surprised. I took the subway back to Brooklyn, bought the Saturday-morning edition of *The New York Times* at the newsstand, and walking down Carroll Street I opened to the theater page. where I found, in heart-halting black-and-white, Mel Gussow's unmitigated rave for *Torch Song*. I leaned back against a brownstone's wrought-iron fence to read the review over and over again. It was real. *The New York Times* called a four-hour play about the life of a drag performer "an infinitely rewarding evening." I ran the last two blocks home and phoned John and Lawrence, who not only had read the *Times* but were screaming about a simultaneously published, similarly ebullient review in the *Daily News* by Rex Reed. John Simon's *New York* magazine rave followed the next day, shooting us into the stratosphere.

I don't talk a lot about reviews. I try not to read them until late in or even after a run. If they're good, I figure I'll see them plastered across the theater. If they're bad, your loved ones will make sure you hear every disparaging word. Not meaning to be disrespectful of how another person earns a living, but my career has already outlasted those of twenty-odd *New York Times* reviewers. When I want to know what a show is like, I ask someone who paid for their ticket. Theater is a place you should attend for healing and not healthcare.

But on that bright morning I loved theater critics: three of them saved our asses and changed the course of *Torch Song Trilogy*'s history and my life. How's that for a self-serving turnaround? Overnight we became such a big hit that Harvey Milk himself had to watch the show from the lighting booth. Yes, reservations went nuts, and so did our producers.

"We want to move the show to an Off-Broadway theater for a commercial run," John said.

My head began to throb. "We just averted complete disaster Off-Off-Broadway. Wouldn't the smart thing be to extend this run, hopefully break even, and call it a day?"

But Glines presented a plan to refurbish the Actors' Playhouse, located in a basement on Seventh Avenue in the Village, specifically to house the show. Rumor has it the place was originally built as a speakeasy during Prohibition. Against my better judgment I agreed, and we immediately told the cast we were moving. What the hell . . . we began this whole thing underground, moved up to the fifth floor, so we might as well finish in a basement.

Joel Crothers took me aside and said that he couldn't stay with us. The double duty of early-morning soap-opera shoots followed by evening stage performances was taking a toll on his health. Earlier that year he'd traveled to Africa, where he picked up a stomach bug that he was still fighting to shake. He was sorry, but he needed to put his health first. Laughable as it sounds, I was so smitten with Joel that it felt less like replacing an actor than a romantic breakup. The few people who saw his performance can tell you that he was remarkable in the role: sophisticated and aloof one moment, dangerously angry the next, then seductive and sensual, all in the blink of an eye. Did I mention the gold piercing of a snake he had through the head of his penis? I'd never seen one before. I asked what you were supposed to do with it, and he said, "Start by making friends."

Of all of us, Joel and Estelle were the only ones with day jobs. This move from Off-Off to Off meant union paychecks for the company. Compared to Joel's TV salary, it was chump change. For Estelle it meant quitting her bookkeeping job. To the rest of us, most especially me, it was everything.

Court Miller's audition to replace Joel is imprinted on my brain. All Ed applicants read Ed's bar monologue, so they began with their backs to us, turning around when accidentally stepping on Arnold's foot. Court's back, fully clothed, swaying to imaginary music, was one of the sexiest things I'd ever seen on a stage. I wanted to jump up and take a bite out of his ass. The rest of his audition was marvelous as well; but charming and delightful as he was, the producers worried that after Joel, he was simply too young. Thankfully I was able to convince them that his thinning hairline would tell the story, and he was cast. As different as he was from Joel, Court slipped easily into the role and made it his own. Where Joel had been aloof, Court was cuddly. Where sadness made Joel's Ed shut others out, Court's grief invited you in. But one thing the actors had in common was a bad stomach. Joel had his African bug and Court had everything else. His hypochondria was soon a running punchline among the company; headaches, heartburn, rashes, and muscle aches. We made a game of it: Name That Symptom.

Court Miller and me celebrating in the
wings after our first Broadway curtain call

When Court and Matthew met, they set fireworks off over the Statue of Liberty. Not romantic . . . musical! They both harbored dreams of becoming song-and-dance men in a Broadway show. During rehearsal breaks the two of them would take the stage and invent soft-shoe routines. I loved sitting in the house and watching them, but Matthew often brought this annoying friend of his along to rehearsal—an intense but adorable curly-headed boy who wore glasses and asked too many questions. He told me that he was going to be a playwright. I waved him away with "Sure, kid. Sure."

When Matthew starred on Broadway in *How to Succeed in Business Without Really Trying,* I don't think I saw more than a few moments of it through my happy tears, remembering him and Court dancing together. As for his friend, that vexing child grew up to be award-winning playwright and Academy Award–winning screenwriter/director Kenneth Lonergan.

During the months off while they readied the theater, I found myself frequenting the Trucks and backroom bars more than ever. Idle hands? One night I was engaged in a group activity in a bar called J's when I suddenly realized that I was bored. I wasn't there because it was exciting or inspiring or even naughty. Sex had become a habit. A quote came to mind that I've ascribed to Colette, although I've never found it again: "When he and he and he became them I gave up men." I eased my way out of the cluster and never engaged in anonymous sex again. For those doing the math, this was the autumn of 1981, so boredom was most likely the reason I escaped the oncoming plague.

During an earlier period of unemployment, I found myself haunted by a story I'd seen on the TV news about a sixteen-year-old boy who had committed a string of heinous crimes, from larceny to rape. His mother hollered at the news camera, "That's not my boy. He's not my son. He's the monster that you turned him into. Take him—he's yours!"

Studying for my teaching license had exposed me to the over-reaches of judges and social workers into child rearing. I wondered if there was a play here. I began sitting in on family court sessions in downtown Brooklyn. Armed with harrowing stories of judges overruling parental rights, schools forcing kids to take drugs like Ritalin, children removed from their homes, families destroyed for the sake of expediency, I began to write a new play, *Spookhouse.*

Torch Song Trilogy reopened in January at the Actors' Playhouse and proved an immediate sensation. From day one ticket reservations were almost impossible to book. We became one of those must-sees. Boldface names filled every performance: Shirley MacLaine, Anne Meara, Ann Miller. I'll never forget the outrage on John Glines's face when Madeline Kahn flashed her NYU ID card at the box office and demanded the student discount.

"You're Madeline Kahn!" the ticket seller told her.

"With so much more to learn," she replied.

A favorite, Carol Channing, came backstage and proclaimed, "This is the gay *Raisin in the Sun*."

The show was such a hot ticket that John Glines immediately began investigating a move to Broadway. I ignored him. I had a hit Off-Broadway show and I was dating Lonnie, that actor I'd met at auditions. I was happy enough. Lawrence and John, Lonnie and I fell into a pleasant domestic routine. Lonnie would pick me up after my Sunday-night performance. We'd buy sandwiches at Smiler's and hop a cab to John and Lawrence's Brooklyn Heights brownstone, where we'd eat, drink, and play board games until we could no longer distinguish the playing pieces. UNO was almost always the final game that greeted sunrise. The cards were big, the game was simple—and who cared who won?

One day, about this time, I was checking out at the grocer's when I remembered I needed rubber bands. I went back and grabbed a plastic bag of assorted sizes. I don't care how stupid this sounds—that was the moment, for the first time in my adult life, that I felt financially secure. I actually had enough money in my pocket to purchase a bag of rubber bands instead of hoarding discarded ones or picking them up off the ground. I studied the multicolored, multisized treasures in my hand and I felt rich.

25

TORCH SONG TRILOGY—
OFF AND ON BROADWAY

Not long into our Off-Broadway run, Matthew took me aside. After seeing him in *Torch Song Trilogy,* Neil Simon offered him the lead in his new Broadway show, *Brighton Beach Memoirs,* but before that he'd star in Simon's movie *Max Dugan Returns.* The problem was that he'd have to leave us soon. He asked what I thought.

"Go!" I laughingly said. "You have to."

"But Larry said we might be moving to Broadway."

My mind flashed to the boy who'd originated Matthew's role at La MaMa. After seeing him in the show, Mike Nichols offered to develop a TV series around him. Thinking he was above weekly television and that this offer was just the beginning, the kid turned it down, and that was the end of that career. Matthew's brass ring was within reach. Everyone knew he had to snatch it, but I loved that he asked my opinion.

Fisher Stevens was a disarmingly funny-looking kid with a raspy voice and an assured way. With his explosive charm and open heart, he slipped seamlessly into the company. We had great luck with actors playing David. Almost every one of them went on to a big career: Matthew, Fisher, Jon Cryer, Patrick Dempsey, Grant Shaud, and Jonathan Del Arco among them.

I was coming out of the Sheridan Square subway station one afternoon when I saw that the line of ticket buyers snaked from the box office, wound around the corner, and disappeared from view. I panicked on two fronts. First, if we were this kind of hit, would I be stuck doing it forever? The second fear was more worrisome. My voice was disappearing. I'd had vocal strain before, but this felt different, and no matter how gently I treated my voice it kept getting worse. Our pianist, Ned, was our company's quintessential Jewish mother. He worried that I could have that gay-cancer thing that the *New York Native* was writing about.

"Stop, Ned. That thing has to do with flight attendants. I have laryngitis."

Lawrence wasn't taking chances. He made an appointment for me to see a famous voice doctor and insisted on coming along. They sprayed and scoped and snipped and X-rayed and told me they'd be in touch when the lab results came back, but in their opinion I should prepare myself for a diagnosis of throat cancer. I went numb. We left the office and I asked Lawrence if he'd mind giving me a moment alone. I walked across to Central Park, where I unleashed a wail of despair that shocked even me. I had no idea that I cared for my life that much. Worse still, I didn't want to be another awful theater-history asterisk: "He climbed the ladder of success only to slip on the top rung and fall to his death."

Rumors spread quickly through the cast. That night Matthew's father, the accomplished actor James Broderick, came to see me. He had been diagnosed and treated for throat cancer himself. With a father's care he assured me that all would be well. The man was the dearest. My illness turned out not to be cancer but merely an infection that had settled down into the nice, warm, moist nest of my vocal cords. Meds would take care of it, and my voice returned with time. Not so for Mr. Broderick. I'm sorry to say that this sweet man lost his battle with cancer just six months later.

The New York Public Library for the Performing Arts at Lincoln Center wanted to record Matthew's performance for their archives. Hoping my voice would heal, they waited and shot his very last appearance. Sadly, my voice was still in rough shape, but I'm glad they captured Matthew as David.

With Fisher and Court settled into their roles and my throat on the mend, John and Lawrence resumed their campaign to transfer the show again. John saw this as a landmark effort; the first openly gay play with an openly gay lead on Broadway. What's run-of-the-mill today was run-for-the-hills back then. There were plenty of producers buzzing around the show. John thought introducing me to the right one would change my mind. It did. After rejecting half a dozen, along came Ken Waissman, who had produced *Grease*. Well, not just Ken, although he was a very nice man; but it was his partners with whom I fell in love. Betty Lee Hunt had been a press agent since the early 1950s. She told me that her first assignment was tending to the needs of Lana Turner, which she did with gusto. She was a tough, old-school broad who knew everyone, had most of them, and could point to where all the bodies were buried. Her partner was Maria Pucci, a fun and flirty gal who ran their household and social lives. I was nuts for these two from the moment we met. They would handle the press and coproduce with the Glines, Ken, and Marty Markinson, who owned the Little Theatre. That was the space where, years ago, Dick Briggs had stage-managed *The David Frost Show*. This was feeling like a homecoming.

No sooner had I okayed the plans than the producers came back for more script cuts. Broadway stagehands would go into expensive overtime unless the curtain came down by eleven o'clock. They were willing to start the show at seven thirty, but I still needed to cut twenty minutes. Estelle was so protective of every one of her lines that for anything of hers I cut, I had to show her two of my own being chopped. And then Diane cornered me to say that she loved playing Laurel but was tired of protecting her voice just to sing the four songs in *Stud*. She missed her daily swims at the Y. Next time an actress tells you that she wants to play Broadway, be sure she's willing to give up swimming at the Y. Instead of hiring an understudy for her, we added a singer to the cast, and the two would cover one another. Everyone happy? Not quite. Off-Broadway I performed only six shows a week. The uptown budget demanded adding matinees. Understudies were hired for Court and me with the understanding that they'd play the matinees and that, as with Diane, we'd all cover for one another.

As it happened, I never missed a performance, but my understudy did. I was asleep on a Wednesday morning when my phone rang. It was our stage manager. "Harvey? Wake up! You've got to go on for the matinee."

"What are you talking about?" I croaked.

"Richard's got a boil on his ass. He's getting it lanced. Meanwhile, you've got to play the matinee."

"A boil on his . . . ?" I pulled my unboiled ass out of bed and got to the theater in time. Union rules called for an announcement to be made. I assumed the house would cheer to hear that instead of the understudy they'd be seeing me. I would be wrong.

The stage manager announced, "At this performance the role of Arnold will be played by Harvey Fierstein," followed by the audience groaning their disappointment vociferously. Leave it to a house filled with theater-party ladies to keep your ego in check.

Most shows try to open as near to awards season as possible, hoping any nominations will translate into ticket sales. We opened in June, meaning we'd have to survive an entire year before getting a crack at awards. The first few weeks on Broadway were delicious for this outsider. I fell immediately in love with the community. I began to meet people, learned the lingo and the lay of the land. It was 1982—not yet the golden age of Broadway. Theater, along with the rest of the city, was struggling. Rather than lighting empty marquees, Betty Lee came up with the idea to post signs reading "See a Broadway show just for the fun of it" on all of the vacant theaters. Still, for a kid who grew up watching this world from the cheap seats, being on the inside was magical. We were surrounded by shows that weren't bait for tourists but aimed themselves toward real New York theater lovers: *Amadeus; 'night, Mother; Plenty; Good; K2;* and *Agnes of God,* to name a few. The musicals included *Nine, A Chorus Line, Barnum, The Pirates of Penzance,* and *My One and Only.* And I was part of it all.

Ted Hook's Backstage became my favorite hangout. Ted had begun as a Hollywood extra in 1940s musicals. He moved on to the job of personal assistant to Joan Blondell and then Tallulah Bankhead. These days he ran his namesake restaurant/piano bar with a singular gusto that made every night a party. Each white-linened table held a small lamp with a removable shade. Each shade bore the name of a celebrity and was placed on their table when they came in. If a new celebrity arrived, a waiter was dispatched to the cloak room, where the name would quickly be applied to a blank lampshade with press-on type. Silly as it sounds, it made the celebrated feel special, and the tourists loved taking a slow stroll to the loo, reading the names of all who might show up. I still have my lampshade somewhere. On any night you might see Anthony Perkins, Liza Minnelli, Stiller and Meara, Rip Taylor, Barry Manilow, and Lauren Bacall all dining, drinking, and relaxing. One of Ted's closest friends was Chita Rivera. We often sat together laughing until closing. The food was awful except for the burgers, but the booze was served in the largest glasses Ted could provide. My goldfish-bowl-sized snifter of Southern Comfort arrived at my table before my ass hit the banquette. Broadway is a club whose members stick together. Who else would understand our particular woes? When regular folks are home in the evenings, we are at work. When they are celebrating birthdays, we are at work. Holidays and weekends, we are at work. Six days a week we're at work and the rest of the time we are nurturing our bodies, babying our voices, or doing press and charity events. Having a place to let off steam where you're surrounded by others like you is essential. My first Thanksgiving on Broadway found me down at the prospect of missing my family dinner. Ted invited me over to have a bite with him. I arrived to find my entire family waiting around a traditional turkey with all the fixins that Ted organized just for us. Show people!

I have to tell you this one story of a night at Ted's. Debbie Reynolds was playing in *Woman of the Year*. She wandered into Backstage on a Saturday night and got "happy" quite quickly. Before long, she was performing her nightclub act for the crowd. When I left at three a.m. she was still impersonating Marlene Dietrich atop the white grand piano bar. I awoke around noon to a TV news bulletin announcing that Hollywood legend Debbie Reynolds had been taken by ambulance to the hospital. EMS workers feared a heart attack. I leapt to my phone, dialed her daughter, Carrie Fisher, and said, "Relax. It's a hangover."

For all the shows I saw, for all the cast albums I sang along with, Broadway was never even a fantasy I'd entertained. The first time I turned the corner of Forty-Fourth Street and saw my name on the marquee—"Harvey Fierstein's TORCH SONG TRILOGY"—I moved out from the sidewalk to lean against a delivery van where I had a clearer view, and wept. No big deal. No heaving or sniffles. Just tears of *what the fuck?* rolling down my cheeks. And I'll tell you a little secret; after almost forty years it doesn't get old.

26

THIS IS A JOB FOR
A DRAG QUEEN
1982

When the movie *La Cage Aux Folles* was released, my phone began to ring. Everyone wanted to turn it into a musical, and as the gay writer du jour, I got the calls. The problem was that I couldn't stomach the movie. In the opening sequence, in order to get his lead drag queen/lover onstage, the club owner punches him in the face, giving him a black eye. The lover takes this as proof of affection. I was done, and never did watch the rest of that film until years later.

My agent, George Lane, called with yet another offer to write *La Cage*.

"How many times do I have to say no?"

"This is Allan Carr, the producer of *Grease*, and he wants to adapt the original French play, not the movie."

"So?"

"Listen to this team he assembled: Jay Presson Allen writing the book, Maury Yeston the score, Mike Nichols directing, and Tommy Tune choreographing."

Even a know-nothing like me was impressed. "So, I'm impressed," I said. "What's it got to do with me?"

"They've all left the project and he is offering the show to you."

"If the best in the business couldn't make it work . . ."

"Meet with him!"

Allan lived in a glass-enclosed penthouse atop the St. Regis Hotel. The door opened and there he stood, modeling one of his famous floor-length caftans, flanked by two men, each bearing a bouquet of yellow roses. Allan held out a piece of paper. "Here's a check for seventy-five hundred." He looked at the gaffer's tape holding my down jacket together and said, "Buy yourself a coat."

Fritz Holt and Barry Brown were a theater couple brought on to shepherd this production. Fritz was known as one of the strongest stage managers on Broadway. Allan handed me a big fat manuscript. "This is a literal translation of the original six-act French farce. They tried to sell me the movie rights as well, but I wasn't born yesterday. This is all we need."

For the record, the money he saved by not dealing with the owner of the movie rights cost us each millions later on, when Mike Nichols snapped them up to make *The Birdcage*.

I looked at this as a project I could play with on my daily subway rides into the city. I read the translation to figure out what I might do. The story began to come alive for me. It was a classic French farce, as if I knew what that was, with attitudes *of their time*. The last team had moved the action from the South of France to New Orleans. I knew I had to move it back to Saint-Tropez, where people can get away with singing and dancing in the street. That wasn't happening on Broadway at the moment unless you were a cat, auditioning for a chorus line, or had been voted Woman of the Year. And the gay politics were causing real battles here. People would be taking sides before they took their seats. Leaving the story in Saint-Tropez kept it exotic and safe. Who cares who's fucking who in France as long as it's fun?

I began by stripping the story down to its basics. The show would be about a hard-working couple who owned a building. They ran a business on the ground floor and lived over the store. Who can't relate to that? They would be respected members of their community whom everyone knew and accepted. I fancied their nightclub like any theatrical venue, glamorous by candlelight but a seedy mess by day. I imagined their residence to be clogged with the debris of past productions: feathered fans, glittery props, tasseled pillows, and the like. Whatever didn't fit backstage was dragged up and left in the apartment. As for the plot, I broke it down in black-and-white: a man struggles to keep the selfish son of his first marriage and his preening second wife from killing one another over the boy's engagement plans. Simple. Human. Relatable. The fact that this couple is gay and that they've raised a straight son who is now engaged to a girl whose parents are antigay bigots would be the coloring. And I would tell the story from the gay couple's point of view. In this world homosexuals are the norm, and heterosexuals the rare birds. I felt I was on to something.

Another call from George: "How would you feel about working with Jerry Herman?"

"Jerry Herman? The man who wrote *Mame* and *Hello, Dolly!*? You have to ask?"

The next day I was ringing the bell of Jerry's East Side town house. The door was answered by Damien, Jerry's houseboy. I thought I'd walked onto the set of *Mame*. Jerry was known for the impeccable restorations and decorating of his homes. This photo-ready abode was done in beige with pops of color in the artwork. His studio was a large sunlit room on the fourth floor; a trapeze hung from the ceiling, and a grand piano stood in the center. The walls held giant three sheets of his hit shows. Jerry greeted me with a mile-wide smile that could only be challenged by Carol Channing's. Before I could speak, he asked if I would listen to something he'd just written. He sat at the grand and performed his musicalization of Arnold's opening monologue from *Torch Song Trilogy*. I laughed and applauded like a fool. Eventually the song found its way into *La Cage* as "A Little More Mascara."

There was no getting around falling in love with Jerry. Sweet, funny, enthusiastic, and dishy, he glowed with the delight of an eternal optimist. I, who had never written a big-budget, high-profile Broadway musical, was completely outclassed partnering with this man who gave us songs the entire world knew by heart, but I swear that he never made me feel out of place.

George called again. "What do you think of Arthur Laurents directing?"

The collaborationists—Arthur
Laurents, Jerry Herman, and me

Really? He was actually asking if I'd want to work with the legendary author of *West Side Story, Gypsy,* and *The Way We Were?* "Send him over!" I said.

What a gutsy little queen I was. Still in my twenties, I had the nerve to claim a place at the table with two of the theater's greatest talents. Unbelievable! Arthur proposed a structure for our sessions. We'd work scene by scene, meeting once a week at Jerry's. We began each session with me reading aloud the new scene I'd just written. Arthur would edit it on the fly, barking out, "No jokes— cut that!" He demanded that all dialogue be true to the characters, without setups or punch lines. I teased Arthur, telling him he sounded like a barking dog. From then on, his order became "It's a dog. Take it out!"

Second item of business had us discussing how Jerry might musicalize that particular section. Sometimes it was a totally new idea, as with "The Best of Times," but more often he would cannibalize my dialogue into his lyrics, as with "I Am What I Am" or "Cocktail Conversation," resulting in the song and the scene melding into one.

Next, we'd discuss where the plot was going and what the next scene should be. Arthur was a genius at construction. Whatever he didn't know instinctively he'd learned at the knees of great directors and producers like Jerome Robbins and Hal Prince. Believe me, I listened to every word the man said, knowing full well that it came from the best in the biz. I was privy to lessons you could not get from any textbook or college class. The man knew his shit. Following his lead, our show took very few wrong steps.

Each week's final task was the most exciting. We read aloud the prior week's scene until we reached the point where Jerry's song would begin and then he'd sing us that new Jerry Herman tune for the first time. Can I possibly describe the thrill of hearing the heart wrenching "Look Over There" or the excitement of listening to the vamp that would become our title song for the first time? Unforgettable, thrilling, theater magic—that's the only description I can offer.

After hugs all around and one piece of chocolate doled out to each of us by Damien from a porcelain plate, I'd go off to write the next scene, Jerry would stay behind to compose the next song, and Arthur . . . ? I have no idea what Arthur did with himself.

When I got the call about Arthur I had immediately phoned his old and my new friend, Shirley MacLaine, with the exciting news.

"Call them back and tell them no!" she snapped.

"But why?" I asked. Arthur had written *The Turning Point,* one of my favorite of Shirley's films. I thought she'd be ecstatic for me.

"Let's say it's your birthday and a hundred of your favorite people are throwing you a party. You're surrounded with love and support and appreciation. Then the door opens and in walks Arthur, who, for reasons you will never understand, is cross with you. The love and support of one hundred friends will not protect you from the cruel intent of that man. By the time he's done, you will be sorry you ever thought of having a birthday."

Fast-forward three years to find us all standing together on the stage of the Uris Theatre, where *La Cage* has just won six Tony Awards. It's the finale of the broadcast, and everyone who'd participated in the evening is lined up together on bleachers singing "The Best of Times" from our show as the credits roll. On this happiest occasion I turned and gaped in horror at what was happening right in front of me, right in front of America, on live television. There, center stage, stood Arthur giving Shirley MacLaine notes on what was wrong with the one-woman show she'd done earlier that season. Forget a hundred friends. Millions of eyes could not protect her from Arthur.

A photographer from the *New York Post* heard me tell this story and sent me this photographic evidence. My favorite detail is Raquel Welch wondering what the hell was going on.

When photographer Dan Brinzac heard me tell the story, he
sent this photo as proof of the tale. You can clearly see Arthur
lecturing Shirley; even Raquel Welch looks disturbed.

Following Arthur's lead, we wrote *La Cage Aux Folles* in mere months. The process he laid out was so logical that progress was almost guaranteed. There were clashes and disagreements that left me in tears some days, but the longer we worked together, the more unified our vision grew. In under a year we were ready for production.

We held the backers' auditions in Jerry's studio and they were a breeze. Every theater owner who heard the show wanted the show. Every producer wanted a share. I nicknamed Arthur, Jerry, and me "the collaborationists," considering that this endeavor was subversive. We came from different eras but were united in our aim to see a Broadway audience cheer a man declaring undying ardor to his same-sex partner with a universal love song and a revolutionary kiss. This was the dream we shared. Or so I thought.

Before I say anything more, I want to clearly state that although I disagreed with him at the time, I believe Arthur may have been right about every one of his choices for the production. Under his direction *La Cage Aux Folles* became a blockbuster hit that is perpetually produced all over the world. My less yielding vision of the show might have shuttered us during the out-of-town tryouts. Still, it was a shock to see Arthur muffling the more outrageous aspects as much as he did. I understood his wanting to make it commercially viable. My fear was that he was making it sterile. His production was beautiful and theatrical but not sexy. Nevertheless, he made it an undeniable seismic attraction. I wanted the show to change the world, but you ain't changing nothing unless you're putting asses in the seats.

The set was the first surprise. Arthur followed my stage directions right down to flying Albin in on a trapeze inspired by the one in Jerry's studio, but instead of the hodgepodge apartment of a drag queen we had a pink marble mansion complete with carved columns and satin-upholstered furniture. When I expressed my concern, Arthur said, "This isn't campy enough for you? Have you seen them?" pointing out a pair of life-sized porcelain animals as part of the decor. The male was a giraffe, the female a kangaroo, complete with plush baby in her pouch.

"Arthur," I said, "can't they at least both be male?"

"They are," he replied. "The kangaroo is in drag" and he had the designer add one crystal earring as proof.

Jerry tried to jump in and help. "Don't worry. I'm going to add a whole bunch of stuff to the glass shelves."

A display of Murano glass was hardly what I had in mind. And I don't care if Arthur did add an earring. Male kangaroos don't have pouches!

I provided what authenticity I could from my own experiences. The gimmick of the performers revealing their true genders by removing their wigs during their bow came from an unhappy incident I'd survived in Montreal. Performing at a club, I was ordered to take my wig off at the end of my act. It was the law. Law or not, I didn't wear a wig. I had my own long hair. The manager shrugged; "It's your ass," and left me to my own devices. At the end of the second show, I bowed and exited the stage to find two policemen waiting for me. Luckily, they let me off with a promise to at least ruffle my hair as I bowed. In the show Zaza attempts to pass himself off as the boy's biological mother to the anti-homosexual parents of the boy's fiancée. We needed a clever way to unmask Zaza as a man. I remembered that incident and wrote it right into the show. At the end of each production number the drag queens would line up, bow, and then remove their wigs to reveal themselves to be men. It became a routine in the show's rhythm. And so, when Zaza, disguised as the mother, finishes entertaining his dinner guests with a song, it is a totally natural move for him to bow and whip off his wig to the shock of all in attendance. It never failed to elicit applause and screams of delight from the audience.

Casting was the next hurdle. I thought I had Arthur's trust and that he'd let me slip a few real drag performers into the show. Arthur had his own ideas. Not only did he reject the use of actual female impersonators, but he announced that two of the club's drag performers would be women.

"Women dressed as men, yes?" I asked hopefully.

"No," he replied sternly. "They will be part of the line. This way, should a straight man feel attracted to one of the performers, he can ease his guilt by telling himself he was looking at one of the real girls."

He also thought it would be a publicity getter, which it certainly was. Authenticity be damned. The audience would try to figure out which ones were the biological females before the wigs came off. Even then, Arthur had one of our male ensemble grow his hair long so the reveal showed a blond mane longer than the wig. Audiences loved it. I loathed it.

Next came my argument to cast gay men in the leads. I pleaded: "The greatest young actress in the world cannot fully express the role of a grandmother. There are things that life has simply not taught her—the gravitas of age, the price of getting older . . ."

Arthur waved me off. "Do you know what your problem is? You are a heterophobe," he pronounced, as he cast two of the straightest men who'd ever trodden the boards —Gene Barry, television's Bat Masterson, and George Hearn, Sweeney Todd himself.

Arguing with a man who knows everything is futile, so I pulled back and tried to enjoy the ride without bumping heads with Arthur again. Good luck with that. Arthur got a kick out of splitting people into cliques. You were either part of his inner circle, whom he bathed with attention, or you were a derided and ignored castoff. No sorority girl ever enjoyed dismissing outsiders more than he did. For example, when our costume designer, Theoni V. Aldredge, measured us three for personally designed tuxedos to wear on opening night, Arthur made certain that he and Jerry got theirs and I would never get mine. It wasn't just my questioning his authority that had me kicked to the curb. The press was beginning to buzz around the show, and Arthur didn't like the amount of attention I was getting. Jerry teased me, saying, "Welcome to the club." He went on to explain, "It's not what you did, it's who you are." And then he borrowed an old movie line: "There is only one star in an Arthur Laurents production."

I was being courted by Brandon Tartikoff to create a sitcom for myself on NBC. Lunching in a Midtown restaurant, we discussed the odds of an American audience embracing an openly gay man playing an openly gay character in prime time.

He opined: "When I put Jim Bailey on a show to impersonate Judy or Barbra, we make him first appear in a tuxedo, smoking a big fat cigar, to prove he's all-man before he straps his tits on. Even then I drown in letters complaining, 'How dare you put that singing fruit on TV?'"

I said, "This season we only put acting fruits onstage in *Torch Song*. They'll have to wait until next season for singing and dancing fruits."

Do waiters still make extra cash feeding items to gossip columns?

They did back then, and my words made the morning edition of the *New York Post*'s Page Six. When I walked into the studio, Arthur halted the rehearsal with a gesture. On his signal the entire company stood as one and turned their backs on me. Arthur then spoke: "You may call yourself anything you like, but we'll thank you not to refer to any of us as a fruit."

He then dismissed the company for a break. I stood for a moment in utter shock and then ran to the office to hide. Arthur came in and stood over me. I swear that little man had grown six inches with this maneuver. "You, better than anyone, know how I feel about our people," I said through tears.

"And you know they'd all call us queers if they could get away with it. You just let them get away with it."

"Arthur, we're doing a show called *La Cage Aux Folles*. Poiret himself"—Jean Poiret, the author of the original French farce—"told us that he named the show 'The Fag Cage.'"

"You're not downtown anymore," he said. "If you want to play in the big leagues you'd better learn to watch your mouth."

I certainly had a lot to learn and got an important lesson that day. It might not have been the one Arthur thought he was teaching, but it's a lesson that has served me over the decades. I never allowed Arthur to hurt me again.

During the next few days some members of the cast apologized for taking part in the shaming. Most did not. But I will always remember the genuine kindness of Elizabeth Parrish, who said that whenever she recited her lines in the show, praising Zaza as someone who brought joy wherever she went, she was always thinking of me. Elizabeth was playing Jacqueline, a character named for my mother.

As for dear, crusty old Arthur, late in the run, when he finally cast two gay men in the leads, he phoned to say, "I do not do this often and I do not do this lightly—you were right. Gay men make all the difference." And the prick hung up.

27

TORCH SONG TRILOGY ON BROADWAY

orch Song Trilogy opened on Broadway at the beginning of
June 1982 and immediately became a symbol of the struggle
for gay rights. That same week, the New York City Council
was debating a gay rights bill for the tenth time in as many years.
Community leader and friend Andy Humm asked me to appear
at the hearing. Also speaking in support of the bill was another
friend, Charlie Cochrane Jr. Charlie was a sergeant in the NYPD at
a time when few police officers were out of the closet. He founded
a national organization called GOAL, the Gay Officers Action
League. I remember breathlessly listening to him as he addressed
the council, refuting the testimony given by the Archdiocese of
New York, the Knights of Columbus, the Central Rabbinical Congress, and the Union of Orthodox Rabbis, among others. "It is not
a contradiction that I am a gay cop," he said. "We gays are loathed
by some, pitied by others, and misunderstood by most. We are not
cruel, wicked, cursed, sick, or possessed . . . Why must others be
so concerned with my sexual activity and choice of consenting
partner?"

We in the peanut gallery gave him a standing ovation.

Later that evening, Jay, my spasmodic boyfriend, and I met up
with Charlie for drinks at the Ninth Circle. I asked how his father,
Charlie Cochrane Sr., was dealing with this public pronouncement.

He told me that they'd negotiated an agreement. His dad would support his work for the gay community if, when he retired from the force, he went into the priesthood. "How the fuck is that going to work?" I asked.

"Like you don't know?" Charlie laughed. "Mother Church is more than aware of how many gay men join the clergy. All they ask is that you refrain from having sex during the period when you're taking your vows."

Charlie moved to Florida and we lost touch over the years. He died in 2008 at sixty-four. In 2013 a small street in the Village, not far from the Stonewall, was renamed in his honor. As far as Charlie knowing me well was concerned, he was right. I slept with more than my share of priests in my day, although I've yet to bed a rabbi. There was, however, a pair of young Hasidic men who would ditch their black coats and hats somewhere, stuff their *tsi-tsis* into their pants, and venture into the back room of the Stud. With their identical white shirts and black slacks, their ringlets tucked carefully behind their ears, they reminded me of a pair of salt and pepper shakers. I thought they were adorable and almost irresistible as their bodies convulsed and they sighed in otherworldly relief. Anyway, Jews are great kissers. Fooling around with them made me feel wicked but at the same time grounded as my worlds linked together. Their vacation from sanctity didn't last long. Others in their sect discovered their escape route and one night set upon the joint with biblical indignation. They smashed the windows and pelted the patrons with rocks and bottles. I mourned their happiness, as these young men never returned. I'm sure someone who loved them prayed for their contentment. But what do I know about the lives of the devout? Last year I ran across a set of keys in a drawer that unlocked the rectory of an Episcopal church in Brooklyn and smiled, remembering how I came to have them.

That first year of *Torch Song* on Broadway was not easy. We had a couple of great weeks, a few good weeks, and a whole mess of marginal ones.

Ken, John, and the others did a masterful job keeping us running, never taking their eyes off the calendar as they looked a year ahead toward awards season. The question was, having been around all this time, could we now make the critics, the award voters, and the arts editors remember how much they once loved the show?

Betty Lee came up with a brilliant idea. She asked if I'd mind switching one of the torch songs for the standard "You Made Me Love You." I had no problem with that. So she called in favors from celebrities and columnists and created a series of advertisements picturing the celeb within a heart and saying, "You made me love you." Sometimes she even included an actual quote from their review. One of the people she called was her dear friend Ethel Merman, who said she couldn't do it unless she saw the show, so . . . she came. Knowing this legend was in the house had me a wreck all through the performance. Afterwards, I rushed back to my dressing room to get cleaned up. Suddenly there she was, in all of her glorious Mermanificence, live in my doorway.

"Oh, Miss Merman, I am one of your most devoted fans. I'm so honored you came to see the show. Please, I'm dying to know what you thought."

She took a beat and then, loud enough to be heard in Pittsburgh, "I thought it was a piece of shit. But the rest of the audience laughed and cried, so what the fuck do I know?"

Our awards campaign invited reviewers back to see the show again. In those days, theater critics could be Tony voters. Frank Rich of *The New York Times* favored my friend Jules Feiffer's terrific piece *Grown Ups* in the race for Best Play. Betty Lee complained to the committee that never having seen us, he should not be allowed to vote. With full knowledge that I didn't perform matinees, Mr. Rich showed up one afternoon, watched the first act, and as he walked out of the theater, snapped at Betty Lee, "There. I've seen your show."

Betty Lee then told me, "I am going to make you do interviews with every school newspaper and grocery handout there is. By the time you're done with the small-poke stuff, you will know exactly how to give a great interview for the big guns."

She was right. She transformed me into someone who spewed quotables and sold tickets. Betty Lee worked every angle she could and, before she was done, we had been nominated for every theater award that season. I'm sorry to say that neither Court nor Estelle received the attention they both deserved. Court and the others took the snubs in stride, but not Estelle. When she won her Emmy for *The Golden Girls* she told me she'd trade it in a heartbeat for a Tony.

My relationship with Ron Tavel became more and more strained. Although he was doing great work with residencies at Yale and Cornell and Albee's writing retreat, he found my move to Broadway a challenge. I understood. He was genuinely happy for me while at the same time resentful of the attention and success I was achieving. We hardly spoke anymore, and according to Harvey, Ronald spent a good deal of energy running me down. I hated that I was coming between the brothers. One night I arrived home from work to find a note from Harvey concerning their mother. "Flo is getting older and I worry about her living alone in her house. I would like to move her in here with me. Please start making plans to move out of your apartment."

There was no arguing. He was right. It was time for me to move on. He had done more than raise and shelter me all those years. I wrote "Thank you" on the back of the note and left it for him.

A parking garage was being renovated into co-ops a few blocks away. I made arrangements to buy an apartment there. I was so busy at the time that this rather momentous rite of passage was almost passing me by: I was getting my own legit flat. Harvey Tavel, who'd retired from teaching, now worked part-time for a designer showroom in the city. He gave me the name of a woman he thought I should hire to design my place. I laughed when I read her card: "Judi Schwarz Interiors of Parsippany New Jersey." In another of life's coincidences, Judi was a zealous fan who bombarded my dressing room with gifts every few weeks. She took the job of designing my apartment and we became friends.

That spring got even crazier. Every morning I stopped at the construction site to check on my apartment. On to the city, where I watched *La Cage Aux Folles* rehearsing for the Boston tryout. Next to my dressing room for a nap or an interview about either *Torch*

Song or *La Cage*, and then my three-hour performance in *Torch Song Trilogy*.

It was finally the night of the Tony Awards. The play had already won the Drama Desk Award and the Hull-Warriner Award from the Dramatists Guild earlier that season. I didn't know what to expect of this night. Even after a year, Broadway still felt unreal to me. In my heart I was still this kid from La MaMa who suited up in a tux. The first presentation that night was for Best Play.

When Diahann Carroll announced our win, John and Lawrence, Betty Lee and Maria, Marty, Ken, and I all ran up to accept the award. I spoke first, blathering some incoherent nonsense, but then John, sensing the historic significance of the event, spoke, calling it a stupendous moment and accepted the award in the name of his brothers and sisters, and his partner and lover, Lawrence Lane. If you watch the tape you can actually see Betty Lee whisper "Let's go!" afterwards. She knew that a cultural landmark had just occurred. Truthfully, I did not. I mean, why wouldn't John thank Lawrence for doing all the work? And as half of a married couple, why *wouldn't* he mention their relationship?

The world read about John's speech in headlines the next morning. Later that night, on *The Tonight Show,* Johnny Carson thanked his lover and partner . . . Doc Severinsen.

Folklore has it that I was the first to thank my boyfriend, but as you see, not true. I didn't even thank him while accepting my acting Tony later that night. It was the following year that I took up the cause. I'd been nominated for writing *La Cage Aux Folles* and sat comfortably in my seat sure that having won the year before, I would not win again, which was fine with me. James Lapine was nominated for *Sunday in the Park with George* and I was rooting for him to win. Alexander Cohen was producing the evening, and before the show went on air, he spoke to the crowd about proper TV etiquette. Among the usual admonitions about going to the loo or falling asleep he said, "And please, no one repeat the embarrassment of last year's Best Play winners."

I felt the eyes of the room turn toward me. Suddenly I wanted nothing more than to win. When my name was called, I took to the stage and thanked my lover for helping to type the script. The world did not end. Johnny did not thank Doc again. In fact, the only criticism I saw was from columnist Liz Smith. I was shocked. Not only was she a friend, but she was a lesbian friend. Sometime later I was on some talk show and I told this story, saying that the only bad press I got was from a closeted lesbian. I named no names, gave no publications. Still, Liz considered this a declaration of war and held it against me for decades. Almost thirty years later she put pen to paper and acknowledged her error in a beautiful note. I am happy to say that we found time to kiss and make up before she died.

That first Tony night happened to take place on the eve of my birthday. My brother, worried that I would not win and wanting to ease the letdown, arranged for a birthday cake to be delivered to my table at the Tony ball. It was one of the dearest gestures ever, but when the cake arrived, my mother was nowhere to be found. We hadn't seen her for half an hour. Everyone went off in search of her, and she was finally discovered in the ladies' room, sitting on the sink, chatting with Eydie Gormé and Mary Lindsay, wife of former New York mayor John Lindsay.

It was morning by the time we got back to my apartment. The phone machine was filled with messages. My boyfriend, Lonnie, nearly jumped out of his skin at the sound of Katharine Hepburn's voice congratulating me on the twin wins. I never had the heart to tell him that it was just a female-impersonator friend and not Ms. Hepburn at all.

Before getting into bed, the newly crowned double Tony Award winner let the dogs out and rummaged through his mail only to find a letter from the New York City Board of Education. It seemed, a decade after graduation, I had finally been assigned a job as an art teacher at a high school in the Bronx. Everyone else on the waiting list must have used connections or found other ways to jump the line and snag a teaching gig ahead of me. I, who obeyed the rules and waited for an assignment, had finally reached the top of the list all these years later. It was a very good lesson as to why one should never obey the rules of a bureaucracy.

The applause that greeted my first entrance in *Torch Song* the next night was so overwhelming that I could not speak my opening lines. I simply sat in place, alone in the spotlight, tears rolling down my cheeks, bathing in the celebration. It was only then that I began to feel the weight of this achievement for our community. For many of my brothers and sisters it was the first time they existed as real people. They weren't an illness or a disorder or an aberration. They were award winners.

28

LA CAGE AUX FOLLES
IN BOSTON

I floated through my final week at *Torch Song*. Leaving the new cast behind, I hopped the shuttle to Boston and before checking into the hotel I rushed to the Colonial Theatre hoping to catch whatever I could of *La Cage*'s final rehearsal. I made my way around to the theater's alley, where stagehands were wrestling a large piece of scenery.

"Oh, no," I said. "Are you still loading stuff in?"

"Out!" the man grumbled.

"Out?"

He nodded toward a huge pile of scenery clogging the alley. "The director keeps pointing at things and hollering, 'It's a dog—take it out!'"

I went around to the front of the theater and opened the door of that magnificent hall. There I saw, heard, and felt the life-sucking thud of a technical rehearsal grinding painfully on. Actors stood around in their costumes, bored and nervous, while lights were being focused and furniture adjusted. Designers were scattered throughout the mostly empty hall, chewing their fingers and giving orders to their assistants. Stage management checked with stagehands to see how much longer they'd need. It was impossible to imagine we'd play to our first audience in twenty-four hours—and we didn't.

"Tomorrow . . . maybe . . . dress rehearsal" is how Marvin

Krauss, our general manager, greeted me as he rushed by on his way to the box office to cancel our first preview. Jerry wasn't there. Arthur didn't look approachable. I watched from a safe distance for a few minutes, but it was painfully clear, even to a newbie like me, that the last thing anyone needed in that theater was a starry-eyed book writer. I retreated to my suite in the Park Plaza Hotel.

Near-hysteria was the general mood of the hundred or so of us scattered around the theater that next afternoon. Designers, assistants, tech folks . . . we were about to witness the first-ever full dress rehearsal of a brand-new musical. The orchestra was warming up in the pit when Fritz Holt stood leaning against the proscenium, looking to Arthur for the final okay. Arthur nodded; Fritz ducked backstage and within moments called the first cue. I could feel my face flush as every muscle in my body contracted. Don Pippin, the legendary musical director, took to the podium and gave the orchestra its downbeat. The overture sounded spectacular as the curtain rose on a Saint-Tropez street scene. Center stage stood a pink building with a glowing marquee, "La Cage Aux Folles." On cue the building began its journey downstage toward us and . . . fell over! Yes, it lurched and toppled flat on its face, stopping the show dead in its tracks. My brain began to chant the mantra "Bad dress rehearsal, good opening night. Bad dress rehearsal, good opening night."

A few hours later they restarted, and the rehearsal went on without another major disaster. Arthur snuck down the aisle to say, "Watch the Dindon house scene. I think it's a dog."

In the story, the girl's father is a right-wing religious bigot. Jerry and I concocted a scene and song for him in the first act. Jerry's ditty was a satiric prayer, a litany of all the kinds of people the father hates, "homos" topping that list. I watched the scene and bade it farewell. Arthur was right. What was gentle ribbing in a rehearsal room was horse flogging amplified on a legit stage. Into the alley that scenery went.

We survived dress rehearsal. We "collaborationists" got together for a little private prayer before our first audience arrived. After telling Arthur what a great job I thought everyone was doing, I took a deep breath and continued, "I love Albin appearing in a suit for the final duet. So romantic. But aren't they going to kiss before the curtain comes down? You told me they would."

"I don't think it's necessary."

"But it would be romantic."

"They walk off into the sunset together. That's not romantic enough for you?"

I dared to push on, "But a kiss would be so sweet. They've been a couple for more than twenty years . . ."

"Exactly. How many couples together that long still kiss?"

"Can we at least try it?"

"That's what I'm asking you. Can't we at least try it this way?" With that, I was dismissed.

I met my brother for dinner at the Union Oyster House before the first preview. He had just flown in and was beside himself. "I'm trying to get them to finish your apartment before you get back, but that Judi . . . now she wants to mirror an entire wall of your bedroom, including the doors."

"I know. It's in the design."

"Do you know how much it will cost to mirror all of that? You are way overbudget already. I told her to stop." Halfway through my salad and my stomach was beginning to flop around.

We headed for the theater. The place was pretty well packed for a first preview of a brand-new show on a Bostonian summer's night. Arthur was sitting in front of us and Jerry behind. The music started and I began to applaud. Arthur spun around and grabbed my hands. "No! If you set off the applause we'll never know what the audience will do on its own."

Thus chided, I tried not to clap, laugh, or breathe unless the people around us did so first. What the hell did I know? I'd never launched a show in a theater with more than ninety-nine seats before. Sitting among seventeen hundred other people, watching a show I wrote for the first time, wasn't just exciting. It was otherworldly.

The orchestra played, the curtain rose, the audience applauded without my help, and *La Cage* went zipping along. Everyone appeared to be having a great time. No one was shuffling their feet. They were laughing where they were supposed to. They were intently following the story as we'd hoped. And then we reached the café scene: Georges and Albin sitting at a seaside café, under the moonlight, romantically reminiscing about the night they first met and fell in love. I looked at the faces, first the ones around me, and then as far across the auditorium as I could see, and everyone was engaged. Onstage a man was singing about his love for another man, and the audience was with him. Directly across the aisle from me, a man took his wife's hand into his. I leaned forward and hit Arthur on the shoulder with excitement. I looked back at Jerry and he was shaking his head in disbelief. At the end of the song the applause was thunderous. Thunderous! A man just sang a tender love song to another man—in Boston, no less—and the applause was thunderous.

The audience stayed with us, completely involved, until the final curtain, which brought a standing ovation and cheers. My brother says I fell to the ground. I only remember crying and shaking and hugging Jerry and Arthur and anyone else who came near. We were, without doubt, a hit in Boston. Back at the hotel my brother called Judi and told her to diamond-stud the bedroom mirrors.

Jerry had a friend in town with a pool. He and Arthur and I swam and sunned and cut half an hour's worth of material from the script before going back to rehearsal. Over the next few weeks we cut and polished and sharpened the show as we readied for our Broadway opening. The word was out: we were the toast of Boston. Jerry and I were even invited to Julia Child's home, where the legend cooked dinner for us herself. Of course, I had to wait another twenty-seven years to get my kiss at the final curtain. When I tried to push him, Arthur said, "Some people just can't accept success."

And then came the matinee of the nuns.

Arthur and Jerry took the time off, but I stopped by to catch a few minutes of the show. I was curious to see how it played to an afternoon audience. The second act was in full swing when I arrived. Looking out across the house I noticed a sea of black. Nuns! Dozens of them, in full habit, seated together in the orchestra. I grinned, thinking, *Wait until they see how the boy has redecorated the apartment.*

To please his in-laws-to-be, the son ditches all of the gay decor and replaces it with monasterial dowdiness. The centerpiece was a life-sized crucifix hanging by the door. I maneuvered my way down along the side wall to get a better view of the nuns for the apartment reveal. The lights came up and the redecoration was met with delightful laughter and applause. I could see the nuns nodding and nudging one another with approval. But as the scene progressed, the son—a young, inexperienced actor making his Broadway debut—was supposed to run about the room ensuring everything was in place. Doing so, he accidentally knocked the crucifix from the wall. It came crashing down onto the floor. In a panic and not knowing what else to do, this young fellow picked up the life-sized crucifix, opened the front door, and heaved it out with a crash. The audience gasped in horror. I ran to the house manager to make certain he'd speak to the sisters as soon as the curtain came down. They were angry, to be sure, but peace was achieved via contrition and a fistful of free seats for a repeat viewing.

La Cage was a Boston phenomenon. We added as many extra weeks as we could. Allan Carr was swatting away investors and eager partners by the dozen. One night, television and movie producer David Susskind was so desperate to talk to Jerry and me about getting involved in the show that he climbed down from a box seat onto the stage during the curtain call to reach us. Word spread to New York, and the box office opened to a healthy ticket-buying line. As a publicity stunt Allan kept the box office open twenty-four hours a day. He also wanted to paint the exterior of the Palace Theatre hot pink. Thankfully, the show needed no such gimmicks.

Opening night on Broadway was one of those rare occasions without nerves or worry. The critics didn't matter. We were a hit, a genuine crowd pleaser that had audiences giving standing ovations in the middle of the performance. As the curtain call began, Arthur, Jerry, and I ran to the back of the house to watch and celebrate together. We hugged and kissed and wept and congratulated one another. Looking out over the jubilant scene, I suddenly felt a hand on my shoulder. It was general manager Marvin Krauss. He leaned into me and said, "Enjoy tonight and then go away."

I looked at him with puzzlement.

"The show is a hit and will be here for years. Some of these folks will never have another night like this, so they'll stay here trying to hang on to this moment from tonight until the closing. You have other things to do. Go away."

29

AIDS

1982 Onward

A man described how it felt when his bungalow was hit by a tsunami. Asleep in bed, the solid earth beneath him began to rumble. He heard what he described as a jet engine. And then he was churning under water, gasping for air, slamming over and around inside an enormous washing machine filled with glass and bricks and nails. It was hours before someone reached and pulled him from a pile of rubble. It was years before he believed he had survived. I listened to him and thought, *I know what you mean.*

Sometime in the summer of 1982 AIDS slammed into us like a tsunami. Until then it was a story we read about and a rumor we passed around. Suddenly it was real. Don't ask me who died first or who was hospitalized when or how I heard that someone was sick. Information traveled on a nameless drone. Unrelenting, constantly crashing against us, we struggled to stay upright.

We simultaneously searched for and hid from information. Newspapers devoted far greater real estate to traffic accidents. Our brains seethed with questions: Is this "gay cancer"? How is it spread? Could I have it? Who do you know? How did you know? Did you hear about him? And the answers were just as unhelpful: I didn't know he was gay. It's God's punishment. Married people don't get it. They all have it. The theater is full of it. I won't go to a restaurant. I can't get my hair done. They spit in your food. Just avoid them.

We were on our own, sounding the alarm, propping up our sick, demanding attention. AIDS was attacking on so many fronts that we didn't know where to aim the meager weapons we had. What did we have? Anger? Fear? Desperation? The louder we screamed "Help us," the faster they ran away. Scientists were alarmed, but who in government cares about what scientists find alarming? "Can I get it?" was the only question they asked. The politicians I spoke with seemed incapable of separating the virus from the people it was attacking. "Sexually transmitted" was permission to judge the worth of the ill. "They bring it on themselves." We fought one another with the same ferocity with which we battled the disease. Should we close the bars? Would shuttering the bathhouses and back rooms help stop the spread? Condoms were protection to some and an attack on our hard-fought freedom to others. We knew it was a virus, but it felt like a judgment.

Ronald Reagan, our first make-believe president, was told that there was no treatment, cure, or vaccine on the horizon. Taking AIDS on meant getting involved in a losing campaign issue. And since it only affected the gay male and drug-using populations, there was no political damage to ignoring the disease completely. Even with his personal friends succumbing, Reagan didn't speak the word "AIDS" publicly for five years. He taught us a reality that had always been staring us in the face: a politician's first priority is to get reelected. Second is to fund-raise. Third is to protect his party. Caring about a disease that is killing a small unpopular minority ranks somewhere below hosting Icelandic dignitaries at the White House.

It's one thing to say, there is no cure, quite another to say there is no hope. We promised one another "We're going to be okay" while we screamed to the world, "Can't you see we're dying?" We stared at one another with suspicion. We studied one another for signs of disease. Makeup disguises just so many sores. Walking with a cane is stylish only if you don't need one. Lust dressed in death's mantle. We wanted and we feared. Some dove headfirst back into the closet. Others were outed by the disease itself. The casual mention of a doctor's appointment became an admission of guilt.

Community leaders emerged with the formation of grass-root organizations, but with goals so disparate these warriors struggled to stay focused: care for the sick, prevent the spread, raise money for research, educate the public, awaken the government, inform the press, demand health care, engage drug companies . . . Our dead lay on gurneys in hospital storerooms. Many funeral homes would not handle AIDS patients. Houses of worship withheld burial rites. Cemeteries blocked access to graves. Parents disowned their children and refused to accept their remains. Others scavenged the bedroom drawers of the dead for valuables while shunning the surviving partners, denying them any rights, respect, or recognition. There was an entire room at Bailey House, an AIDS residence, filled floor-to-ceiling with pornographic magazines and VHS tapes that families donated from their deceased's abodes. Employers fired gays at will. Home-care agencies and nurses hid behind religious dogma to reject patients. Discrimination was given the all-loving God's stamp of approval, and courts of law backed them up. Dentists shoved dental dams in our mouths and covered our faces with plastic wrap, like hazardous waste, before they'd touch us. We were banned from donating blood. Not just banned: outlawed. They criminalized gay men who gave blood, a disgrace that continues to this day. Thankfully our lesbian sisters stepped in to fill that void. Blessed be our lesbian sisters. We were unclean. Unkosher. Unacceptable. Subhuman. Diseased. Thank you for reminding us.

Within our community so many heroes were doing so much good work. I shy from naming the dozens that quickly come to mind because I will leave off hundreds more who deserve to be lauded. Surely you've heard of some; but most, like the masked nurses who held the hands of our friends as they struggled for air or took their last breaths, will remain unnamed but are no less heroic. I'm sad to admit, for all the good uncovered during those years, I have never been able to shake the feeling that the heterosexual community at large let us die. They wished us well, then turned their backs, issuing sighs of relief that they had nothing to worry about. I've buried the ashes of three friends in my yard. I suppose a piece of me is out there as well.

I was meeting Joan Rivers for lunch in the city. On my way out I stopped at my mailbox and there, waiting, neatly boxed and labeled, were my friend Christopher's ashes. His wish was to be buried at my house, and here he was, sitting amongst a few catalogs and charity requests. I couldn't just leave him there, so I dropped the box into my backpack and drove away.

My backpack sat on an empty seat at our lunch table as Joan and I settled into our usual easy gossip. I couldn't help thinking how much Chris would have loved being there. I imagined him calling out for a better view of the table and thought, *Why not? Joan's got her silly-ass lapdog with her. Why can't I have my friend? She'll understand. She only lost her husband, Edgar, a few years earlier.*

I apologized and told Joan about Christopher's ashes as I placed them on the table next to me.

Joan said, "Hey, I get it," removing a small tin from her purse and placing it on the table as well. "I never go anywhere without a little bit of Edgar."

Joel Crothers, Court Miller, Christopher Stryker, Herb Vogler, Richard DeFabees, Scott Oakley, Ned Levy, and Phil Astor are the names of the *Torch Song Trilogy* cast members we lost. From where I sit there are treatments and drugs but still no cure. I sometimes wonder if pharmaceutical companies are even looking, since their financials are so impressive treating AIDS as a chronic ailment. Young men wishing to be sexually active must likewise sign on to a lifetime of taking pills for protection. I spit at the TV screen every time I see a cheerfully produced ad announcing yet one more new drug that will allow you to live as if you were normal. They've turned us into drug addicts, and managing us is a very profitable business.

Richard Hale was an Okie of Cherokee descent who came to New York to be gay. He stripped his shoulder-length hair platinum, and although he usually wore a mustache, he never left the house without a full face of makeup. All Richard wanted was to fall in love. He worked as a receptionist and lived modestly in the East Village. Richard was a lot of fun. He was good natured and good sex and the kind of friend you always wanted to be around. I could never figure out why he had so much trouble finding Mr. Right. And then he did. He met Izad and everything came together at last. Izad was sick, but no matter, Richard made a home for them. The sicker Izad became, the harder Richard worked to keep him alive. Izad's family, as was his wish, knew nothing. Richard's family, as was his wish, were spared no detail. When Izad died, Richard took care of the burial arrangements. He settled any odds and ends, and when all was done he set out to get himself infected. Richard was HIV negative, but he decided he wanted to die as Izad had died. He believed it would bring them back together. Ironically, it was a struggle to get his blood to convert, and even then it took years of debilitating, painful illness until his body finally succumbed and freed him. Years. I had to admire how hard he worked at dying. He approached it with religious devotion. Assuming, for the sake of the poetic, that there is life after death, I wondered if Izad would greet him with open arms or anger.

Surrounded by disease, the world was an uncomfortable place. Beautiful men came with warning labels affixed. There was no longer anything casual about casual sex. It was a subject that could not be ignored. One warm evening my friend Judi arranged to pick Lonnie and me up and we all headed to Little Italy for the feast of San Gennaro. During the drive Judi was talking about her own dating life and how the men she was meeting wanted nothing to do with condoms. I said, "Cheating used to mean the death of a relationship. Now it just means death."

Lonnie, sitting in the backseat of Judi's Benz, began to say something. I didn't catch what it was, but Judi violently cut the steering wheel, pulled the car over to the curb, and ordered both of us out. "Get out now!" she said as she unlocked the automatic doors. Whatever she heard him say must have been bad, and she wanted no part of the conversation that was about to happen.

Lonnie and I got out and she peeled away. I looked at him and he shrugged, saying, "Can we get a drink?"

We arrived back at my place carrying a fresh six-pack of Bud, not the regular size but the tall ones, and a bottle of Southern Comfort. Lonnie tearfully confessed to having slept with his ex. I listened and nodded as he went through the story and the six-pack. With barely a word I sent him off to bed. I then emptied the hamper, did the laundry, fetched a duffel bag from the back of the closet, and filled it with all of Lonnie's belongings. I cleaned the ashtrays of his cigarette butts and put his empty beer cans in a garbage bag and dropped it all down the incinerator shaft before going to bed. The alarm woke him in time to get to work in the morning. After rushing to dress he found the packed duffel bag waiting for him at the door. I'd removed my key from his key ring and left a subway token in its place. So ended our years together.

At that time I'd go in and out of performing *Torch Song* whenever the box office needed a boost. My condo was designed to fit my life, to offer me comfort, but it now felt oddly unfamiliar. I'd thought of it as my sanctuary, but now, no matter how personally it was decorated, the world waited right outside the door. Betty Lee and Maria spent weekends in a small Connecticut town where they had a charming converted barn. I was often an invited guest. I loved swimming in their pool, and Maria was a terrific home cook, and the booze flowed while we sat around the fireplace and gossiped. Heaven. One weekend I was sharing photos of apartments I'd been looking at in Manhattan. I thought a change of residence would help somehow. Maria said, "You already have a place in town. Why not a country house? It could be your quiet place to write. You could have a pool for the summers and your dogs would love it."

I found a Malibu-style beach house sitting on the rim of a New England hill with a hundred-mile west-facing view, and although I've replaced the house over the years, I've made my home there ever since. The world is still outside, but I no longer feel locked behind a door.

I wanted to write a play about what I was witnessing, not one of those Disease of the Month things. There were plenty of Hallmark weepers around already: award bait. Portraying us as tragic victims wasn't helping rally the world to our cause or warning them to be cautious. It only made our community less hopeful and feel more like victims. I wanted to write about our lives and how they were being changed by AIDS. I had an idea for a trilogy. No one in these

plays would have AIDS, but all of their lives will have been trans-
formed by the disease. I called the evening *Safe Sex* because there
was no such thing. You could exercise safer sex practices, but the
danger inherent in sex, with or without a disease, was ever present.

   Manny and Jake depicts a man cruising for sex. He sees another
hot man and approaches.

JAKE: Can you kiss?
MANNY: Do I inspire you to lust?
JAKE: What if I said yes?
MANNY: I'd have to say no.

In a playfully abstract scene, I presented a man whose life was
dedicated to the enjoyment of sex in all of its variety with as many
partners as possible. Now, with the onset of AIDS, he's been told
to restrict his activities to "safer sex practices," which he sees as a
bastardization of this life's purpose. Refusing to alter his behavior,
he swears off intimacy until after a cure is found.

MANNY: And then I will kiss. I will kiss. I will kiss having
learned nothing.

The second play, from which the trilogy takes its title, gives
us two men who'd been partners but had broken up. Now, partially seeking safety in the familiar, they've come back together for
another try. Seeing male relationships as a struggle for dominance,
I set the play on a giant seesaw, one lover on either end. Dressed
in nightshirts, ready for bed, the two maintain balance by staying apart, sticking to their own end of the seesaw. As they argue
about everything from cheating to politics, one of them comes to
the realization that AIDS has unmasked the gay community: even
deniers now see gay men on the nightly news, in the papers, and in
everyday life. He muses: ". . . And all because of a disease. A disease you get, not because you're gay, but because you're human. We
were gay . . . and now we're human."

   The play ends with a miracle. Having declared his love, one of

the men leaves his side of the seesaw and walks the span to his partner as the board remains perfectly balanced.

John Bolger took to the seesaw with me in this shot
from the La MaMa premiere of *Safe Sex*.

As with *Torch Song*, the style of the third play—*On Tidy Endings*—is realistic. Court Miller died leaving a grieving lover and an
ex-wife behind. Taking great liberties with the truth, I presented
this mourning pair to compare their pain, bargain their social positions, aim blame at each other, and finally embrace in healing.

As I said, no one in *Safe Sex* has AIDS but no one in the plays
escapes its effects.

We premiered at La MaMa, where the plays were received almost
with gratitude. The audience was more than with us. They *were*
us, and we were them. It was remarkable. Frank Rich wrote in *The
New York Times*: "There was no doubt that . . . on this night, Mr.
Fierstein had hit the jugular of his entire, sociologically diverse
audience. . . . The communality of the theater offered the transi-
tory balm of shared emotional intimacy to an audience now frightened of physical intimacy."

Once again I had a sold-out hit at La MaMa that begged to be
moved to a commercial production, but after earlier failed transfers
I wanted to be careful. We needed a small venue that was close to

where we began. As it happened, the only Off-Broadway theater available was the Astor Place, which was actually perfect. Located just a few blocks from La MaMa, it seated fewer than three hundred people, and the manager was our friend Albert "Peaches" Poland. Well, it seemed Albert was in a conundrum. He told my agent that he had two projects from which to choose: he'd give the theater either to us or to this mime show where a bunch of guys make music out of strange objects and toss paint around at one another. "Are you kidding me? How could he possibly not choose us? Did he read Rich's *Times* piece?" I asked. "We're good for at least a year. How long will that other thing last?"

Well, Albert foolishly chose the other show. It was some stupid thing called *Blue Man Group,* which as of this writing has been running for thirty-two years. The show's made so much money that they bought the theater.

Seeing our predicament, the Shuberts offered us Broadway's Lyceum Theatre, where we predictably and unfortunately failed to catch on. I could blame the loss of intimacy or the timing or the strange circumstances of our producers, but I think the truth was that the majority of the world simply did not want to be told that AIDS would forever change their lives. To most people, AIDS was a disease that would soon have a cure. No way were they going to have to wear condoms or rely on drugs or in any way curtail the mindless pleasures that the hard-fought sexual revolution had delivered. They were finally getting laid. How dare Fierstein tell us to stop?

Howard Rosenman and Carol Baum were producers with Sandollar. They optioned the film rights to the play and brought them to HBO, a fledgling back then when it came to original movies. Colin Callender was the executive responsible, but his interest was in filming only the third play, *Tidy Endings.* Starring Stockard Channing and myself, it turned out well. But sadly, without the context of the other plays it came off as the Disease of the Month affair I'd been trying to avoid. The advertising slug line said it all: "Even the survivors are victims." Yuck.

30

GARBO AND DOUBTFIRE

1984 Onward

Sidney Lumet had seen me on stage and asked if I would do a scene in his new project. *Garbo Talks* was the first movie I made that didn't leave me on the cutting room floor. Back in 1976 I'd improvised a scene with Woody Allen in *Annie Hall*. Danny Aiello and I were arguing at the counter of a Coney Island diner when Woody came to break up the fight. Recognizing him as a TV personality, I ran off camera to get a pen for an autograph. Not finding one, I returned with a butcher's knife and handed it to Woody.

"What am I supposed to do with this?" he asked.

I pulled up my sleeve, exposing my arm. "Give me your autograph."

"Do you think there's enough room?" he quipped.

I shrugged. "Just write over the stretch marks."

The scene did not make it into the movie. Years later, when filming *Bullets Over Broadway*, I asked one of Woody's trusted crew members about it. He said the outtake often shows up in their Christmas reel, so I'm glad someone gets to see it.

Garbo Talks is remembered fondly for being the first movie appearance of Court Miller, Mary McDonnell, Liz Smith, Dorothy Loudon, and me. Starring in the flick were Anne Bancroft, Carrie Fisher, Ron Silver, Howard Da Silva, and lyricist Betty Comden as Garbo.

Sidney Lumet could not have been dearer. When I was done shooting he asked, "Darling, my darling, where the hell were you when I was casting *Dog Day Afternoon*?"

I answered, "Watch it again. I was an extra in the gay protest mob."

The member of that company I was most enamored of was Hermione Gingold. What an original! I couldn't believe she was having breakfast mere feet from me. I approached as she brushed cake crumbs from her chest. Lipstick smeared, her wig askew, she wore an oversized golden necklace in the shape of a Venetian lion door knocker. I heard her mumbling, "Oh, dear. I've been feeding my knocker again!"

I introduced myself and heard, in that singular voice, "Forgive me for not rising, as I am running late. My maid did not show up today. I certainly hope nothing trivial happened to her."

I sat down for a marvelous chat with this acting legend. I cross-examined her about every role she'd played, and she was completely forthcoming, but one reply was priceless. I asked what it was like working with Vincente Minnelli on *Gigi*. She tilted her head and bemoaned, "I had my ideas, Vincente had his. Mine were left crushed under the horses' hooves."

That same year I provided the narration for Rob Epstein and Richard Schmiechen and their documentary *The Times of Harvey Milk*. Production funds were so scarce that we recorded the rough track in my Brooklyn apartment. The movie went on to win the Best Documentary Feature Oscar. A decade later, I worked with Rob again on *The Celluloid Closet*, but my part in that film pales next to the story of what came before.

Vito Russo's book about the history of homosexuality in film is a treasure. Unfortunately, he lost his battle with AIDS without seeing it adapted into the award-winning film. Lily Tomlin was a great friend of Vito's, and to raise money to make the movie she arranged for herself, drag superstar Lypsinka, and Robin Williams to give a benefit performance at the Castro Theater in San Francisco. Lily called and asked me to emcee. I agreed, thinking all I need do was make introductions, but when I arrived, Lily told me that I had to open the show with half an hour of stand-up. What? I had nothing, literally *nothing*, prepared. Pacing in my hotel room I noticed that my suitcase contained naught but casual travel attire. That gave me what I thought was a funny idea. I would model my plaid shirts, work boots, and hoodies as a lesbian fashion show. Well, it struck me as funny. My lesbian sisters in the Castro did not agree. It's one thing to do stand-up with no laughs, quite another to be booed from the stage. I was so loathed that a newspaper reported that I tried to steal focus from Lily by carrying out a glass of water to her. She asked for it—I swear she did. Robin Williams watched the entire thing from the wings laughing his ass off. All comics are familiar with the anguish of bombing. He felt my pain. Next thing I knew, producer Marsha Williams, Robin's wife, contacted me about playing his brother in *Mrs. Doubtfire*.

We played around with a whole mess of wigs and
songs and stuff while shooting Robin's transformation
into Mrs. Doubtfire. That's comedian Scott Capurro
as my better half in this candid Polaroid.

Working on that movie was a dream. Director Chris Columbus devised a brilliant system of capturing all that was Robin. We did each shot over and over again as scripted until Chris was sure he had what he needed, and then Robin was set loose to improvise. This was especially fun when we worked on the scenes transforming him into Mrs. Doubtfire. But the shot I remember most was the one where Robin knocked on my door and asked me to make him into a woman. I did the line as written a few times until Chris told me he had what he needed. Now it was my turn to improvise. I cannot tell you how many times Robin knocked, said, "Can you make me a woman?" and I reacted. Dozens of takes, dozens of lines . . . until Chris finally said, "Cut. We've got enough."

We were just about to step off set when I was struck with an inspiration. I screamed out, "Just one more." Chris was game. We went back and I delivered the line that has become a meme for all occasions: "Oh, honey, I'm so happy."

Losing Robin was impossible for all who loved him. Cliché be damned, he was like a brother to me. Always generous, supportive, inclusive whenever we could get together. I don't know why, but some people just walk right into your heart and make themselves at home. That's the way it always felt with Robin. As with any true friendship, it was our private time that I cherished most. We were once having dinner in San Francisco when I told him I needed to get back to LA in the morning. As it happened, a studio was sending its private jet to bring him to Hollywood for a meeting. He invited me to come along. We were the only ones in the plane's cabin besides a flight attendant. For reasons I don't recall, there was a guitar on the floor. Robin picked it up and began to improvise. Nonsensical as it sounds, for the next hour I took on the role of Spanish actress Charo and he assumed the role of a chihuahua as we fought over which one of us Xavier Cugat loved best. It was a musical. We were in *cuchi-cuchi* heaven.

Of all questions the press asks I am most often queried about Robin. He is so beloved. People only need to hear his name and they automatically smile. I confess, that was never my reaction to him. Even before considering the torment he must have been experiencing to end his life the way he did, whenever we were together my heart reached out longing to comfort him. My brain reasoned, *What the hell do you think he needs from you? He's got a wife, beautiful children, a great career, more money than he can ever spend, terrific buddies, and a world of strangers who would kill to be his friend. The audacity to think he needs anything from you!*

But that feeling was always there. A tiny voice from deep within called out in pain, and I was never sure he knew that I heard it.

While I don't question my affection for my friend, I can't help wondering if I was just one of the crowd. I sometimes felt that Robin sent out that signal, that homing device, unconscious as it might be, that he was in need of rescuing. Some people do. It's an element of star quality that attracts others, drawing them in, making them almost irresistible. Marilyn Monroe and James Dean both shared that quality. To feel personally needed by someone so powerful is a poor substitute for being loved, but if that's all that's up for grabs, it's as strong an attraction as lust. People say they most admire Robin's outrageous humor, but I wonder. Funny people are a dime a dozen. Even comic geniuses abound. Robin's magnetism earned so much more from his fans. Ask any of them. As I said, it was sensational to be part of his life, to spend time with him, to be under his spell.

31

I'M GONNA BE A
MOVIE STAR

1987

My brother was adamant that I not lose artistic control of the *Torch Song Trilogy* movie. He felt that no matter what else I'd write, this piece would always be my most personal. Can't argue with that. So, backed by George Lane, he went off to assemble a production that would guarantee my vision was fulfilled.

Howard Gottfried was Paddy Chayefsky's producer when he was making films like *Network* and *Altered States*. Good enough for me. He and Ron then struck a deal with Bob Shaye at New Line Cinema. Known for the *Nightmare on Elm Street* movies, Shaye saw us as part of his new lineup to high-tone the company's output. Coincidentally, they were filming John Waters's *Hairspray* when we arrived. As an independent production, we were given a budget of three million dollars. It was going to take a lot of creativity to make this movie for that, but it would be *our* movie.

Paul Bogart had a decades-long career directing everything from *All in the Family* to Arthur Miller. From our first meeting I felt I had met a kindred spirit. He was a little bit Arnold, a bit more Ed, and a lot of Ma! Insisting that every day of filming be filled with laughter, we had only one argument during the entire production. It concerned the song for the final scene of the movie. Years earlier I'd bought an album out of a fifty-cent record bin. It was *The*

Amazing Big Maybelle. I'd never heard of her, but when my needle hit that vinyl a new world opened. Maybelle was a rough-and-ready, gravel-voiced songstress sometimes credited as the mother of rock and roll. Among the extraordinary cuts I found, "I Will Never Turn My Back on You" was so filled with raw emotion that I constructed the final three minutes of the entire trilogy around playing that recording. In the last moments of *Torch Song* I had the son, David, dedicate this song to Arnold on the radio. The final notes of the cut were timed to the final light cue of the play. The effect of Big Maybelle on every audience was palpable. I never considered using anything else. As is done, we shot the movie version without music, but when Paul screened it for me, he had dubbed in a track of Ella Fitzgerald singing "This Time the Dream's on Me." Now, I love my Ella, and that's a gorgeous song, but it ain't Big Maybelle. I threw a fit. He threw a fit. " 'I'll never turn my back on you' sounds dirty," he said.

"Are you nuts?" I exploded.

"Think about how that sounds," he said. " 'I will never turn my back on you'?"

"*You* think about how it sounds!"

Our argument extended out into the hallway of the editing suite. Still fighting when the elevator door opened, I could not believe my eyes: there stood Paul Simon riding down as well. I knew he'd seen the show, and so, with Bogart standing right there, I asked his opinion of switching songs. Without prodding, Simon volunteered: "That song, for me, was the entire story. My favorite thing in the show. Cut it and you cut the heart out."

My grin of told-you-so won no points. Bogart said, "Put that song in and take my name off the movie."

How does a man play so dirty? I conceded. I should not have, and as you can tell from this, I still wish that I hadn't. I wonder if I can swap the song out now . . . I need to look into that.

Adapting the screenplay, I was adamant about only one thing; I did not want AIDS to discolor the story. At that time, there was no writing about homosexuality without including AIDS. To me it was like saying every African-American story has to involve sickle cell anemia, or every Jewish character has to have Tay-Sachs. When I want to write about AIDS, I will do so. That's not this piece. So I moved the story back a few years, ending it just before the consciousness of AIDS. Remaining true to the play, I kept the structure to three sections; but a film audience needs to be shown what a theater audience only needs to be told, so *Fugue* was expanded into a full act with every detail that had been discussed in dialog now coming to life onscreen. Writing that section was a total kick. I added musical numbers in the drag club and more detail to the relationship with Alan. Writing Alan's death scene, however, was not so much fun. Filming it turned out to be pure hell. If you watch carefully you will see, as the ambulance carries Alan away, that my whole body bounces with the same jumpy tic that affected my mother at funerals. It was nothing I consciously planned, but as they did at her funeral, my emotions took control of my nervous system.

If you see a movie with a great gay role, you can be ninety percent certain that the actor playing it is heterosexual. Not only do straight men get all of the great gay roles, but they're almost always awarded for the unbelievable bravery displayed by taking on such an impossible feat. I remember George Hamilton remarking that the press never asked how difficult it was to play a vampire, but constantly questioned the difficulty in passing as a homosexual. I swore that my movie would not be that way. I ordered the casting office to find me a real live homosexual to play Ed. They looked, they tried, they failed. Gay actors, at that time, did not want to be identified as gay. Some of it had to do with the fear of AIDS, but mostly it was that same old self-loathing on display. After many Hollywood casting sessions, I finally pulled out my address book and told Bogart, "If we can't find real gay folk, let's at least hire friends."

Brian Kerwin had played Ed onstage, although never opposite me. With Joel and Court both gone I was grateful to have sweet Brian at my side.

Arnold's best friend and confidant, Murray, never appeared onstage, but I wrote him a juicy role in the movie. Who better to play it than Broadway luminary Ken Page, a large man with a larger voice and even larger heart? If you ever want to feel protected, just tuck in next to this big bag of love.

Charles Pierce had been a famous female impersonator for eons when we became friends. A caustic-tongued Bette Davis was his forte. Wanting his splendaciousness captured on film for posterity, I wrote the role of the older drag queen, Bertha Venation, just for him, and he did not disappoint. My favorite memory of him, as it happens, did not happen in front of the camera. We were shooting the interiors of our drag club at La Cage, a real drag club in West Hollywood. It was early morning. Ken Page and I were waiting in the parking lot, both in full drag, when the makeup trailer door opened and out stepped Madame Pierce, resplendent in head-to-toe red sequins. She motioned us to her side and confided a warning with all seriousness, "Girls, my mother is coming to the set today, so . . . not a word!!!"

I kid you not. After half a century in drag he had still not told his mother that he was gay.

Matthew Broderick was obviously too old to play my son, but more than old enough to play my lover. The problem was that he never gave us an answer. We waited as long as we could before casting another terrific young actor. Just before production, Matthew finally called and said he wanted the part. It was heartbreaking having to let this other actor go. Not that his career suffered; he's done quite well over the years. Still, like the good Jew I was raised to be, I carry the guilt.

Estelle was another matter. Paul Bogart wanted Anne Bancroft to play Ma and had the script sent to her. When she accepted the role, New Line went bonkers with excitement. Estelle was doing *The Golden Girls* at the time, so she had a name and a following as well, just not as legit for selling a movie. Besides, Paul had directed her in several *Golden Girl* episodes and didn't feel her performance would translate to the big screen. I'm happy to note that Estelle's performance was captured and is available for viewing as part of the New York Public Library at Lincoln Center's theater collection, so I don't have to answer when people ask whether she or Anne was better in the role. I will say that onstage, in that original production, in authenticity alone, no one could compete with Estelle. The fabulous actress Barbara Barrie replaced Estelle for a period, and at the end of her run she told me that one of the greatest disappointments of her career was that she could not crack the role of Ma. As for Anne, after watching a screening of the finished film she took me aside to say, "If I knew it was going to come out that good I would have worked harder."

That broke my heart just a little.

Estelle and I remained close despite the disappointment.

As for me, I was hypersensitive of how I'd look on camera and resorted to a starvation diet for a year. Dangerous and unpleasant as it sounds, I restricted my food intake to a few minuscule meals a day along with Diet Coke and, before bed each evening, as a reward, a shot of Southern Comfort. By the time we began to film, I weighed 162 lbs. which today would be the weight of one thigh. Still, I noticed in reviews that I was referred to as fat or overweight. What we girls go through!

I wanted Arnold to display a touch of androgyny even when out of drag so I had my entire body waxed. My dedication was repaid with a staph infection.

During this period two friends of great importance entered my life. Richie Jackson was a young man whose mother took him to see *Torch Song* onstage when he was seventeen. After the show she told him that she would not be like that mother if he turned out to be gay. The play became an important touchstone for him. Soon afterward he volunteered to work with the Glines, and Lawrence brought him to me as an assistant during the production of *Safe Sex*. During the years our relationship blossomed, to say the least. He's been my assistant, my agent, my manager, and most of all we've been almost inseparable friends since. When I went west to film the movie, Richie stayed behind, caring for my life back on the East Coast.

Alan Siegel and I became friends as he was Estelle's Hollywood manager. We began to work together, and he was responsible for all of the TV and movie jobs I got at the time.

Script written, cast assembled, crew set, we all trundled off to

New Jersey to start shooting the movie. Jersey was the location they found to be Ed's farmhouse. Alas, it was raining that morning, and the only interior set ready to go was the haystack where Ed seduces Alan. That meant the very first shot of the movie would be Matthew and Brian, two of the straightest men you'd ever met, kissing passionately. I'm not sure the two had even been introduced before they were brought to the set to rehearse. Brian had no compunction about kissing boys, as I found out later when we shot our own love scenes, but Matthew was not as loose of tongue. When the moment arrived and Brian went in for the big kiss, Matthew stayed in character as long as he could, but eventually, lips still in lockdown, his arms and legs began to flail like a turtle laid on its back. Bogart let the shot go much longer than was needed and we all shared a laugh when he finally called "Cut."

Matthew would not let Brian even stand near him for the next few hours.

Anne Bancroft worried that I wouldn't
look young enough to be her son. I
think we looked great together.

Shooting the movie would qualify as an out-of-body experience. All of these situations and settings and characters that I'd been imagining for years were suddenly made real right before my eyes. I was touching the dishes in my kitchen. I was climbing into bed with my lover. I was having dinner with my parents and brother . . . This life was as familiar as memory and as foreign as hallucination. I was at once completely comfortable and totally unmoored. In this world I was skinny and beautiful and successful and loved and, best of all, the center of the entire universe. It was as close to a dream state without drugs or mental illness as I could imagine, and I never wanted it to end.

We finished shooting and returned home. New Line was very happy with what they saw. They arranged test screenings around the country. There was one in a Jersey suburban mall that I attended with Ron and Paul Bogart and some New Line execs. When the screening ended, Bob Shaye, spinning off the audience's sky-high ratings, threw his arm around my shoulder to congratulate me. "And if a reporter asks," he instructed, "it was a five-million-dollar budget!"

New Line was pumped. Probably *too* pumped: they rushed the release from spring of 1989 to Christmas of '88, when it would compete in that awards season. They arranged a gorgeous black-tie premiere at Lincoln Center. Their hopes of success were high, but I was reading the room differently. Up against the major big-budget studio Christmas releases, we were not getting much traction. No national outlets or TV stations were interested in a small gay film from the makers of Freddy Krueger movies. Because of Matthew we got a few fag-rag covers. Other than those our biggest piece was a feature on me in *Premiere* magazine. The reporter, Bruce Bibby, had pushed his editor hard to get permission to do the story. I was so grateful that I spent the next five years of my life with him. Yes, I met my next lover doing press. Oh, those Hollywood romances!

Sadly, the movie was ignored by most and earned little box office. As I recall, many reviewers attacked me for excluding AIDS. Some accused me of whitewashing the truth, and some said I wasn't brave enough to take on the subject. I think my favorite notices said that I was nowhere near good-looking enough to attract either Matthew's or Brian's character. Nice for Harvey.

There was a political cartoon that best summed up the movie's reception. It showed the exterior of a movie triplex. The titles on the marquee were *Twins, Tequila Sunrise,* and *Torch Song Trilogy.* A straight couple, seeing the queue of gays waiting to get into the theater, walks away saying, "I'm not standing in that line!"

In retrospect I wonder if I made the right choices for the movie. At one point a major studio and top-shelf director offered to make the film, starring Richard Dreyfuss. I considered it for a moment. As a heterosexual he'd be a cinch to win an Academy Award. It's a rule. Funny how it doesn't swing the other way—and I think we play straight much better. Anyway, when we got into discussions, the studio said they wanted to ditch most of the first two acts and concentrate on Arnold fighting with his mother. Smelling Disease of the Month, I walked away. Leave it to Hollywood to turn all of our lives into an *After School Special*. I still wonder whether critics would have said Mr. Dreyfuss in bias-cut satin was pretty enough to attract Brian or Matthew.

32

YES, I WROTE *LEGS DIAMOND*

1988

Robert Allan Ackerman and I became close when I took over the role of Arnold in the London production of *Torch Song Trilogy* from the marvelous, Olivier Award–winning Antony Sher. Bob directed that production for producer Robert Fox. Back in those days pubs and restaurants stopped serving at eleven p.m. Robert and I, along with his partner, Franco, and playwright friend Martin Sherman, would rush to catch a bite at Joe Allen before it closed and then retire to my rooms at the Savoy Hotel to watch the very limited TV available on BBC. Oh, the glamorous life of a West End star!

I was about to leave for Toronto to film *Tidy Endings* when Robert phoned to ask if I'd be willing to doctor the book of *Legs Diamond*. He explained it was a musical he was creating with songwriter/showman Peter Allen. Seems Peter had an undying desire to play the Prohibition-period mobster. It was my turn to ask the question that the world would someday wonder for themselves: "Why?"

"Peter bought the rights to the movie years ago," Bob explained.

"Okay—why? I mean, isn't it an awful grade-C movie?"

"It's Peter Allen."

"And he should know better. Of every character on this earth, why would he want to play a minor American bootlegger?"

Robert begged. "It's Peter Allen! All we have to do is stick him on a stage, let him shake his ass, and we cash the checks."

"So then, what do you need with *me*?"

They needed me because they'd already produced a disastrous workshop employing a script by Peter's best friend, dress designer Charles Suppon. The project was dead without major rewrites. Sadly, Charles was succumbing to the dementia that affected many AIDS patients in those days. He could not continue writing. Bob assured me that all the book needed was tightening.

I said no. I meant no. And to this day I know that no was the right answer. But then Robert pulled an intriguing rabbit out of his ass: The show would feature a very theatrical gimmick. Working with a special-effects company, Robert had devised a production of unique novelty. Whenever a musical number began, the stage switched from incandescent lighting to black light. Everything was underpainted with otherwise-unseen luminescent color. This allowed all sorts of magical effects to take place when the black light was operating. People could appear and disappear in an instant. A character could toss out a feather boa and have it become a staircase. Buildings and furniture could come to life. I began to imagine it as one of those trippy Betty Boop cartoons with dancing props and singing scenery. I thought, *Peter Allen plus this gimmick might work. And I'd only be the consultant: Charles's name would still be on the show.*

I sat down to write an entertainment that was more of a Bugs Bunny feature than a traditional musical. I called it *The Almost Totally Fictitious Hystery of Legs Diamond.* There were chase scenes and getaways and magic acts . . . You bet I was going to make those special-effects folks work their asses off! Marvin Krauss called me. "You did it—you turned it around! Peter, Robert, and the producers all loved the script and want to put it into production. But you have to put your name on it."

How do you like that? I saved the day. I knew I shouldn't put my name on it, but Marvin said I'd saved the day. My ego will always win out over my sense. I agreed.

I went off to Toronto to make *Tidy Endings* and then proceeded to film *Torch Song*. When I returned to New York, *Legs* was already in full rehearsal. Surprisingly and unwisely, because the production was so unwieldy and impossible to transport, they had booked this thing with no out-of-town tryout or even a workshop. They went straight into production. I arrived at the studio, and as the cast worked on a dance number, I drifted over to look at the set model. I was confused.

"Like it?" Robert asked.

"What *is* this? Where are the black-light effects?"

"Oh, we did away with all of that. The lighting designer said it would never work, so . . ."

"But this whole show is conceived around those effects. Without them—"

"This whole show is conceived around Peter Allen, and he's right over there," Robert said. "Relax."

I could go through the gory details of the great disaster of 1988, but why bother? Any Internet search will tell you that after *Legs* the Mark Hellinger Theatre became a church. Some prayers are answered with one-hundred-year leases. As tragedies go, *Legs Diamond* was at least entertaining for us. It was such a lost cause that you couldn't do anything but shrug it off. I used to hide in the lobby during our endless preview period and eavesdrop as audiences left in confused disgust. My favorite remark was made by a woman who caught me lurking: "Oh, Harvey, no, no, no!"

And she was right. We worked on that thing daily, but no matter what we tried, it only got worse. We added songs, we added characters, we cut songs, we cut characters. In the entire show Peter had only one line he could get a laugh with. Act 1 finished with a long chase scene with lots of machine-gun fire (please remember this was supposed to be the black-light gimmick), at the end of which Legs is shot dead. Curtain. Intermission. Act 2 opened with his funeral, at the climax of which Peter jumps up from his coffin, still alive, and greets the mourners.

"You miss me?"

"But you're dead!" says a mobster. "I shot you myself."

To which Peter answered smugly: "I'm in show biz. Only a critic can kill me."

The producers asked me to take it out, knowing that the critics would cling to it, but I argued that it would be one less laugh in a show that had four. One critic did quote the line and added: "Bang, bang, you're dead."

Peter eventually learned to milk the line until he'd get a full round of applause from the house.

I adored Peter; but truthfully, besides the show being a stupid idea, he was the main problem. He was way out of his element. No actor, he exuded a kind of flop sweat that audiences sense and reject. The undeniable proof was that he couldn't get entrance applause from fans who'd paid premium prices to see him. How do you stage a show around that? The producers asked me to do something, no matter the cost. I devised a new first entrance for him. A gigantic electric sign spelling out "LEGS DIAMOND" would fly in with Peter riding on it. He even wrote a terrific new song to go along, "When I Get My Name in Lights." They built the sign, we rehearsed the number, and we crossed our fingers.

We all crowded together in standing room to watch Peter enter atop this mammoth electric beast. It went off without a hitch . . . and still, dead silence. Charlene Nederlander, wife of our theater owner and lead producer, turned to me and shrugged. "I could have bought a bracelet."

Another problem with the show was how many members of the company were ill. Intangible as that may be, how could an audience not pick up on that vibe? Charles Suppon was the only one we spoke of, but Peter himself had AIDS, as did the original choreographer. Joe Silver, our lead gangster, had cancer and was receiving chemo several times a week. I believe we lost seventeen members of that original cast. How could that not affect the mood of the cast no matter how hard they rallied to entertain? Even Peter's standby, Larry Kert, the legendary star of *West Side Story*, was ill.

Speaking of Larry . . . One afternoon during our endless preview period, he was given a full rehearsal just in case he ever had to go on. Curious to hear the material in another voice, we all showed up to watch. Don't get me wrong, the show was still awful, but in the hands of a pro like Larry Kert it came alive. He was sexy and charming and winning. The absurdity of a man becoming a gangster just to get a job in show biz read funny instead of desperate, as it did with Peter. If the script had just been a bit smarter it might have passed for satire. And satire, as everyone knows, delights the critics on Friday and closes on Saturday. Even as it was, with Larry singing Peter's songs, the show was no longer an embarrassment. At intermission I started over to Jimmy Nederlander, who, before I could say a word, held up his hand: "No, Harvey. I only produced this show as a favor for Peter. I won't take it away from him. I won't. I can't."

During the years since, I've had many approaches for permission to resurrect the show and I've always declined. A great chef may be able to make a turned piece of chicken taste good, but it will still make you sick. Most of the songs were eventually cannibalized into Peter's biographical show, *The Boy from Oz*. I think he'd be happy knowing he had a hit show after all. It only took casting the irresistible Hugh Jackman instead of Peter.

33

HANGING WITH MADONNA, HOLLY, AND BRUCE

1988–1992

The next few years were, at best, unfocused. After the exciting letdowns of the *Torch Song* movie and *Legs Diamond* and a less than stellar Off-Broadway production of *Spookhouse* I was feeling pretty cooked—not defeated, but teetering on the vertex of disheartened. Why was I working so hard if no one was enjoying the output? That's one of those questions that separate show biz from art.

Holly Woodlawn sent me the galleys of her autobiography, *A Low Life in High Heels*, and asked me to call. "My diva *daaah*-ling, only you! Only you can turn my life into the Technicolor dream it was meant to be! Please, my *daaah*-ling, you must."

Of the three legendary queens of Warhol, Holly was always my favorite. I could never catch what Candy Darling was talking about, and when I did, it wasn't worth the effort. Jackie Curtis was a genius—absolutely—but she'd steal your lipstick, eat your sandwich, smoke your last cigarette, and get pissed that you didn't have more to swipe. Jackie was a pain. I remember Harvey Tavel arranging for Halston to do a dress for her to wear in *Amerika Cleopatra*. The crazy queen set it on fire, put it out with a glass of white wine, dried it on a hot radiator before deeming it fit to wear. Holly, on the other hand, was genuinely fun, harmless and outrageous and ready to have a good time whenever. This book of hers wasn't awful. It had a lot of gossipy details, and thinking about it, I could imagine the story of the three of them as a kind of insane, *How to Marry a Millionaire*. And Lou Reed's "Walk on the Wild Side," which mentions all three of them, was a built-in record deal. I sent the book over to Howard Rosenman, and he was on it!

"Madonna!" he said. It was 1991. "Madonna is looking for projects for her film company, Maverick. Do you think you could pitch this to her?"

"Wow! I can just imagine her playing Candy Darling. Right?"

Howard agreed and immediately booked a meeting.

We walked into Madonna's Central Park West apartment and I was blown away to see that every white wall of the living room held a magnificent Tamara de Lempicka portrait of a woman. I was impressed. I couldn't imagine many pop stars understanding the importance of this artist's deliriously deco vision of the female persona as machine-age form.

Madonna came in, and after the usual chitchat I described the adventures of Holly, Candy, and Jackie, giving it all the energy I could. She asked what her role in the project would be. I said, "You'd play the gorgeous, glamorous, glorious Candy Darling herself! She was the most commercially successful of the three—she even had Tennessee Williams tailor a stage role for her. And she's the one who gets the big dramatic tragic death scene."

I was working it!

Madonna thought for a moment. "But do you really think I could play a drag queen?"

"Of course," I said. "Everyone's already seen your pussy. It's time to show them your dick."

The movie rights are still available.

Bruce and I were exploring our lives together. With an art education, his interests leaned toward creating abstract iron sculpture. Now, employed as a writer and editor for a movie magazine, Bruce was weighing options, keeping an open mind and searching for his calling. He'd survived two serious relationships. The first was with a married college professor, and his second was lost to AIDS. Much more outgoing and social than I, Bruce had a great fondness for arranging dinner parties and inviting guests up for the weekend.

He forced me to accept travel invitations that I'd normally turn down. We went to Santa Fe, San Francisco, and even took a tour of Scandinavia. A gay cruise company offered me a week's vacation in the Caribbean if I'd perform an hour-long nightclub act. I had no nightclub act, but they said they'd help put one together. Bruce wanted to go so badly. Again, ego over sense, I took the bait, we took the cruise, and predictably, the club act was simply awful. Still, they asked me back time and again. We cruised the islands, the Mexican Gold Coast, and even Alaska. We had the best vacations and met fabulous entertainers like Diane Schuur, Ann Hampton Callaway, Thelma Houston, and Jim Caruso who are friends to this day. Yes, when I allowed him to pull me out of my cocoon, Bruce and I were a fun couple, never without a cigarette or a drink in our hands, he with his vodka and me with my Southern Comfort.

One Friday evening, I picked Bruce up at the train from the city as usual. It was the day before my birthday and he seemed nervous. As soon as we got into the house he sat me down and began to cry. "I'm an alcoholic," he said. "I've finally admitted it and I've joined AA."

I had all kinds of thoughts, but the first thing I did was to tell him how proud I was of him and that he could count on me to help in any way I could.

While he went to wash up, I made a pitcher of lemonade and poured him a gigantic glassful, brimming with ice.

I can't say I really understood what was so bad about Bruce's drinking. I'd never seen him stumble or mush-mouthed or sloppy. He told me that every time he'd take my glass to the bar for a refill, he'd pour himself a drink, down it, and only then refill our glasses to bring back. Even then, I didn't think he drank as much as I did, and I certainly wasn't an alcoholic.

And so we settled into an altered life of sobriety. From the moment I picked Bruce up at the train on Friday night until I dropped him back at the station on Sunday, lemonade, iced tea, and Diet Coke filled our glasses. During the week, of course, I was free to tipple, but being the exemplary human I was, I kept my tippling to myself. It was Bruce's problem, but my sacrifice made it all about

me. Bruce created a wonderful support system through his Twelve
Step meetings. I joined Al-Anon and began to shop for my booze in
other towns. No one ever saw me drink again in public. At home,
once my day was done, I'd pour myself a nice fat tumbler of SC
over a stack of ice cubes and settle in for an evening of television.
Sometimes, when there was nothing more to do, I'd have a cocktail
before dinner. There were also days where I'd begin drinking in the
afternoon, but as long as I waited for the *Judge Judy* show to come
on the air at four it was fine. *Obviously, if you can control your
drinking like that*, I told myself, *you have no problem.*

Bruce wrote for *Premiere* magazine, as I said; and newly sober
and eager for change, he was looking to go beyond feature writing by developing a pseudonymous gossip column. I wasn't crazy
about the idea. I thought our personal relationships with celebrities would suffer if he was apt to publish something someone might
say off the record. It turned out to be so. Several famous friends
began to distance themselves. Bruce was of the Rex Reed school of
journalism, often delivering a line he attributed to his hero: "If a
celebrity picks his nose in front of me, I have the right to report it."

Elsewhere in our world the AIDS crisis was raging, and many on
the forefront had severe burnout. With an ever-growing need for
fundraising and public awareness, they didn't know who to turn
to for help. Seeing closeted gay celebrities skating by with careers
unscathed by AIDS panic, many of our community leaders turned
on them with anger, calling for them to help the cause and thereby
dragging them out of the closet. Outing became a community pas-
time. Interviewers began to brazenly ask if this or that one was gay.
I wanted no part of that mess. Not that I approved of living in the
closet.

Those people collected the big checks, leaving the struggle for
our rights to others, and then cashed in their tales of seclusion and
personal martyrdom when it was advantageous to come out. We
took the beatings and they took the bows.

With love and understanding I say "Fuck you" to them all. But
outing was not the answer. Bruce and I disagreed.

I shared this story once on PBS. I was at my local Stop & Shop buying Thanksgiving groceries when Diane, the checkout person, said, "So, you do the shopping and your wife does the cooking?"

"No, Diane. I do the cooking *and* the shopping. I'm gay."

She laughed. "You are not no gay!"

"Yes, I am. I'm gay."

"Stop. You are not no gay!" she insisted.

"What makes you so sure?"

"Because," she said, "if you were gay you would be too ashamed to say so."

That's when it struck me. Of course she would think that. At work she is surrounded by magazine covers blaring "Ellen Denies Being a Lesbian" and "Elton John Threatens to Sue over Gay Claim." How could she *not* think that all gays are ashamed? All the gays she ever heard about were.

For the record: I used Ellen and Elton because they both know they are gay. Now.

I used to tell reporters that if they saw me with a celebrity, it was proof that that person was straight. No closeted gay actors wanted to be seen with me. Even sweet Rock Hudson insisted we meet either at a friend's apartment or at a discreet neighborhood restaurant when he was in town. I nearly broke my mother's heart when I told her he was gay. Straight people used to be totally blind to our existence. In any case, a resentful, embarrassed celebrity in denial was proof positive that there was something wrong with being gay.

Bruce's sobriety rekindled his love of life. He was suddenly more energetic and adventurous than ever. I, on the other hand, already immobile and stagnant, only grew more so without my cocktails and quiet evenings. I was growing resentful. Sometimes I couldn't wait for Bruce to catch the train back to the city so I could drink. Still, I had to work. With Lawrence Lane's help, Eric Concklin and I mounted another revival of Robert Patrick's *The Haunted Host* at La MaMa and then moved it Off-Broadway. It didn't click.

Sadly, my relationship with Bruce was also failing. We saw one another three days a week, and I don't think they were the best days for either of us. Bruce had been reborn. His mind was clearing and his goals were reforming. With his survival instincts kicking in, he knew it was time to get out.

He'd done the hard work of getting sober. Now it was time to reclaim his life.

With Bruce gone I was now free to drink 'round the clock if I wanted, and why wouldn't I?

My boyfriend just left me.

34

ALL TALK AND NO . . .

C an we talk? As the most economical way to sell tickets, books, or careers, talk shows are an inescapable tool of the biz. Most are silly wastes of time. Hold up your tell-all— show a clip from your movie—deny the rumors of your death— and hope to escape with your dignity. The guest pays the host back with an item of gossip or a silly bit of nonsense. It's entertainment to sprawl by. There's no need to mention, let alone remember, most talk shows or their hosts; but there were some . . .

The best of the best, anyone who's ever mounted a couch will tell you, was Johnny Carson. I appeared on *The Tonight Show* a mess of times with Joan Rivers and Jay Leno hosting, but only once with Carson himself, and there was no comparison. He was the greatest audience. He cared only about making you look good, which he accomplished by effortlessly appearing to have the best time with you. No one thought you were funnier or more interesting or more important than he did. Most hosts ask a question and then, as you begin answering, they are already looking at their cheat cards for their next question. Carson made you feel he was with you 100 percent of the time, and for a performer who improvises, that is nirvana. I remember saying something to him to which he remarked, "Oh. So you're gay."

And I ad-libbed, "You couldn't tell from the socks?"

It was a totally senseless remark that sent him into a fit of laughter that I recall to this day.

A funny thing happened on the way to *The Tonight Show* stage one afternoon. Joan Rivers was hosting and another guest on that episode was that star of 1930s and 1940s musical Hollywood, the one and only Ginger Rogers. I'd been a fan of hers since those *Million Dollar Movies* in my bedroom, so when I heard she was there, I snuck down the hallway in search of her dressing room. The door was partially open, and I could see a segment producer speaking with her. Waiting politely outside the door, I heard her tell him that she wanted to be offstage when I was introduced.

"Oh," he said, "do you have somewhere you need to be?"

"No," she answered.

"In that case, Joan loves for all the guests to stay after their interviews. It makes for a more partylike atmosphere."

"I understand," she confided, "but this guest after me . . . he's a homosexual?"

"That's true," the producer confirmed.

"I can't chance that. I'm not saying he has it, but I can't chance catching AIDS."

The producer, duly embarrassed, said he'd bring her off during the commercial break. I can't describe the shade of red he turned when he saw me standing in the half-open doorway. I smiled and entered, rushing to Miss Rogers's side, where I took her hands in mine and planted a huge kiss on her cheek. "Miss Rogers, you'll never know how many hours of pleasure you have given me over the years. I only hope I can give you back something in return."

She thanked me and asked, "What's your name, dear?"

"I'm Harvey Fierstein, the guest following you. I'm sorry we won't be sitting together, but at least we've had this moment to connect. A moment that will always be part of me."

I'm going to preface this next story with an excuse—I was drunk. It was Johnny Carson's final appearance on *The Tonight Show*. Loving him the way I did, I was a blubbering mess before he even stepped through his multicolored curtains. During the show he included a joke about gays. I bolted straight up in bed, *No. Please, no.* I adored and worshipped this man. He couldn't go out that way. He couldn't. I picked up my telephone, dialed information—I kid you not—and got the number for NBC Studios in Hollywood. I dialed it, asked for the Carson stage, and got through to a PA, whom I asked to please put me through to Carson's producer, Freddie de Cordova. With the wrap party blaring in the background, Fred got on the phone and said, "Harvey, what can I do for you?"

"Please, Fred. I beg you. The West Coast broadcast hasn't aired yet, please take out that antigay joke. Please don't let Johnny finish with that as part of his legacy. This episode will be aired and studied long after we're all dust. It's already a cultural landmark. Please don't let that joke remain. I beg you."

Fred listened to it all and said, "Thank you for calling," before putting down the phone.

I've always felt like an asshole for making that call. And as much as it's been aired, I've never been able to watch Carson's final show again.

My second favorite host was Arsenio Hall and not just because he gave out the best gift baskets, although I still have three or four of his embroidered bathrobes in my closet. Arsenio was another true gentleman who labored to make his guests feel welcome and special and supported. He would actually lean into you while you spoke, never losing eye contact. It was almost like being on a date with him. A lovely man.

I was performing *The Haunted Host* Off-Broadway in 1991 when a call came inviting me to appear on the show. It meant I'd have to fly out from New York to LA that night. Lawrence Lane, my producer, practically shoved me onto the plane, but with such short notice I had nothing appropriate to wear on a national TV show. In one scene of *Host* I wore a kimono. We had picked up a few to choose from and the extras were still racked backstage. I chose the most beautifully elaborate one, black satin with a huge gold dragon embroidered on the back. I figured that I'd at least be colorful wearing it as a jacket over my shirt and slacks.

Our onscreen interview was going very well until I mentioned, as I was apt to do, that I was gay. The audience, almost as one, groaned their disapproval and there were even a few boos to be heard. Arsenio turned on them, blasting them, saying something on the order of: "Harvey is my guest, and you will treat him with respect. You are also guests in my home, and I expect you to act better than that."

We finished the episode and I thought that would be that. But Arsenio had me back to do his show, flying me in from New York, two or three times a year until he went off the air. I became part of his TV family and it was wonderful.

But that ain't the end of this story. Arriving back in New York the next day, I got a phone call from Lawrence saying that the organization Queer Nation did not like my appearance on the show. It wasn't what I said; they objected to my wearing the kimono. They judged it a gay stereotype and called for a boycott, complete with picket line, against my Off-Broadway performance. I was speechless. An organization that called themselves Queer Nation thought I was too gay. It was only activist and reporter Andy Humm's speaking out as the voice of reason that canceled the protests. I still find it remarkable. A men's kimono worn over men's slacks and a button-down shirt had activists taking to the streets. So much for the loving support of my community.

My only TV appearance to be banished was a profile that Lesley Stahl put together of me for *60 Minutes*. It was produced around the time of *Hairspray*'s explosion on Broadway. She and her producers did their usual stellar job of gathering materials and information and clips in preparation. My brother was fine about giving an interview, but my mom was so nervous that Lesley had to take her and her friend Roz out to dinner to convince her to go on camera. I remember Lesley and I walking and talking around the streets of Broadway together while theatergoers called out their greetings. She jokingly dubbed me the Mayor of Broadway during that shoot. We settled down for the meat-and-potatoes interview, which I remember went quite well. Some weeks later I was told that Lesley was apologetic but the piece had been killed by executive producer Don Hewitt. He'd originally okayed it as a light-entertainment spot about that guy who ran around the stage in dresses, but when he saw a rough cut and realized how politically immersed my work actually was, he pulled the plug. Despite Lesley and her producer reediting it three times, he shelved the piece during his last weeks with the show. Lesley tried to revive it, but the moment had come and gone.

Of all of my TV appearances, I am most often asked about doing *20/20* with Barbara Walters. That thing has been online since there was a line for it to be on, but just in case you can't find it, here's the tea. *La Cage* was the hot ticket in town. *Torch Song* was packing them in a few blocks away. Legendary broadcaster Barbara Walters scheduled me for a feature. They shot the usual B-roll backstage and on the street before we settled down on the set of *Torch Song* for the interview. I went into this shoot relaxed, as I'd known Barbara socially and, having done a ton of press over the past few years, I was armed with a slew of "off-the-cuff" comments I could fall back on. Roll tape, I'm ready. But as soon as we began, Barbara questioned me as if I were an interstellar alien. I was no longer the Harvey she knew. She was interviewing some creature she'd never met before. What is this thing called homosexuality? I was dumbfounded. If you watch the tape, it's clearly visible on my face. *Who the fuck is this woman and what did she do with my friend Barbara?* Although shocked, I was never speechless, as I clearly and methodically explained the world to her as if to a five-year-old: Love, commitment, and family are human words. They belong to all people. Monogamy is as prevalent a disease in homosexuality as heterosexuality.

She innocently queried, "What's it like to be a homosexual?"

"What's it like to be a heterosexual? I'm just a person. I assume everyone is gay unless told otherwise."

But the kicker was when she asserted, "A few years ago I would not have been able to do an interview like this and put it on the air."

To which I answered, "You could have done it, and you should have done it."

Mic drop.

Whatever brought it on, the experience was totally unexpected. Furthermore, I had no idea how it would play in America. I guess the fact that it's still talked about forty years later says more than I can about its impact. I suppose we'd done an important thing. When people tell me how good I was in that interview, I always make the same point: Credit Barbara Walters. She could have edited that interview to make me look like an asshole and for her to come off as a brilliant reporter. Instead, she made me look great, while she appears uninformed. She aired a discussion that to us seems conventional but back then was groundbreaking. I am grateful when considering the generations of children and adults who've watched that interview and finally discovered that they are not alone. From the volume of mail I've received over the decades I'd say that millions found comfort and strength in that conversation with Barbara. We can all learn a lot from that lady.

Once upon a time there was a comedian who took himself way too seriously. He had a fun show on basic cable called *Politically Incorrect*, during which a lively panel of four comics, politicians, or exposure-seeking celebs would sit in a circle and discuss the latest news. I confess to appearing a bunch of times and enjoying myself. Well, it was basic cable, so you didn't have to be polite or even truthful. As long as you were subservient to the host, Bill Maher, you were always a welcome guest. Time came when the show moved to network TV—late-night but network. It might have been my first appearance on this iteration, I don't recall, but the guests were my friend actress Lynn Redgrave; ex-punk-rocker Johnny Rotten; conservative radio mouth and adopted son of President Reagan, Michael Reagan; and me. A discussion of AIDS got heated and, sick of listening to Michael Reagan defend his father's criminally negligent record, I blurted out, "You know what? Fuck you and fuck your father!"

This would have been nothing but a naughty glitch on cable, but here we were on Disney-owned ABC. Maher summoned me to his dressing room for a dressing down. I didn't see the big deal, as the show was pretaped and bleeping those few words would take under a minute's time. Anyway, I apologized and flew home. Overnight the shit hit the papers. *Hollywood Reporter* reporter Army Archerd called me for the scoop. It seems Michael Reagan had gone on his radio rant and called for a complete boycott of me. Furthermore, Bill Maher claimed that I cost the show and network a fortune because they had to reedit the episode. I spilled my side of the story, which Mr. Archerd found amusing, and that was that. There was no boycott. I wasn't banned from TV. Nothing. On the night of the broadcast I tuned in. (I don't usually watch myself on television—it adds fifty pounds.) I was curious to see how they cut those words out. Well, no big deal, they simply bleeped the two seconds. *But* . . . as I watched, I saw a much bigger edit to the show. During that taping Lynn Redgrave, another frequent guest, had accused Maher of being a male chauvinist. Maher always had four guests. She complained that the majority of them were always men. She said that she had never seen the show when all four of the guests were female, while there were plenty of times that all four guests were men. And she'd never even seen a show with three women and one man. Women were always the minority, because even when he hosted two women and two men, his sex threw the balance to male. She held this as proof that Maher was indeed sexist. Well, guess what was cut out of that show! Mr. Liberal Standard Maher censored Lynn's entire accusation. Gone with his whim. I assume Maher told ABC that the editing costs were due to my mouth, but they were actually to save his own ego from critique. For the record, they've called and invited me to appear with him a few times since, but I said I'd only do it if he'd fess up. I have no plane reservations in waiting.

35

SITCOM HOLLYWOOD

1992–1996

I was never great at impersonations, but it turns out I did a pretty good Harvey Fierstein. Good enough to hide what was actually going on inside me. I was tired all of the time. Not sleepy but unmotivated, uninspired, and uninterested. Somehow I never figured I was depressed. Fueled by booze, I remained in motion. I never had a hangover because I was never sober. It was smooth sailing on calm waters, and nobody was getting in my way. As the old-timers say, all your disease wants is to get you in a room alone and kill you. I was making up the bed in that room. I was dying. Slowly dying. And no one, including me, guessed.

Hollywood's a great place to be an addict. It's almost expected. A rite of passage. Sitcom hours are short most days. Movie hours are long, but you have lots of down time napping in your trailer. I never drank during working hours, but as soon as I was back at the hotel the ice was clinking in the glass. I remember my friend Judi once saying, "When I hear the ice tinkling in your glass, I know you are okay." Oops.

Alan Siegel was working hard to get me a television series. I'd performed guest spots on *Miami Vice; Murder, She Wrote;* and even one on *Cheers* that earned me an Emmy nomination for supporting actor. A show of my own still seemed to elude us. I had lots of meetings, some of which turned into development deals with me writing the pilot scripts. None ever got beyond that stage.

Jeff Sagansky was head of CBS and a fan. He had green-lit a pilot for the marvelous comic actress Julie Halston and offered me the role opposite her. In this precursor to *Will & Grace*, Julie's character left an unsatisfying marriage in Long Island to move in with her gay best friend in Manhattan and become an actress. Academy Award winner Eileen Heckart played Julie's mother, and *Maude's* Bill Macy played the mute role of her father. We even had sitcom royalty directing us—*That Girl's* sweeter-than-honey Ted Bessell. If only we'd had a script! Our scribe, one of the creators of *Kate & Allie*, sat on a stool day after day watching us struggle. Whenever one of us would ask for help, he'd discount us: "CBS loved the script, so the problem has to be with you."

The problem was with him. What's great on the page may not be so great on the stage. Sitcoms are about chemistry. All elements have to come together to make an audience—most of whom are watching in their underwear—look forward to their weekly visit with you. Even if you've got great jokes, if they don't enhance the character or sound right coming out of the mouth of an actor, they are useless. We didn't have great jokes. We didn't have characters you wanted to visit every week. We didn't have a chance. We taped *Those Two* in front of a live audience who were the first and last humans to see the show.

Somehow, after that failure CBS was more convinced than ever that I should be on TV. Dudley Moore had a sitcom about to go into production called *Daddy's Girls*. Dudley would play an LA dress manufacturer raising three daughters, his wife having run off with his best friend. There was the role of the company's dress designer, an ersatz mother to the girls, that they thought would be a great fit for me. This show had a twelve-episode on-air deal, so the offer was tempting. I was promised that if I did the show and it was a hit, CBS would spin me off to my own sitcom after the second season. If the show did not get picked up but I got the kind of notices they thought I might, they'd give me my own show the following fall. How could I say no?

The show was produced by Witt/Thomas, the company that gave us *The Golden Girls, Empty Nest, Blossom,* and *Soap.* These folks owned that TV formula. *Daddy's Girls* was cute but stale and predictable at a time when TV was getting Seinfelded. Most days Dudley and I would hop into his new convertible (he'd driven his last one into his swimming pool a few weeks earlier) and take a short ride to the Ivy for lunch. I loved this man, and we had a lot of fun together.

At some point it was obvious that the show was going nowhere fast. We'd already shot three or four episodes, and you'd have to be blind not to notice the forced smiles on CBS execs when they'd visit the set to watch rehearsals. One day at lunch I asked Dudley bluntly, "Is this the show you wanted to do?"

"Not sure what you mean," he answered.

"Not to embarrass you, but I've been a devoted fan since I saw you do the one-legged-Tarzan sketch in the sixties. You've always been smart and edgy and dangerous. Our show is so . . . safe."

"I guess."

"Have you ever spoken with them? Maybe given them a few ideas or nudged them to take chances?"

"No."

"But Dudley, this is *your* show. They'd not only listen to you; I think they'd be thrilled to have your input."

"I would, but . . . Harvey, I don't care."

"Say again?"

As blankly as you can imagine, he restated, "I don't care. I want a place to go to get out of the house. After that, I don't care."

It never occurred to me that he was ill or depressed. I didn't recognize it in myself, so why would I see it in someone else? I knew he wasn't telling the truth about not caring, because every day, sitting around the set, we'd wildly improvise and tease one another with abandon. Stacy Galina (who played the eldest daughter), Dudley, and I were the worst culprits. Our wild antics were funny and outrageous. They were everything the show needed, but that spirit never made it beyond the rehearsal breaks. The producers kindly invited me to sit in on writing sessions, but I was less than useless. I didn't understand this kind of formulaic joke writing. I was of no help. We shot eight episodes, three of which CBS aired before canceling us. I don't know that it's noteworthy, but thanks to this show I was the first openly gay actor to play an openly gay role in a sitcom. If there was any backlash, CBS never told me.

If *Daddy's Girls* is remembered for anything, it would be as the series debut of Keri Russell. All of eighteen, she was remarkably poised, beautiful, self-possessed, and kind. She played the youngest daughter, and no matter what she was asked to do, no matter how silly or self-deprecating, she did it with a smile and positive energy. There was no doubt that this young actor was going to be a star.

As for me, I was hot on a Hollywood health kick. I worked out with a trainer three times a week, ran on a treadmill in my dressing room, and ate a plant-based low-calorie diet. At the end of each day, I'd return to my hotel suite and drink myself into oblivion. Sadly, I was suffering from another disease, commonly called "drink and dial." Once I had a good buzz going, I'd pick up the phone and call our sitcom director to bitch about how terrible the scripts were. Greg Antonacci and I were friends from our La MaMa days. Audiences remember him best for a recurring role on *The Sopranos*. Greg was good-natured and so gentle with me. Happily, I had the opportunity, years later when I got sober, to apologize to him for being such a pain.

As for CBS, I did receive good notices and positive feedback from the viewing public, but by the time we were cancelled, Jeff Sagansky was moving on from CBS, so . . . farewell to *The Harvey Show*.

Over the next few years I was courted by, or had actual development deals with, NBC, Fox, Showtime, and HBO, none of which ever got beyond pilot scripts. Aaron Spelling once saw me on a talk show and called me to his mansion for an audience. Now that was a trip. Alan Siegel and I arrived in the limo he'd sent. The chauffeur pulled around the circular Belgian block driveway to the front staircase, where we were met by a butler who held a parasol over our heads so we wouldn't burn on our walk to the front door. Another butler opened the massive portal and motioned us in. The front hall was the size of most homes. Twin staircases led to the private quarters above. I had to pee. The comfort station was under the staircase on the right. Sometime later I learned that Candy Spelling's legendary gift-wrapping room was under the staircase on the left. I won't bore you with a description of the facility beyond telling you that it was made up of three separate rooms—one for handwashing, one for waste elimination, and the third for . . . I don't know. Finally, in Mr. Spelling's office, I could not help noticing that the books on his floor-to-ceiling shelves were all arranged by color: a case of yellow books, one of green, then one of blue . . . well, you get the idea. Being cute, I tossed off, "So, Aaron, have you read any of these?"

To which he answered, "No. But I wrote them all."

Yes. These were the bound scripts of his many TV series, each in its own colored binder. Mr. Spelling made me a more-than-generous offer for my own series. We shook on the deal and left Candyland. I never heard from Mr. Spelling again. Seems he tried to sell the series and, finding no takers, simply moved on. It took me a little longer. There was no malevolence to the slight. It's just the way of Hollywood. If someone can't do you any good, why waste your time?

Years later, when I was on Broadway playing Edna in *Hairspray*, a TV producer asked to meet with me and my then manager, Richie Jackson. He was anxious to develop a sitcom for me in which I'd play a suburban housewife, but was nervous about my being openly gay. Yes: he wanted a man to play a woman but not if he was gay. I volunteered to claim that my homosexuality has all been a publicity stunt, but cautioned that we might encounter a few legions of men willing to provide evidence to the contrary. They developed a pilot script that went nowhere. It may have been because after slavishly working to create a believable mother of two teenaged children, the episode ended with her dancing on a pole in a strip joint.

Before we leave Hollywood, I'd like to say a few words about *Independence Day*. Beyond *Mrs. Doubtfire* it's the project I'm most asked about, although I don't have much to share. I worked on the film for two days. Director Roland Emmerich was a complete doll and joy. Truthfully, the set was so lighthearted that I had no idea this would become a sci-fi classic. I thought it was a comedy. We certainly played around on set as if it were. In my first scene, when Jeff Goldblum repairs my company's cable feed, Roland took me aside and told me to give Jeff a big kiss on the mouth when he's succeeded. I don't think it made the cut, but the look on Jeff's face was not shock. It was closer to wonder, as if he were thinking, "That was interesting. Now where are we going?"

Jeff is totally enigmatic in his simplicity. I adore him. If you watch the film (which I have yet to do), you might notice that my lips do not sync with the words coming out of them in the famous "Oh, my God" scene where the alien plot is revealed. The ratings board allows only so many curse words before slapping an adult classification on a film. We were right on the edge of the curse count, and so, when it was time to dub lines in post-production, I was given alternate dialogue. Although any lip reader will tell you I say "Fuck my lawyer," the soundtrack plays "Forget my lawyer," and just before the Empire State Building falls on me again the soundtrack says something less egregious than my mouth. Hollywood!

36

GETTING SOBER

1996

Once upon a time a boyfriend took me home to meet his mother, where in response to my polite "How are you?" she answered, "I'm dying," to which I replied, "Aren't we all?"

I returned to my life in my small fictional Connecticut town, but there's no going backwards. Harvey's Boozer Express had left the station and was running on a well-greased track to no place good. I learned not to drink and dial, proving that I still had a few brain cells firing. Mornings were filled with whatever needed to be done: cooking, shopping, phone calls, correspondence, etc. I even made it to the gym to work with a trainer three times a week. Afterwards I'd stop for lunch at my friend Barbara's Southwest Cafe, making sure that everyone had seen or spoken to me, which left me free to begin my more important work. I poured a nice big celebratory cocktail, turned on the TV, and by four I was passed out for the first time that day. Regaining consciousness in the evening, I'd air the dogs, feed them, feed myself, and then, accompanied by the joyful tinkling of ice in my glass, I was back to bed, television on and unconscious. No one on my team would dare question my taking time off, since I had just worked so hard on the sitcom. I was flush with TV money and left to my own devices. No one ever saw me drink. Neighbors did not drop in. Good dogs tell no tales. Southern

Comfort had me all alone in a room and was working on taking me out of the game, but there was no rush.

During that period, I started a few projects that went nowhere. I acted in a couple of movies that no one saw. Still, even failure can spawn a memorable moment. Somewhere in a box I have a compilation CD that the incredible Rosemary Clooney sent over when she heard that I was making a movie with her son Miguel Ferrer. She wrote across the insert, "Take good care of my little boy and be kind to my sweet nephew." The sweet nephew was George Clooney. *The Harvest* shot in Mexico City, and I'm embarrassed to say that the moment the airplane doors opened I was struck down by altitude sickness. I had no idea that such a thing existed until I barely made it onto my hotel bed before passing out. The telephone rang incessantly. It was Miguel, calling from the bar downstairs, begging me to join him for a drink. He would not take no for an answer. I finally managed to clothe myself and stumble down to the bar. There, he and George were having a marvelous time. I wish I could remember more of the goings-on. They were both so adorable, kind and funny. Years later I heard George talk about that evening on *The Tonight Show*. He said that I called him "Stella by Starlight" the entire time. And why would I not? In this silly movie I played a straight villainous character and George played a transvestite stripper. Maybe the casting director had altitude sickness as well.

I accepted another stupid role in another ignorable film because I'd have a scene with one of my character-actor heroes, Stephen Tobolowsky. *Dr. Jekyll and Ms. Hyde* starred Tim Daly and Sean Young, with whom I had my first and last heterosexual sex scene. I must say that Sean was so game that she insisted my body be covered in kisses, placing each one on me herself. Tobolowsky's comic genius was a joy to observe up close. The three of us had a scene playing footsie under a conference table. It's a textbook example of bad movie comedy, but oh, did I have fun shooting opposite that man!

I didn't have much on my plate when I was invited to perform at the Edinburgh Festival. Ellen Stewart used to tease, "I cannot send you to festivals with the rest of the children. Not everyone speaks English and your work got too much conversin'."

My big bro disagreed. He was always sending his musical artists around the world. If I could cobble together ninety minutes of material, he'd arrange Edinburgh and a few other English-speaking destinations. Ninety minutes of me singing? Ha! A concept popped into my head and I called songwriters Ann Hampton Callaway and Lindy Robbins to expound my theme. Together they penned a most amusing opening number for my act. And the best part was . . . it was a tango!

> Before I start the show
> There's something you should know—
> This is not going to be pretty.
> I've really got no choice,
> I've really got no voice—
> Oh, this is not going to be pretty.
> I don't sing Sondheim songs or wear a tux—
> I can't believe you just paid twenty bucks.
> I cannot belt an A or trill a C—
> You should have rented *Torch Song Trilogy*.

I contacted Lenny Babbish, the pianist who'd played for me on the gay cruises, and asked how he felt about adventure. He was game. We went through a mess of music, I put together a few monologues, I bought an American flag as a costume, and we flew off across the sea. We played Edinburgh, Dublin, London, and Amsterdam. I choose to remember that audiences enjoyed the show, and we certainly had fun.

Dublin provided my greatest culture shock. Asked what I'd like to do on my evening off, I said, "Let's go to a gay bar."

"Oh, I'm sorry," our host said. "We've none of them in Dublin."

I guess my outraged countenance alarmed him. "No, no, don't misunderstand. We legalized homosexuality years ago and so have no need to segregate."

It was the first time I felt as if America was a third world country.

We followed that tour up with a gig at New York's famed music venue the Bottom Line. Again, Ron produced these shows. He and his business partner, Steve Addabbo, also arranged to record the performances for a "Live at the Bottom Line" CD appropriately named *This Is Not Going to Be Pretty*. A server at the club told me that I was the first openly gay act to ever play there. I found that almost impossible to believe in 1995, but when I thought about gay folks who'd performed at the club, I realized that none of them had been out of the closet at the time. Should you ever feel the need to sample the show, I have a few hundred unsold CDs in my basement. They make great coasters, or wired up and hung as a mobile, they scare critters from vegetable gardens.

Not long after the tour, with nothing better to do, I fell in love again. It's a good time killer, and it kept me from having to examine myself. Sam was someone I'd met years earlier when Bruce and I were still a couple. We were introduced at an AIDS benefit I threw with my friends Barbara and Steve. I can't say he made much of an impression then, but on second meeting I found him intelligent, funny, complex, and challenging, so I pursued him. I folded myself into his world, made friends with his friends, set social engagements I knew he'd enjoy; I did his laundry and assigned him closet space. I can't remember giving him much choice in the matter once I decided we'd be a couple. Looking back at photos of us from that time, I can't say that I ever looked happier. I had my man. Ever together with him, I had what I wanted: someone I could hide behind. There are photos of us in all of his favorite places, where we traveled to be with all of his favorite friends. We went to flea markets and county fairs and the Cape and the Catskills. I treated him like one of those finicky babies that you toss into the car and drive around until they are lulled to sleep. He wasn't close with his family, so, as the perfect partner, I took care of that by inviting them to be with us. We spent most of our time with his friends or his family, doing whatever he wanted to do.

What was it that *I* wanted to do? I was doing it. I was in a relationship with an adult man, being a supportive partner, and had

everything, including my drinking, under control. The more I con-
centrated on his life, the easier it was to ignore my own. I passed
the booze off as festive, which was easy at first, but he'd come from
a family with a history of alcoholism. As we spent longer times
together, I grew certain that the alarm bells would eventually go
off, so I called upon some of the secret drinking tactics I'd used
during my years with Bruce. I'd wait until bedtime or even after
Sam fell asleep to sneak off to the kitchen for my Southern Comfort
fix. I had convinced myself that I could not sleep without a drink.
I'll just have this one drink to put me out and that will be that.

The truth is that I hadn't slept in years. What I did was pass out.
I wanted my buzz, that warm, calm feeling that settled in my gut,
banishing the world's sharp edges and numbing me to anything
bad. At home I hoarded cigarettes and Southern Comfort as end-
of-the-world supplies. If we went anywhere overnight, I slipped a
flask or two into my luggage. He caught me at my game, but an
alcoholic and the son of an alcoholic defines stalemate.

My intake of one-hundred-proof Southern Comfort grew to
almost half a gallon per day. I hadn't had a solid bowel movement
in months. My legs were in pain almost all of the time. An online
search pointed to gout. Gout! How 1930s movie tragic! I cared less
and less about the pain and more and more about the numbing.

Sam was the only one who knew what was going on with me. My
ploys weren't fooling him. He saw right through them, and me, and
finally rebelled in ways that would end our relationship. His actions
were neither healthy nor helpful, but what are you supposed to do
when partnered with an addict in the final throes of his disease? I
had the bottle. All he had was childhood nightmares of fear and
disappointment. Our relationship went loudly, abusively, painfully
south. I did everything I could to keep us together. I thought I was
fighting to change his mind but learned that I was fighting *not* to
change my own. He escaped, and just as with Bruce, that alcoholic
part of me was relieved. The bottle at last had me all to itself. It
held me and comforted me, *What is this all for? Haven't you strug-*
gled hard enough, achieved enough, made your mark and left good
behind? No one cares that you're in pain. No one cares that you're

alone. You are the only one who can put your foot down and say you've had enough. And you have. You have had enough. There is no need to continue this suffering. For what? For who?

You know people are serious about suicide when they don't bother leaving a note. What's the point of an explanation? If they didn't understand when you were standing right in front of them, why would they understand now? Anyhow, who cares? Whoever reads a suicide note is only going to disagree.

I straightened up the house, then drove my car around back and pulled it into the garage that I almost never used. I closed the door behind me. Back up to the kitchen for my favorite, biggest drinking glass. I put a nice amount of ice into it, grabbed a pack of cigarettes, my lighter, and a half gallon of booze. Nursing that absolutely vital and delicious drink, I turned on some evening lights, let the dogs out for a last pee, fed them, washed out their bowls, and headed back to the garage with my booty. I wasn't numb. If there were tears on my cheek, they were as much relief as anything else. I had no anger, no thoughts of revenge, no thoughts of anyone other than myself. Simply stated, I was done. Finished. Over. I turned the car on, popped one of my "suicide tapes" into the cassette player, settled back with my drink and a cigarette, and waited for nothing.

I have no recollection of how long I was there. I remember awakening to the feeling of an itch. A bad itch. A mosquito was biting me. I shook my head awake and realized that there were several mosquitos biting my arms, my legs, my neck. I beat them off as sense of place returned. I wasn't dead. It hadn't worked. I was drunk and drowsy, confused and dizzy and itching like mad. I turned the motor off, got out of the car, and climbed the stairs to my bedroom, where I collapsed.

I came to the next morning, still cloudy, but very aware of all that had happened. I reached for my phone book, looked up the number of my friend Julie Janney, who I knew had some experience with Twelve Step work, and when she answered the phone I said, "You've got to get me to a meeting. Please."

The two of us ran around trying to find an AA meeting. It was actually pretty funny. In a world filled with alcoholics and drug addicts, we could not find a safe place to be this peaceful Sunday morning. We finally found one, but they wouldn't let us in. It was a men-only meeting. I said, "Don't you understand? I just tried to kill myself!"

"Rules are rules," one of the men offered.

In my years of Twelve Step I have never allowed someone who showed up to be turned away, no matter what the condition or circumstances.

Coming home, the house stunk of exhaust fumes. I began to air the place out as best I could while also calling the fantastic folks I knew in program. Everyone I reached out to rushed to my side in support. Even a few of Sam's friends were there to help. I had just tried to off myself, and yet the overall feeling was one of celebration. Erase a few fiddly details, and I'd died the night before in my garage only to be reborn that morning. Walking into a meeting and having someone ask if I was ready to surrender my will was almost amusing to me. My will, and everything I had done, led me into that garage. I was so ready to let someone else call the shots. I began to pray daily. Sometimes I prayed hourly. Not believing in a deity, I called my god "Group of Drunks" and let them guide me. Whoever was going to make my decisions from then on had to do a better job than I had. They couldn't do worse.

Those first few sober months were a true balance of pain and joy. The joy was feeling free for the first time in decades. The sleep! The undrugged rest that my body and brain had been begging for was delicious. I was finally mourning all of the disappointments, the failures, the attacks, and the losses I'd suffered but never allowed myself to feel because I numbed my brain out. What an ass. I'd avoided none of the unpleasantness. Every bitter bit of it waited patiently for me to awaken. Now, like it or not, it was time to process and make peace with my own life. Two times a day for the next year I sat and cried through AA meetings. But I was smiling. I was acknowledging and saying goodbye to the ghosts and all the other scary shit hiding in my closet and under the bed. Sitting in a meeting room is the safest place in the world. The people there know who you are. You may never have met, but you passed one another in the darkened hallways of the torture maze, and you all made it out. You've nothing to hide from one another because they knew it all.

A circle of friends began to grow as I awoke. Lauren was someone who saw me at my first Early Bird meeting and swooped me up. She did that with every newcomer, but I swooped back. Patty was one of Sam's best friends who I happily inherited during the divorce. Meg and Justine were an incredible lesbian couple, also friends of Sam's, who surrounded me with healing love and watched over me until I could stand on my own. You may have noticed that I'm only mentioning women. Don't get me wrong, I love my male friends. But when it comes to emotional honesty and acceptance and patience and support, the women in my life have always been the rocks I could count on. Hopefully, I've been the same for them.

Before I forget to mention it, I still had the rest of my life to deal with. Since I had no idea that I was about to hit bottom, I had accepted a role in a movie that was filming in Croatia, on the Dalmatian coast. The director told me that there would be boats to ferry us to Venice on our days off. "Bring your boyfriend. Have a dream vacation on me!"

I was less than two weeks sober. Sam and I were barely speaking, but off we went to Croatia to film another of my best-forgotten movies, *Kull the Conqueror*, starring a very sweet Kevin Sorbo. Arriving late at night, we found our lodgings to be less than the dream hotel promised. We were filming in a deserted summer camp. Our beds were cots, our showers were cold, and, to the shock of this newly sobered person, a bottle of water ran three times the cost of wine. Furthermore, because this was a European crew, wine was served with every meal. *Salud!*

One reason I had accepted this job was because Sam wanted to see Croatia. I thought of it as a paid vacation we'd be taking together but here we were, broken up and barely speaking, only going because the trip had already been arranged. I saw my dream of this honeymoon drifting away on the Adriatic until surprisingly, Sam sparked to the adventure. Not working for the first few days,

I was able to focus my attention on making him happy: "What do you want to do? . . . What would you like to eat? . . . Should we go for a hike?"

Sam loved hiking, swimming, and exploring new places. We spent a few beautiful hours climbing amongst the endless walls that farmers had fashioned by piling the stones they pulled prepping the soil, separating the grape and olive orchards. We sunbathed nude on the shore and swam in the crystal waters. There was much to call idyllic about those first few days. Sadly, once I was called to work, Sam and his desires were shifted to the backseat and all attention was placed on me. He was not at all comfortable with the demotion and made certain I felt his displeasure. By the time he headed back to the States for work we were again estranged.

Meanwhile, there I was in the middle of the Adriatic Sea, playing a pirate. How absurd is that?

There was a scene that called for me to be thrown off my pirate ship and left behind to drown. As they readied the shot, they asked me to please remove pieces of my costume as they needed to dress my stunt double for the shot. Out came an old man—I mean an *old* man—dressed and bewigged as I was. This was my stunt double? I said, "You've got to be kidding me. You can't make that guy jump off the ship. You'll kill him."

"Well," the director said, "you can always do it yourself."

I looked over the edge of the ship. It really wasn't that high And I'm a pretty good swimmer . . .

"You're the only member of the cast not doing his own stunts. Even the girls do theirs," he purred into my ear.

Should you ever have the misfortune to see this movie, you now know that it really *was* me tossed like Yom Kippur sins into the sea. That, too, is me struggling to swim after the ship in the water. And that's also me tearing my rotator cuff doing my own stunts.

I returned home sore but sober, my arm in a sling, and predictably nervous as to what I'd find. The relationship did not survive, although I tried to hang on. Another favorite Twelve Step concept: "I've never let go of anything without leaving claw marks."

I asked Sam if he'd be willing to try therapy. He said yes, so I arranged a session with a couples counselor conveniently located close to his job. She asked him what he'd like to get out of this and he said, "Myself," and stood to leave. "Therapy would involve opening a whole can of worms. I'm not willing to do that. Not for him. Not for anyone."

That was that.

For the next ten years I awoke to daily heartache at the thought that Sam was gone. No shit—ten years. I always thought the rule stated you could mourn for half the length of the relationship. So, if you were together for ten years, you were completely over it after five. A six month fling earned you three months in solitary. But here I was stuck grieving a two-year affair for a decade. That seemed like unreasonable punishment. At first the pain was stabbing, a piercing punch as remembering ripped my gut open. Then it became more of a burning, a soreness, a tearing like that of an overextended muscle. Eventually it was the routine of pain that made awakening fearful. He was gone and an echoing emptiness ached in his place. I carried a wound that I thought might never heal completely. Who knew heartache actually hurt? Leaving booze behind meant starting each day ritually ripping the scab off my heart and moving through *la peine du jour*. I guess I just wasn't used to being alive.

Having been only semiconscious for decades, I never learned how to deal with rejection or loss, or anything else for that matter. I had a lot of emotional catching up to do. I had to wonder, *If I never learned to let go, did I ever really learn to love? Was this just about Sam or was I actually mourning all of the relationships I'd never been able to grieve until now?*

Putting down the glass was so much easier than being sober.

37

IDLE HANDS ARE
A NO-NO

1996 and Onward

I t is suggested that you make no major life changes during your first year of sobriety. Makes sense. You've just awakened from a coma. Emotionally raw, your first instinct is to try and clean up the mess you made while using. Truthfully, you're barely in shape to do the dishes. It's much wiser to reengage with life in small doses. Do the laundry. Answer the mail. Reset your sleep schedule. All else can wait. The promise is that after five years of sober living you will get your marbles back. That's actually how they put it, and you know what? They're not wrong. It takes that long to sift the real from the imagined, assess the damages, mourn the losses, and develop new aspirations.

During those first years I acted a bit, I wrote some, but mostly I healed. They said, "Wear the world like a loose garment," and I tried. Thankfully the royalties from *La Cage* and my other plays plus the fees earned doing voice work were enough income to keep me solvent.

Inspired by watching a TV show on the subject, I began to make quilts. More than a craft, quilting can be a challenging art discipline or can provide a low-pressure activity for achieving a meditative state. A completed quilt imparts a sense of pride along with beauty and warmth. And they make great gifts, especially from a person currently eating crow. Face it, when you give someone a painting you've stuck them with a thing they have to hang whether they like it or not. Even if they only drag it out when you visit, you've burdened them with one more duty. But a quilt? Who can't use a quilt? If you love it, you throw it on your bed or drape it over the sofa for comfort on chilly nights. If it isn't your taste, you can fold it up for the dog to sleep on. Even the ugliest quilt can still cushion an old bike in the garage or protect the dining-room-table leaves in the basement. And quilts have two sides, doubling the chance you'll find something you can live with.

On the occasion of her work being put on display in the Smithsonian, a quilter was asked for comment. She shook her head and smiled, "It's amazing how far a needle can take you."

I had a more personal reason to learn to quilt. Under the remarkable leadership of AIDS activist Cleve Jones, family and friends of people who died with AIDS created coffin-sized quilt panels representing their loved ones. The panels were then joined together into a huge quilt of remembrance and mourning. The Names Project AIDS Memorial Quilt was about to be displayed for the first time in Washington, DC, and I was asked to be among those who'd read the names of our dead out loud as the quilt was unfurled. I wanted to make panels for my friends Court and Christopher but I didn't sew and so my dresser, Larry Tarzy, and I spray-painted their names onto their panels graffiti style. Although I was proud to see their names represented on the National Mall I promised that I'd someday make proper fabric testaments to their lives. Learning to quilt was that first step. I'm sorry to say I've yet to complete that promise.

I'm not crazy about children, but I love doing children's television. I appeared as the Easter Bunny in *Elmo Saves Christmas*, and I sang "Everything's Coming up Noses" on *Sesame Street*.

HBO had an award-winning children's series called *Happily Ever After: Fairy Tales for Every Child*, featuring classic stories reset in alternate cultures. In a retelling of *Thumbelina* I voiced Mrs. Leaperman, a *yenta* frog, who Thumbelina befriends in her Amazonian rain-forest home. The following season producer Donna Brown Guillaume asked if I'd like to write an episode for the series—maybe Jewish, maybe gay. I'd read a children's book called *Oliver Button Is a Sissy,* a well-meaning little tale with an ending that really pissed me off. All through the story this little boy's classmates taunt him for being a sissy because he likes to sing and dance. At the end of the story, when he shows everyone how good he is, they cross out the graffitied word "sissy" and write, "Oliver Button is a star." Fuck them and fuck that!

I sat my ass down and wrote *The Sissy Duckling.* In my retelling of *The Ugly Duckling* Elmer loves to do all of the things I loved doing as a child: play with dolls, make sand castles, put on puppet shows, and the creative like. Elmer isn't looked down upon by just the other ducklings. His own father calls him a sissy and turns his back in shame. By the end of the tale, Elmer has earned the respect of all, who declare that he is no sissy. But unlike Master Button, Elmer declares, "I *am* the same sissy I always was and am proud of it!"

That's the message, right there.

HBO green-lit the project and assembled a fabulous team. Voices included Melissa Etheridge, Sharon Stone, Ed Asner, Kathy Najimy, and Estelle Getty. They went on to hire the number-one animation designer in America, who just happened to be Daniel Haskett, who just happened to be a friend from high school. What a thrill to work with this childhood acquaintance! When designing Elmer, he based the character on memories of me from our school days.

Thirty years after graduation, the two of us shared an even bigger thrill: meeting up at the recording studio, we sat listening to Dionne Warwick record the original songs for our project.

"Daniel," I said, "could you ever have imagined that you and I would be sitting here together with Dionne Warwick asking us if she did okay?"

Director Anthony Bell and the rest of the team did such a phenomenal job that we were awarded the prestigious Humanitas Prize. That was the good part. The bad part was me. I was so anxious to jump up at the ceremony to deliver my own pro-gay statement to the audience of Catholic clergy that I shot my mouth off, got back to my seat, and only then realized that I had thanked *no one* for their work on the show. I thought about jumping back up

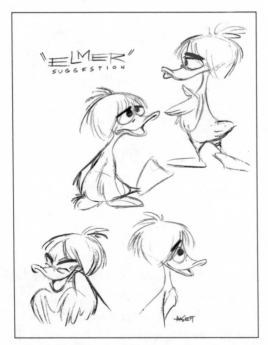

Daniel said he used his memories of me as
a kid for inspiration when designing Elmer.
Here are his original concept sketches.

and making it right, but they already were on to the next award. I
sat there, open mawed, with a now smudged list of names I'd prepared to read growing moist in my hand. That ego had gotten the
best of me again. I sent flowers and regrets the next day, but there is
nothing that replaces doing the right thing at the right time, which
is why I still carry that guilt.

The following year I adapted the story into a picture book for
Simon & Schuster that has been reprinted time and again over the
years. A few children's-theater companies have also adapted the
story into live musical productions.

I never wanted to be a children's book author, but I can't imagine
what my life would have been like had I found *The Sissy Duckling*
waiting for me on the library shelf. It may not have made my journey any shorter or less painful, but at least I would have known
that I wasn't walking the path alone. Maybe I could be a pre-adult
author.

38

HAIRSPRAY

2000

*H*airspray was on the money with the AA prediction: you get your marbles back in five years. After avoiding life-changing decisions as best as I could, I was in shape for a good game of marbles. Along came the musical *Hairspray*. In John Waters's original movie, the role of Edna Turnblad had been created by the singular actor Divine. We weren't close friends but knew one another from the downtown scene.

We were once sitting together waiting for a wash cycle to finish spinning his sheets at the laundromat on Christopher Street when he looked at me and said, "You and me—both cared for by the same abusers."

When I designed my poster for *Flatbush Tosca* I came up with the slug line "Men call her diva. Women call her devil. Police call her daily." A few seasons later Divine was appearing in Tom Eyen's *The Neon Woman,* and their poster ripped off my slug line. I complained to director Ron Link only to have him lie right to my face, saying that I gave it to him. I told Divine about it and she made sure that the ads and posters were redone without my purloined prose.

Sadly, he passed not long after the success of the *Hairspray* movie.

Theatrical producer Margo Lion had optioned the stage rights and assembled a stellar team to adapt *Hairspray* into a Broadway tuner. Composer Marc Shaiman and his partner in lyric writing and life, Scott Wittman, were fluent with the themes, melodies, and genres of 1960s pop music. The transgressive humor they'd displayed in projects like *South Park: Bigger, Longer & Uncut* proved they were up to musicalizing John's offbeat world vision. I actually broke the back of the seat in front of me with convulsive laughter the first time I saw those little South Park animated characters singing "You're an uncle fucka. I must say, We fucked your uncle yesterday." Cartoon and humor writer Mark O'Donnell was signed to write the book, and the multitalented and totally adorable Rob Marshall was nabbed to direct and choreograph.

Sticking to the original concept of a man playing the role, they reached out to most of the obvious character actors for Edna. None felt exactly right. Richie Jackson tried and failed to get me seen by the casting office. Frustrated, he phoned Shaiman directly. As Marc recalled, "I thought you were a great idea. Edna's first entrance happens with a stage full of singing and dancing teens. What better voice than yours to cut through all of that?"

When Richie told me I had an appointment to audition, I thought, *The female lead role in a Broadway musical? Me? Hysterical.*

I hadn't auditioned for anything in decades. Most jobs came my way because the director or writer knew they wanted me in advance. Richie would tell potential employers that I was too well-known to audition, but the truth was that I was too embarrassed by my dyslexia to read out loud. What would people think, hearing me mispronounce words or stumble or yabber senselessly on? Fear cost me a good many opportunities, including a shot to replace a role in *Love! Valour! Compassion!* How well I remember the look of displeasure on director Joe Mantello's face when he gently asked, "Can't you read a few lines for us? Just so we can hear the language in your mouth?"

My terror surely appeared as arrogance when I said, "Sorry." Happily, that role went to Mario Cantone, who made his fabulous Broadway debut.

Now that I was a sober person, fear was no longer an indulgence I allowed myself. Scared or not, auditioning was part of an actor's duties. I walked into the room, faced the banquette of theater pros, and smiled, "What can I do you for?"

I think we began by reading a scene or two. The table laughed, which helped me relax.

Then it was time to sing. I called Lenny, my pianist extraordinaire, into the room and we performed a silly Cole Porter ditty, "The Tale of the Oyster." Once again the table was receptive. They briefly whispered among themselves before Rob Marshall asked, "Do you have anything more melodic?"

"In my throat or my repertoire?" I answered.

A quick look to Lenny, who waved his portfolio: "Honey, I brought it all."

We settled on the ballad "Happiness Is a Thing Called Joe." Polite applause and smiles met Lenny's final arpeggio as I said "I can't thank you enough" and headed for the door.

Again Rob spoke: "How about something more uptempo?"

Something more? I was bewildered but willing. Lenny suggested the raunchy blues classic "Frankie and Johnny." Before I began I warned them: "This thing's got a dozen verses and they're pretty much the same, so, no insult, feel free to cut me off anytime."

They didn't. They let me sing right to the man's demise.

Roll me over, Frankie,
Roll me over slow,
Roll me over on my right side, Frankie,
Why'd you shoot so low?

This time I was sure I was done, but no: before I got out of there I sang damn near everything in Lenny's portfolio. I left exhausted but filled with pride that fear had not won out. This was a new day for me. I dialed Richie from the pay phone on the corner.

"Oh, Cookie, you would not have believed how sweet they were! I was almost crying. I think they wanted me to feel I had a fair shot, so they let me sing damn near every song I know. Please call Shaiman. Treating me that way was above and beyond. Thank him for me and tell him I'll be there cheering for them on opening night."

"Are you done?" he asked.

"Yeah. Why?"

"They already called and offered you the part. Congratulations!"

I bought a VHS copy of the movie but decided not to watch it again. I remembered Divine's performance vividly. She was beyond. Playing a Baltimore housewife was in her DNA. But if I wanted to make this character my own, I had to begin anew. I had a pretty good start. I knew what it was like to be overweight and what it was like to be ruled by fear, immobilized by how the world views, judges, and ignores you. Still, I dragged my ass to the mall and tailed large women to see how they moved, how they negotiated their surroundings. I sat in my car and watched these women order meals at fast-food drive-up windows before squirreling off to a spot at the far end of the parking lot to eat. As for the specifics: Edna hides in her second-floor apartment, taking in dirty laundry to support the family. Her husband follows his dream of running a novelty joke shop on the first floor. They have a rebellious teenaged daughter. The girl is overweight, which makes her mother want to shield her from the cruelty of the world.

But this isn't the story of a mother hiding her daughter. It's about a daughter opening the world up for her mother. Edna's transformation from agoraphobic hausfrau to self-assured woman is the stuff actors dream of playing; Eliza Doolittle, Cinderella, Edna Turnblad. Iconic. I was excited.

Hairspray's first adventure was a workshop of act 1. Belonging to a cast can feel like getting adopted into a new family. Watching these folks arrive, I couldn't help thinking that these strangers saying hello for the first time might be one another's best friends a year from now. Some could even fall in love. Theater isn't just magic for the audience. Most of these actors were young, in their twenties, getting their first break. Being introduced to Marissa Jaret Winokur, the actress who was to star in the show, was an event. A funny little thing, short and round and exploding with energy and a thousand-watt smile. She spoke at a breathless pace in a pitch that rose with excitement and lowered with intimacy. She was happy, she was frightened, she was sure that she'd be fired, and all I could think was, *If this fireball goes down, she's taking the building with her.*

Shaiman was teaching "Timeless to Me" to me when Rob brought someone over to join us. He was a skinny thing, bent a bit this way, twisted a bit that, sporting a shock of white hair that crowned a wonderful Old World Italian face.

"Meet your husband," Rob said.

I was already a fan from afar. I'd fallen in love with his assured belt when I'd heard him sing "(You Gotta Have) Heart" in *Damn Yankees*. Dick Latessa and I were a team from our first hello—no exaggeration. He never treated me as a man playing a woman. I was always his wife. We were partners. Over the years I played opposite a number of wonderful gentlemen, but there was only one Dick Latessa. At one point we were Broadway's hottest couple. Invited to perform at benefits, we sang all of the great older-couple duets: "It Couldn't Please Me More" from *Cabaret*, "I Remember It Well" from *Gigi*, along with Frank Loesser's "Baby, It's Cold Outside." There was even chatter of us recording an album together. We were a matched set. When Broadway contracts were negotiated, the producers claimed that Dick demanded too much money and they were moving on. I said I wouldn't do the show without him. I even offered to take the extra pay from my salary. They folded. When they asked me to extend my contract, I agreed only if Dick would stay on. When they offered me the Las Vegas company, I said I'd only do it if Dick Latessa was part of the deal. I've got to tell you, we both did Las Vegas because the money was so insane. It paid for rebuilding my entire house, and Dick bought his daughter a Manhattan apartment. Those shows in Las Vegas were our last together, but the memories I carry of them are more precious than any paycheck.

Some shows fall into place effortlessly and some take years of hard work, struggle, rewriting, and recasting until they finally find themselves. *Hairspray* was one of the latter. Soon after our work-

In rehearsal, in performance, the affection
between Dick and me was real.

shops, Rob Marshall left to direct the movie of *Chicago*. Margo
offered to change our production dates, but Rob was out and the
director/choreographer team of Jack O'Brien and Jerry Mitchell
were in. There were cast changes and song adjustments, and like
most shows, troubled or otherwise, *Hairspray* had second-act problems. After establishing the plot and characters, the Waters movie
shifts styles and veers off into a lavish farce. There's a minicar race,
a bomb planted in a beehive hairdo, and the sudden introduction
of the beat generation. Mark O'Donnell faithfully followed that
blueprint, and that led to an unproduceable mess. Margo asked if
I'd join the writing team to help get the show back on track, but
I declined. For the first time in years I was just an actor, and I was
loving it. Playing Edna, I felt I'd taken on about as much as I could
handle. Margo turned to Tom Meehan, who had a reputation for
book fixing, to assist Mark. Together they gave the show an over-
haul of new jokes and song ideas but did nothing to address the
structure, characters, or storytelling.

The plan was to present one final workshop/backers' audition before going into rehearsals for our out-of-town tryout in Seattle. As I recall, we did two performances in a theater at Westbeth for backers, producers, theater owners, and friends. Everyone showed up—everyone. We gave it our all, but the reception was less than stellar. People found much to love, but the show just didn't add up to anything. What's promised in the opening number must be delivered before the final curtain. It's a theatrical journey that's as true of *Hello, Dolly!* as it is of *Sweeney Todd* or *Hamilton*. *Hairspray* lacked that drive, that marksmanship. Richie put his foot down. "You can't commit to this show. You've waited this long to return in the right property. You'll wait a little longer."

I halfheartedly agreed. I wanted this so badly.

Jack O'Brien asked to meet with me. I sat down at home, went through the script, and made notes of how I thought it all could be fixed. I brought my notes, all neatly typed out, to our meeting, but Jack waved them away. He insisted that the writers had been working and that there was a new script addressing all of the shortcomings.

"Oh, great. Can I read it?"

"No," Jack said. "You need to commit to the process."

I'd been doing workshops of this show for nearly two years and still the problems persisted. How could I commit?

Shaiman called me at home that Saturday morning and I gave him the same answer: "How can I sign a contract when you won't even show me the script?"

"I'll show you the script," he said. "But I've got to tell you that it's not there yet."

This was 2001, when our technological capabilities were not what they are today, but we each had a fax machine. Marc began to fax the script to me, page by page. As they came through, I retyped each one, rewriting as I went along. Being slow of finger as I was, I couldn't keep up with the machine, and so I finished my rewrite the next day. It happened to be Easter Sunday. I memorialized the date in the script by having the TV show host, Corny Collins, ask one of the girls if she's ready for the big dance contest and had her respond, "Ready as a rabbit on Easter."

I dropped lots of other little Easter eggs into the script so that if anyone ever denied my contributions, I could point to a reference and ask why it was there. For example, who but I would place the finale on June 6th? But it was my birthday, so . . .

I faxed the script back to Marc, page by page, and I think he sent the pages on to Jack. A flurry of phone calls followed, by the end of which I'd been hired to ghostwrite the show. I'd forgo my name appearing as a writer, and I'd have no say in production decisions or movie rights, but I'd receive royalties, etc. O'Donnell's lawyer asked that I never disclose my participation, but that I refused. I did agree to remain silent through the awards season so as not to hurt their chances of winning something. Sobriety had put me out of the lying business.

All of Jack's years of running the Old Globe theater in San Diego taught him how to get the most from a team. Whenever a script problem arose, Jack presented the challenge to Tom, Mark, and me as a group before sending us off separately to develop solutions. Best idea won the day. Jack was one smart cookie.

One evening, after a long day of rehearsal, I was grabbing my dinner in our Seattle hotel lobby restaurant. Tom and his wife were seated at the bar. Suddenly Tom was at my side.

"Jack cut my last line today," he said. "Did you realize that? I don't have a single line or idea left. Nothing of mine is left in the show."

"I'm sorry," I told him. "No. I didn't know. That's not something I keep track of."

"Now you know."

"Sorry," I repeated as he stood staring down at me. "So, what do you want to do? Will you take your name off the show?"

He stood quietly, unsteadily, for a moment and then walked back to his barstool.

He did not remove his name, but he did graciously mention me when accepting both the Tony and Drama Desk awards for writing the best book of a musical.

Hairspray, you might remember, tells the story of racial discrimination in 1960s Baltimore. African American teenagers were segregated at school socials and prohibited from appearing with the white kids on the local television dance show. We had an interracial cast, but due to the nature of the plot the white cast and the Black cast often rehearsed apart. One morning, early on, I stepped out of the rehearsal room to find most of the African American cast members mulling about in the hallway. Some were bored, some angry, and most feeling a degree of disrespect. Although we all held the best intentions, our creative team, with the exception of orchestrator Harold Wheeler, was all white. Add the fact that the story was being told from a white family's perspective; no matter how much love and respect we felt creating them, the Black characters were presented as the outsiders. A number of our African American cast members felt this acutely, especially when sitting, unused, in the hallway for days while the white kids rehearsed their dances. Jerome Robbins manipulated a similar situation to legendary advantage when creating *West Side Story,* but these were different times. No one wants to feel like an outsider. As I recall, Jack, ever the loving father, sat the cast down and did his best to address the history we were representing, and why it might be affecting the experience we were having in rehearsal. We were all artists together, but we were also individuals. The audience needed to perceive us first as Black and white cliques. Our job would then be to open their minds and engage with us as one human family made up of unique individuals. Problems arose every now and then, but I think from then on people were for the most part heard and respected.

When African American director Kenny Leon helmed the live television production of *Hairspray* in 2016, I felt those tensions greatly reduced. I believe that the African American cast experienced their roles as equal in all ways. Was the difference Kenny or the times or the fact that *Hairspray* was now a known quantity? I'm not sure but I was glad to be conscious of my coworkers's perceptions and sensitive to them. The lesson learned back then is not so different from the one I struggle to remember today; sometimes it's best to shut up and listen. You could learn something.

Halfway through rehearsals in 2002, we experienced an incident that's become Broadway legend. The young actor playing the romantic lead left the show for a movie role. When the producer announced that we'd replace him through auditions, Marissa stepped forward and advocated for another member of the ensemble. She said, "He's a great dancer, a terrific singer, and absolutely gorgeous. What else are you looking for?"

Matthew Morrison was promoted from the ensemble to play the male lead and from there went on to have a stellar career.

Creating Edna was a team effort. Makeup, hair, and clothing were all part of the illusion. William Ivey Long was our costume designer and a willing playmate. We spent hours in a studio messing with foam and undergarments until we hit the right volume for Edna's body. At first he had her shaped like *The Jetsons'* Mrs. Spacely, with protruding chest that met a large tummy in a straight line down.

"No, my darling." I shook my head. "Edna is a mother. A voluptuous Botticelli nude gone wild. Think Etruscan fertility goddess!" I quickly sketched a round bosom and undulating stomach along with an ass you could serve drinks upon. William needed no more. His creations for Edna, from simple housedress to a Chanel suit to a flaming-red gown, are each unforgettable. I wore every one of them with pride. William is a genius.

The Seattle tryout was pretty damn triumphant. The weather was unusually warm, and the theater, of course, had no air conditioning, because they swear it never gets hot in that city. But it was a completely different kind of heat that radiated from that stage to the audience and back again. From the first drumbeat of "Good Morning, Baltimore," the joint was on fire! The show was far from perfect, but you could not tell that from the reaction. The audience laughed at every joke, hooted for every song, applauded every exit, and cheered every dance number. When we caught sight of one another backstage during costume changes, all we could do was smile, wide-eyed, shaking our heads at one another before rushing back onstage for more. It was the kind of reaction you only dream about.

As it was the first preview, our bow at the end of the show was rudimentary at best. We all held hands and bathed in the applause before rushing back to our dressing rooms to change. My wig, dress, and undergarments were being stripped from me when Marisha Ploski, the assistant stage manager, knocked on my door. "You've got to get back out there."

"What are you talking about?" I asked.

"Just get your ass out there."

I pulled my robe on and followed her. Almost immediately I heard a sound, a throbbing, thumping disco beat, as she led me toward the stage.

Hands over her ears she said, "They won't stop. Not until they see you."

I realized that thunderous sound was the audience stomping their feet and clapping their hands.

Marisha pushed me out onstage. I stood there in my robe and slippers taking in that overwhelming uproar. It clicked in my memory that a large portion of the audience was made up of members of the Seattle Men's Chorus, a group I'd performed with many times over the years. They were giving me a joyous welcome home. Sissy-Mary-Lala that I am, I waved and wept and blew kisses. From that moment on I felt I no longer had anything to worry about. I suddenly believed that Edna was going to take care of me, and I was going to take care of her, and together we were going to make a mark on theater history.

We arrived back in New York as a conquering army. There was real excitement on that street of dreams. *Hairspray* promised to be more than a hit: it was going to be an SRO smash! Considering that 80 percent of Broadway shows lose money, just being a hit should be more than enough. But *Hairspray* was embraced by its audience with a devotion and energy that were absolutely thrilling. Performance after performance, standing in place backstage, waiting for the curtain to rise, we'd hear the first notes begin to play and the audience was already screaming and applauding. For my first entrance I was hidden behind a sheet that I held in front of me. Dropping it, I almost always had to hold for long entrance applause before beginning my dialogue. The poor ensemble was stuck, bent over, in a repetitive dance position until the applause

Marissa Jaret Winokur, Dick Latessa, and
I were invited to perform at every function,
every fundraiser, every event that year.

died down enough for us to start the scene. From the corner of my eye I could see them shaking their heads and rolling their eyes my way.

Sometimes I'd be walking down the street on my way to work when I'd suddenly catch the photos of Edna on the outside of the theater. I'd stop to clear my head from disbelief. Me, Harvey Fierstein, singing and dancing on Broadway! Quite an ego booster. Which reminds me: We were recording the original Broadway cast album, the entire company huddled around microphones singing "Welcome to the '60s," and when they yelled "Cut" I laughed, gasping for air. "It's so much easier to sing that without having to dance at the same time!"

Our musical director, Lon Hoyt, looked at me curiously and said, "Why are you singing? Your microphone is off."

All this time I'd been killing myself, straining to keep up with the ensemble, only to realize now that they didn't want my voice messing up the harmonies.

For years before this I felt like a visitor to Broadway. I was a downtown person who'd been invited to the party but didn't really belong. More than once my friends mocked my return with Susan

Hayward's speech from *Valley of the Dolls*: "So, they drummed you out of Hollywood and you come crawlin' back to Broadway. Well, Broadway doesn't go for booze and dope!"

But I wasn't Neely O'Hara crawling home drunk and destroyed. I was Dorothy Gale awakening in her own bed in Kansas, now filled with the true meaning of home and overflowing with gratitude to have another chance. The fanfare wasn't all about me. I was part of an elixir brewed of John Waters, Divine, Shaiman, Wittman, Mitchell, O'Brien, O'Donnell, dressed in clothing by William Ivey Long, hair by Paul Huntley and Jon Jordan, and makeup by Mark Manalansan, and slapped together eight times a week by my dresser, Keith Shaw. This old witch had finally found her magic potion. Stand her up center stage, hit her with a hot-pink spotlight, and you had the promise of Charlie Brown's Christmas tree, the Statue of Liberty, and Ethel Merman all rolled into one.

Audiences, critics, even other performers embraced Edna in astonishing ways. Legendary caricaturist Al Hirschfeld drew her; glass-ornament designer Christopher Radko created not one but two Edna ornaments; I wore a ten-million-dollar canary diamond around my neck and a specially designed gown to appear on the arm of Rod Stewart as we presented Robin Williams with a Grammy. Edna was photographed by Annie Leibovitz, Steven Meisel, and Richard Avedon. Matt Lauer flirted with me; Katie Couric courted me. Edna and I appeared in trade shows, Bloomingdale's windows, and on magazine covers. Most memorable of all was riding atop a float in the annual Macy's Thanksgiving Day Parade. Oh, yes, the singing trio of girls from the show and I rode atop a mock convertible car and, with me dressed as Mrs. Santa Claus herself, sang a special song created for the occasion, "Santa Knows." It was all in good fun and made for a most unforgettable holiday. Never being one to miss an opportunity, I wrote an op-ed that *The New York Times* published the day before Thanksgiving. Inspired by the fantasy of playing Mrs. Santa, I opined on the notion that we really know very little about Santa. What would happen if we suddenly found out he was gay? I wondered if people of faith would shoo him away and ban him from the holiday. I thought it a question worth asking. You can imagine how Macy's phones began to ring, but they stood steadfast behind my appearance. They simply said that I was playing Edna and *not* Mrs. Claus. They underlined it by having a woman costumed as Mrs. Claus ride along with Santa when he appeared at the end of the parade. Most amazing was the general public's reaction. Along the route there were no boos or catcalls. There were only happy, smiling faces and waves. The only negative feedback I received was from a gay member of the *Hairspray* team: no one hates us like we hate ourselves. But this world, on that Thanksgiving morning, was a loving place where I wanted to spend the rest of my life. I was very proud of Macy's.

Legendary clown Grandma posed with me before I climbed aboard the float in the Macy's Thanksgiving Day Parade.

Tony Award day was one for the books, or at least this book. Up at five a.m. to shower, shave, and get my ass into the dressing room so my "glam squad" could get me into full Edna drag. The entire *Hairspray* company was set to perform our finale on the Tony broadcast. We were due to arrive at Radio City Music Hall dressed and ready to go by nine a.m. We got there, were shown our way around, put through the entire number for the cameras, and then taken back to the Neil Simon Theatre, where we got out of

costume, wigs, makeup and had breakfast. By noon I was back in
my dressing room to get into drag again because we had a matinee to perform. The matinee, I should note, was wild. The company was on fire with excitement, and the audience knew we were
going to the Tonys, so they were pumped as well. After the matinee I scrubbed Edna off again and got into my tuxedo. Richie and
my press agent extraordinaire, Rick Miramontez, loaded me into
a limousine for the ride back to Radio City Music Hall to walk the
red carpet. I posed and gave interviews, trying as hard as I could
to let all of this soak in. It had been twenty years between Tony
ceremonies. There were a lot of emotions churning around in me.
Barely through the press line, I was whisked backstage and into a
dressing room, where my glam squad was waiting. They stripped
me down, slapped the makeup and wig back on, and before I knew
it we were live on national TV performing "You Can't Stop the
Beat" to a raucous theater audience. The number ended and again
I was scurried away to the dressing room, where, for the third time
that day the makeup was scraped from my face and my girdle was
replaced with a tuxedo. Finally, they sat me in my place in the auditorium. Marissa was seated in front of me, Richie at my side. Theater producer Daryl Roth and her son, Jordan, sat across the aisle
from us. For a few moments I was able to center myself before the
category of Best Actress in a Musical was announced and Marissa's name was called as the winner. She leapt to her feet, I leapt
to my feet, and I grabbed her, whispering something into her ear
before pushing her off toward the stage to accept her award. Many
have asked what it was I whispered. I'll tell you. I said, "Your name
has just been changed from Marissa Jaret Winokur to Tony Award
Winner Marissa Jaret Winokur, and they can never take that away
from you."

A few more moments to breathe before my category came up.
When my name was called as the winner of Best Actor in a Musical
I was definitely launched into another state of being. Lightheaded
and buoyant of foot, I arrived onstage and immediately sought out
the faces of the other gentlemen in my category—Antonio Ban-
deras, Brian Stokes Mitchell, Malcolm Gets, and the divine dancer

John Selya. I looked out at them and off the cuff said, "Boy, am I glad this wasn't a beauty contest!"

Richie was crying; the cast members I could see were hugging and crying as well. I tried very hard to focus and thank everyone I needed to thank. I've never watched the tape of the event, so I can't tell you if I succeeded. I can only tell you that I tried.

More press backstage. More photos, hugs, and kisses. Awards over, Richie rushed me outside, where Rick flagged down our limo. The car door closed, the limo pulled out, and for the first time since five a.m. the world was quiet—marvelously quiet. I looked over at Richie and then down to my hand, where I saw the Tony clenched in my fist. I read it aloud: "2003 Best Actor in a Musical." Richie and I stared at one another and then, in tandem, we burst into laughter. The relief was so great that I actually fell to the floor of the limo and rolled around in hysterical joy. What a ride this had been, from the audition to this night! I had no idea that I was capable of such euphoria.

Sidenote: When I left my place to accept the award, a seat filler was installed next to Richie so any TV shot wouldn't include an empty space. Not interested in speaking to this stranger, Richie kept to himself until the broadcast cutaway to commercial break, at which time he stood to stretch his legs. Seeing Daryl across the aisle, Richie went over to say hello. He introduced himself to her son, Jordan, and the pair have been together ever since. Married with two children, Richie and Jordan owe their happiness to me and/or Edna. Or maybe the Tony voters. Or the seat filler. Or maybe just to the magic of theater.

As for how Edna made me feel about myself . . . well, we had a complicated relationship. I fell in love with myself as Edna. I came to feel most at home when I was her. Maybe it was the role, maybe it was the costumes, maybe it was those enormous rubber tits, maybe it was all just a joke played on me, but I believed in Edna. I became Mama to the company and was, on some level, perceived as the mother figure in the theater. Everyone hung out in my dressing room as if hanging out at home. They ate in there. They napped in there. They came to me with their troubles and complaints, expecting Mama to take care of them. I like to think I lived up to those expectations as best I could. I went so far as to write a Mother's Day op-ed for the *Times* about my theater children. The kids are all grown now and have moved on with their careers, but I'm proud to say that many of them still call me Mama. Hearing that makes me swell with pride.

I performed *Hairspray* for two years without a holiday or vacation, missing only half of a performance when swatted down by food poisoning. In any case, history had been made by Edna. She was now as iconic a Broadway dame as Mame, Dolly, or Miss Adelaide. Entering its third year, the show was still packing audiences in, but it was time to pass Edna on to other performers. I begged

It broke my heart to leave my *Hairspray*
family. Here I am holding up the "I Love
You" sign as Kathy Brier looks on.

them to replace me with Lainie Kazan. I thought she'd tear the place up in the role. After her, they'd be free to cast whoever they thought might be fun. They could switch back and forth between men and women; anything would be possible. And what a great press getter that would be! But they insisted on continuing the line of strictly male actors in the role. Oh, well.

The week after I left *Hairspray,* I grand-marshaled New York City's Gay Pride Parade for the umpteenth time, and then put myself on a strict diet. It was time to say goodbye to all of Edna. I could hear the ghost of Marvin Krauss whispering in my ear, "Enjoy tonight and then go away." As much as it pained me, I knew his was the right advice. As with playing Arnold in *Torch Song,* I knew there would be times when we'd be together again. For now it was time to move on.

39

LA CAGE'S FIRST REVIVAL

2004

It was towards the end of my run in *Hairspray* when I heard that Jimmy Nederlander Sr. wanted to revive, *La Cage Aux Folles*. The original production was shuttered prematurely to allow for the construction of a hotel in the airspace over the Palace Theatre. They offered to relocate us to another house, but we'd just lost Fritz Holt, who was the hands-on producer and the only member of our team who could have captained such a move. We let the show go after a four-year run. Seventeen years later, Jimmy had an opening at the Marquis Theatre and thought it was time to bring *La Cage* back. I needed convincing. I mean, why? Did they have a new concept or some big star asking to do it? Not really. Jerry Zaks was contracted to direct, so they sent him over to my dressing room for a chat.

"Darling, it's going to be a beautiful production," he said.

"That tells me nothing."

"We're going to do the show. What else do you want to know? Scott Pask is designing, and William Ivey Long is doing the costumes. You trust them."

Realizing that Jerry had walked in halfway through this movie, I filled him in on my original ideas, hoping to get him onboard for something different and exciting. No one does what Jerry Zaks does. He is precise and professional and polished, but cutting-edge doesn't interest him. Reinventing the wheel only eats into the energy he needs to perfect the wheel he's been given. He listened politely, waving an "I've got this" hand at me like one of those smiling cats sitting by the register of a Chinese-takeout counter. He told me not to worry. I worried.

I called Jerry Herman and heard a familiar tune. "Harvey, I don't know how much longer I have to live."

Jerry had been HIV positive for twenty years, and as it turned out, he practically outlasted us all before passing in 2019 at eighty-eight (the same number of years that a piano has keys). He asked me to let him have this production of our creation so he could hear it one more time before he died. He went on: "I understand what you want, but Zaks will do a beautiful job. He will make us both so proud. You'll see. It's going to look and sound glorious. They've promised me a twenty-two-piece orchestra. Please, let me have this one and the next revival is all yours."

I loved that man. I wouldn't have denied him this, even if he hadn't offered that last promise, but with it I was already dreaming of my production in the future. Meanwhile, the three Jerrys went to work: Jerry Zaks directed, Jerry Mitchell choreographed (his cancan was one of the most insane feats of athletic and comedic dance ever seen on a Broadway stage), and Jerry Herman bathed in the sound of the orchestra accompanying a wonderful group of singing actors. Jerry told me that this was the best cast of singers he'd ever had in one of his shows. I dared to ask, "Are you saying that you'd trade the brilliant comedy of a Carol Channing for the operatic voice of a diva like Montserrat Caballé?"

"Absolutely," he answered. "I'm a composer. I want to hear my music."

I was never certain how seriously to take that conversation, but it absolutely floored me, so I'm passing it on to you.

It also made me consider my own situation. There's no denying the universality of music. Depend on the English language and you're speaking to less than 15 percent of the population. But express yourself in song and the world opens up to your message. If I was given the choice between music or language I would, I think, choose music. No doubt I wish I had a beautiful voice. When I sing, being more than familiar with the limitations of my instrument, in my head I hear notes that are strong and on target. I can float a tone with the delicacy of a feather on a breeze, and belt a final note that leaves no doubt of whose song has just been sung. But then, of course, I hear a recording and situational reality returns, *Oh, well,* I muse, *at least one person on the planet hears beautiful music.*

The production fulfilled my wish for—both leads to be played by openly gay actors. In an embarrassment of gay riches, even the thoughtless son was played by an openly gay actor. That gay dream didn't last long. It's a funny thing about unhappy people: they're only satisfied once they've made everyone else miserable. During my career I've suffered two leading ladies of that ilk. One of them actually came to me on closing night of our show and said how sorry she was for torturing me. She said, "I do it on every show. I pick a man, always a man, and I use my position to make him suffer as best as I can. It's not you. It's about my relationship with my father."

I'm not kidding. A well-known Broadway actress said that to me during a closing-night party. I could think of no response. I stared at her for a moment or two and then simply walked away.

At *La Cage* it was Gary Beach, who was being mistreated. Our wonderfully humane producer Susan Bristow brought in matinee idol Robert Goulet to return the fun to our show. Robert was a love and a half, an absolute joy to be around and watch onstage, even if he wasn't gay. He presented another drawback. For some time age had been chipping away at his memory. Knowing that the show must go on, he'd trained himself to keep a scene going even when his mind went blank. This resulted in many amusing ad-libs, but my favorite happened while he was accusing his son of betrayal. Instead of calling out "You Judas! You traitor! You collaborationist!!" he pointed his finger and shouted, "You traitor! You collaborator! You . . . Buddhist!!"

The production won both the Tony and the Drama Desk Award for Best Revival of a Musical, and Jerry Mitchell won his first Tony and Drama Desk Awards for his choreography.

40

FIDDLER ON THE ROOF

2004

My phone rang one morning and it was my friend Susan Bristow saying, "Don't answer before you've thought it through, but promise not to shave until then."

"What the hell . . . ?"

"I want you to take over *Fiddler on the Roof*."

My brain shot off at supersonic speed: *Is she kidding? No, wait—she once teased me about playing Golde. But why ask me not to shave if she wants me to play Golde?*

We were close enough friends for me to ask, "What the fuck?"

"Fred is leaving in January, and you should replace him."

"Oh, honey. I just finished two years of *Hairspray*. The last thing I want to do—"

"This is Tevye!" she shouted.

When I was that kid attending all those classic Broadway shows, I enjoyed nuns in *The Sound of Music* and orphans in *Oliver!* until one day, to my amazement, the curtain of the Imperial Theatre rose on an entire stage filled with Jews. I rubbed my eyes to make sure I wasn't hallucinating men wearing *tsi-tsis* onstage. Not only wearing them, but the lead actor talked about them: "We wear these prayer shawls to show our devotion to God."

In an age when common consensus dictated you change your name and get a nose job if you wanted to be in show biz, here were

Jews singing about being Jewish. And now, on my phone, a producer offering me the chance to be that lead Jew.

This revival had opened at the beautiful Minskoff Theatre nine months earlier and was met with a ridiculous controversy over the great British actor Alfred Molina playing Tevye. A few boobs, led by my friend columnist Michael Riedel, derided the production for its lack of Jewishness. This was, I'll admit, a new *Fiddler*. Director David Leveaux ditched the cute little motorized houses from classic productions and instead populated the landscape with trees and lanterns to represent these lives lived mostly outdoors. Rather than present the Germanic or Polish images we knew from our ancestors, Leveaux gave us the *shtetls* of Russia, the villages that author Sholem Aleichem would have known and written about. I found the production breathtaking to watch, but if they bucked against Fred, what the hell were they going to say about me? I sought advice from Jack O'Brien.

"You have two choices," he said. "You either do it or spend the rest of your life trying to convince people that you turned it down."

I called Susan. "What does David think?"

"He loves you. He wants you to do it."

Yes? No! Yes! *NO!* No? Oy!

"I'll do it under two conditions," I said. "I want a meeting with Leveaux. If that goes well, I want the authors to hear me sing the entire score."

"They saw you in *Hairspray*."

"'Timeless to Me' is not 'Do You Love Me?' The entire score."

The book writer, Joe Stein, the lyricist, Sheldon Harnick, and the composer, Jerry Bock, had all consulted on this production. There was no way I would have the gall to get up on a stage and sing "If I Were a Rich Man" without their express approval. At the very least I didn't want them to be able to say, "If I knew he'd sound like that, I never . . ."

"I'll set it up," Susan said. "Meanwhile, no shaving!"

The meeting with David was wonderful. His mind, his imagination, his love of this piece and of theater as a whole inspired me.

And then it was time to sing for those geniuses. We met in a rehearsal room. The music director took his place at the piano. The authors sat together at a table and I began. I sang "Tradition" and they were still there at the end. I sang "Rich Man" and no one left. "Sabbath Prayer," "To Life," "Tevye's Dream," "Sunrise, Sunset," "Do You Love Me?" . . . but when I reached "Chavaleh" my voice cracked with emotion. I could not hold back my tears as Tevye sings of the daughter he's lost. I looked over at these men, these men who had been listening to actors sing this song for more years than Moses wandered in the desert, and they were moved as well. I had their blessings to do the show. Jerry Bock told me that he always looked forward to my "Chavaleh." He felt I'd turned it from a plaintive cry to a prayer. The three boys, as I called them, visited the show and my dressing room quite often during the run, but almost never together. Boys will stay boys. Sadly, I was the last actor to play Tevye with the approval of all three of its creators. We lost Joe and Jerry in 2010.

What's more iconic than Tevye talking to God just
before singing "If I Were a Rich Man"?

Tevye demands everything an actor has to give. You must perform comic scenes, dramatic scenes, monologues, slapstick, athletic choreography . . . and let's not forget the singing. The mark of a truly great role is that it's open to interpretation and strong enough to survive the stretching of an actor's ideas. We each discover our personal path. As Tevye, I was particularly proud of my relationship with God. Surrounded by a wife, five daughters, milk cows, chickens, and even a female horse, God is Tevye's only male friend. I made our conversations intimate, as personal and as present as speaking to another character onstage. I wanted there to be no doubt that God was real. Only then could the audience feel Tevye's loss when he turns his back on God. In the second act, when his middle daughter elopes with a non-Jewish boy, Tevye declares this daughter dead. He sings a prayer to her and then never speaks to her again. Studying the script, I realized that he also never speaks to God again. I wondered if he turned his back on God because he was angry or because he was now too busy trying to hold his world together to waste time talking to a God who never answered. I thought this was a detail that served the play and the character very well. It is almost a statement that a relationship with God is a luxury he no longer had time to indulge. With that idea in mind, I held back looking to the spot above the theater balconies where I'd carefully placed God for all of our encounters during the evening. I avoided looking up to see if God was there until the last moments of the show, and then I glanced up—only to find him gone. God was gone and Tevye had to move to America. I joined my wife, Golde, at the wagon, now filled with all of our earthly possessions. Leveaux had carefully staged the entire show without us ever touching one another. In this last moment, I reached out and touched Golde's hand. The world they were born into was now gone.

I discovered another favorite moment during dress rehearsal. After saying goodbye to my daughter Hodel at the train station, I began to walk away. Putting my hands in the pockets of my coat, I discovered a pair of gloves that wardrobe had placed there in case I wanted them. And so, as I walked, I put them on. The staging called for Hodel to cry out and run back to Tevye for one last goodbye. When she did, I hugged her, let her go, and then, instinctively, I took off my gloves and pressed them into her hands. We then parted for the last time. It was a lovely discovery, and, dare I

Here is the one moment Golde and Tevye actually touched during *Fiddler*. That's my darling friend Rosie O'Donnell's expressive back.

say, I've seen at least one more Tevye adopt this moment into his performance.

The day before I took over the role, they changed the signage on the building. I was crossing Broadway, east to west, when I looked up and saw my name and photograph two stories high on the glass facade of the Minskoff Theatre. I nearly shit. I also nearly got mowed down by a pedicab. Two stories high . . . my name . . . my face. It was so unreal.

I had my dress rehearsal with the company that afternoon. Many members of the *Hairspray* cast came to cheer me on. I remember seeing Bruce Vilanch sitting dead center, first row of that huge, empty auditorium. Bruce had played Edna in the road company and was now doing a stint playing her on Broadway. I'm sure he was there to support me, but it was intimidating to speak my first line, one of the most famous in all of theater, directly to someone I knew so well. Still, I somehow spat it out: "A fiddler on the roof. Sounds crazy, no?"

The dress rehearsal went as dress rehearsals go. Surviving is the only goal, and that I did. Marc Shaiman grabbed me afterwards: "Why are you singing in the basement like that?"

"I thought I'd sound more masculine in a lower key."

"Don't be such a coward," he laughed. "You can hit those notes. Raise them up!"

We took his advice and raised the keys upward. He was right.

I hurt myself early in rehearsals. It wasn't even the dancing. It was the singing from the diaphragm that split my groin open, and that was in the lower key! I didn't need a doctor to tell me I had a hernia. There was no way I was giving up this opportunity, so I kept the injury between myself and my faithful dresser, Charlie, who had to know just in case there was an emergency. The muscle tear grew over the months until my intestines, quite often, would protrude through the tear and I'd have to manipulate them back into place during the show. Charlie would see me lying down on an offstage prop and say, "Hey, you! Shove your guts back in and get the hell out there!"

The company was so wonderful to me—accepting and supportive and loving and patient as anyone could possibly be. I was touched the first time a member of the company addressed me as "Papa" outside of the play. How do you like that? I went from being Mama to Papa, and I loved both designations equally. The audience response never ceased to move me. We weren't only entertaining folks; we were enriching them with a story so universal that audiences around the globe swear it's about their own family history. The critics also responded positively, surprising even themselves. I'll confess that no one thought it crazier than I did to have a downtown experimental theater drag performer who'd arrived on Broadway having anal sex center stage and, most recently, won a Tony for playing a three-hundred-pound housewife, now take on one of the most revered male roles in all of the theater's canon. It was a cultural touchstone, even earning a joke on the TV show *Will & Grace*. A character asks a cop, "Can you help me get rid of a ticket?"

"For parking?"

"No. For Harvey Fierstein in *Fiddler on the Roof*."

The stage door of the Minskoff has an underpass allowing the audience to gather for autographs. Wednesday matinees usually saw a large number of Hasidic Jews in attendance. After one particular matinee I noted a young boy in his black suit and *yarmulke* staring up at me. His gaze was so intense that I finally stopped signing and asked him, "Is everything all right?"

His eyes bored into me. "Are you really Jewish?"

I fought back my tears and smiled. "Yes, son. I am a real Jew."

I was the boy. The boy was me.

Tevye and I had come full circle.

Seen here for their last time together, Sheldon Harnick, Joseph Stein, and Jerry Bock—the creators of *Fiddler on the Roof*. I bowed to their genius at our final curtain call.

Long before the offer to do *Fiddler* I had been contracted to open *Hairspray* in Las Vegas. It was not a deal I could break, so I stayed with *Fiddler* until the very last day, closing that production. I gave more than four hundred performances, helping make that Leveaux production the longest-running revival of *Fiddler* thus far.

One last Tale from the Shtetl. The Tonys had a category for Best Performance by an Actor or Actress in a Recreated Role. The rules required that the Tony Award administration committee's vote be unanimous. Going through the list of eligible performers, each was voted down until it came to my name. As it was told to me, the show of hands appeared to be unanimous until one member of the

committee spoke up. "I'm sorry, but I did not see Harvey's performance, and so I cannot in good conscience vote yes."

It should be noted that I was still performing at that time.
That committee member could easily have caught me in the show.
Instead, by one vote, I was denied that Tony. Who was the person
who blocked it? *Hairspray*'s lead producer, Margo Lion. She was
indignant that I'd told her I was too tired to continue in *Hairspray*
and here I was doing *Fiddler* instead. She thought it an act of dis-
loyalty. A year or two later we talked it over, made up, and I did
indeed return to the Broadway production of *Hairspray* for the last
six months of that run.

41

AND THEY CALL HIM
SONDHEIM

2005

Who didn't want to write with Stephen Sondheim? Whenever I had an idea for a show I always began my thinking with *Would he go for this?* It's no insult to the other composers I've worked with or will work with, but there was only one Sondheim and I wanted to watch his brain at work.

Driving home one night after a performance of *Fiddler,* I had the satellite radio tuned to the Broadway Channel; they were playing the entire original Broadway cast recording of *Follies.* Listening to those songs about love and regret and roads not taken brought a movie to mind: *A Letter to Three Wives.* It's one of those wonderful 1940s dramas about love and regret and roads not taken. Three Long Island housewives are chaperoning a group of children on a day-long picnic to a remote island. Arriving at the meeting point, all three receive a letter from a fourth woman, an old flame of each of their three husbands. The letter claims that she has run off with one of the men but doesn't say which, leaving the women to wonder, in flashbacks, who will come home to an empty house. I watched the movie over again. I even watched an impossibly tacky 1980s TV movie adaptation. And then I read the tawdry paperback novel on which it was based. All in preparation for a meeting with the Great One. I called and set a date and time, which happened to fall on an ice cold, rainy, winter Wednesday between matinee and evening performances. Steve welcomed me into his East Side town house and led me downstairs to sit by the fireplace. After some cursory chatter about his beautifully presented magic card collection, I finally got up the courage to say, "So, let me start with—"

At which point he cut me off. "No."

"No?"

"I love that movie. And you're right, it has everything I enjoy. I could probably sit down and play you a song right now. I could probably write the entire score in a few days, that's how familiar this material feels to me. But . . . no."

"Can I ask why?"

"It's simple," he said, jiggling the ice in his glass. "The title. *A Letter to Three Wives*. No matter how much they love the first story, most of the audience is going to look at their programs and say, 'Damn, we've got to sit through two more!'"

That was it. How the hell are you going to argue with that? If I was smarter I would have sat back and laughed, but I tried to sell him on the idea until it was time for me to head back to Anatevka.

Later that year I had a more pleasant romp through Sondheim-ville. The occasion was his birthday and, as with every one of his birthdays, an all-star tribute concert was being planned. Each of these outings instigated the same Battle of the Divas over who'll get to sing "Rose's Turn" this time. The musical director, Kevin Stites, asked if I'd end the battle before it began by taking it on myself. How could I refuse? He came up with a stupendous musical idea. I dressed as Tevye and Kevin led the orchestra in the "Rich Man" vamp as I entered: *BOOM bada-boom-bah, BOOM bada-boom-bah* . . . The audience laughed, unsure what was happening. Reaching center stage, I looked up above the balcony to speak to God as Tevye would but, instead of his usual lines but still in Tevye's rhythm, I launched into "Rose's Turn":

Why did I do it?
What did it get me?
Scrapbooks full of me in the background . . .

By this time the house was mine, totally into it, as I belted "I had a dream . . ." with all of my heart.

Sondheim was famous for answering every letter written to him and sending thank-you notes whenever due. I have the note that followed this performance framed and I've kept it in every one of my dressing rooms since that day:

"Thanks . . . for contributing so hilariously to the occasion. So why did it make me cry?"

Coincidentally, I'd gotten to sing "Everything's Coming Up Noses" to a mob of Muppets on *Sesame Street* the year before.

Even in our casual run-ins I always felt Steve had some sort of bad feeling toward me. I guess I can figure why, but the fault is not mine. As previously noted, *La Cage* opened the same season as *Sunday in the Park with George* and took the Best Musical Tony. Those things happen. But the first revival of *La Cage* opened the same month and year as the revival of his *Pacific Overtures*, and again *La Cage* came out on top. And then, in the 2009–10 season, Steve's *A Little Night Music* was revived with a glittering cast of stars. That same season was the third coming of *La Cage*, which amazingly made it three for three in the Tony department. I just want to say that I am *not* a Tony voter. I have never been asked to be a Tony voter. I've never been asked to be on any Tony committee. So, Maestro Sondheim, I can only offer a quote from some play of mine in apology: "In matters of taste there is none."

I still think that if I had only worked harder on my *Letter to Three Wives* pitch I could have gotten him there. Before giving up and getting up to leave I did offer one more angle to the story: "Who finds love? I mean, a love that you can trust and live with and never question? Isn't that the goal?" Steve took a reflective sip from his cut-glass tumbler and softly offered, "Oh, Harvey, you'll find him some day. Don't give up. Not yet."

42

SHOOT ME OR THE DICE!

2006

"Hey, honey, where do you wanna go on vacation this year?"

"I don't know. You got any ideas?"

"Well . . . I heard about this tomb. It's a thirty-story, black, windowless Egyptian pyramid. There's plenty of parking, the pool is surrounded by gigantic cement gods, and down in the basement they put on *Hairspray*!"

Who the hell thought it would be a good move to stage *Hairspray* at the Luxor Hotel in Las Vegas? People go to Vegas to gamble, ogle titties, and watch aging recording stars lip-synch "My Way." They pack into Cirque du Soleil shows because they are brilliantly conceived displays of athleticism draped in amazing costumes, accompanied by fantastical lighting, ear-splitting music, and lyrics sung in alien languages. You don't have to think, understand, or even remain conscious to enjoy a real Las Vegas show. So, what the fuck were we doing there?

The Luxor's theater was built as home to the *Ben-Hur* chariot race. Yes, my friend, the arena was big enough to stage live horse races. It was so big that the crew parked upstage. Our entire orchestra sat on a truck unit that traveled downstage during the bows. The stage was so wide that I'd run from the wings, barely arrive center in time to turn around, and retreat back to change for my next appearance. I don't care what Shakespeare said, the play was *not* the thing. In Vegas, gambling is the thing. *Hairspray* was the attraction to lure suckers over to the Luxor Casino, where they would hopefully gamble before and after the show.

For all the fountains and laser-light extravagance of the Strip, Las Vegas has one goal: empty the tourists' pockets before they can board their flight home. Don't believe me? There are slot machines to snatch that last nickel at the airport gates. So, as much as management admired our theatrical prowess, they didn't want the audience idling for three hours in a theater. We were given orders to cut the show down to ninety minutes. And we performed that show, not the usual eight times a week, but *ten* times a week. I tell you that this fabulous company worked their asses off giving wonderful performances to half-empty houses, but we never had a chance to make it on the Strip. Our producers and the casino owners, management, and staff treated us like visiting royalty. They wanted the show to work so badly, they put so much effort and money into the endeavor, it was heartbreaking to see how slim the odds of success were. The production ran through my contract and the show closed a few weeks after I left. I went home and finally got my guts sewed back together.

43

LA CAGE IN LONDON

2008

David Babani is a wonderfully creative theatrical force in the London fringe theater. He's artistic director of the Menier Chocolate Factory, a 180-seat venue in an old chocolatier that has become famous for staging pared-down versions of Broadway musicals. He asked to meet with me to discuss a revival of *La Cage*.

Hubris had consumed the original London production in 1986. Certain that they had a smash on their hands, Alan Carr and Arthur Laurents conspired to book the twenty-two-hundred-seat Palladium Theatre, where it limped along for less than a year. I was in London performing *Torch Song Trilogy* at the time, so I could have seen, but never did, a full performance. Why? There's an unpleasant image burned like a strip-mall tattoo onto my hippocampus. Having overslept on the morning I was to watch the dress rehearsal, I hustled from my apartment at the Savoy over to the Palladium and entered through the back of the house. There, onstage, seemingly a mile and a half away from the last row of the stalls, I saw this teeny-tiny set on this enormous barren stage. These fools simply reproduced the New York production in London without reconsidering the aspects of the theater. The Palace in New York, for all of its outsized glory, is a third smaller and was designed to highlight a featured performer center stage. It almost magnifies a person standing there. The Palladium, on the other hand, was built to house huge theatrical productions. Our set was swallowed by the hall. I needed to see no more to conclude that our tender loving comedy would be lost in that barn. I said my hellos to everyone and made my way back to bed.

So here comes David Babani armed to present the case for a scaled-down production and expecting an argument from me. With Jerry Herman's promise singing in my ear—"the next production is all yours"—David found an exuberant partner. I'll confess that I stopped to consider Arthur's feelings in the matter, but, as he had taken hold of both *Gypsy* and *West Side Story*, redirecting new productions as he'd always envisioned, I felt he'd understand this Harveycentric approach. And so producer Babani, director Terry Johnson, and I agreed . . . The club would be small and "home-made," the apartment would be "overthought and overstuffed," the orchestra would be of a size and sound appropriate for a nightclub, and the drag queens would be men who really loved their time as women. Only one detail gave me pause. He had a heterosexual actor in mind to play Zaza. He assured me that Douglas Hodge was a brilliant choice for the role, and since I was being handed 90 percent of my dream production, I gave my approval. *Hell,* I thought, *if it's no good it's only being done in this tiny fringe theater. Take the leap. Besides, this actor is English. None of them come off as straight. What's gayer than Hugh Grant in a rom com?*

Tied up with other productions in New York, I never crossed the Pond to see it but the photos, the videos, the reviews, and the personal reports of friends were phenomenal. The show was a wowser and a total triumph for the theater.

The Chocolate Factory's production transferred to the West End, where it was such a smash that they were beset by celebs begging to replace the leads. At long last *La Cage Aux Folles* showed its authentic face in London. Jerry Herman asked if I thought he should fly over. Pretty sure that he would not approve of an orchestra of ten, I encouraged him to remember the last revival instead and to enjoy our progeny's success from afar.

44

A CATERED AFFAIR

2007–2008

Back in my *Million Dollar Movie* days I saw Bette Davis in *The Catered Affair*. Originally a 1955 television play by Paddy Chayefsky, a year later the story got an MGM movie rewrite by Gore Vidal. Taking place in the 1950s, it's the story of a taxi driver who is torn between buying his own taxi with his life's savings or spending the money on a wedding for his only daughter. After years of working on big musicals, I loved these uber human proportions. Intimate and relatable, the richness of these characters was irresistible to me. Who can't understand a man wanting security for his family, or a mother wanting to give her daughter a wonderful sendoff as she leaves home? Unrequited love, doubts, regrets, hopes . . . These were characters that could sing. I was almost tempted to call Sondheim again.

I'd been a fan of John Bucchino's songwriting for years. His compilation album, *Grateful*, was perpetually in my CD carousel. Completely in touch with his emotions, he writes without embarrassment or self-editing. His heart is available. I hoped he would be as well. I made contact, and after a few discussions he joined the project. As usual, my brother was in charge of licensing the rights. He reached out to Paddy Chayefsky's son, Dan, and they became fast friends. Dan was onboard and eager to see what I'd come up with.

Every story has its own way it wants to be told, and I think adapters need to listen for those cues. Bucchino and I started to work together scene by scene, song by song, feeling our way with each other and into the material. With John living in Manhattan and me in Connecticut, we usually worked over the phone, but John was spending this one weekend at Stephen Sondheim's country home, so we decided he'd stop by my place on his drive back to the city and we could work face-to-face for the day. As it happened, I was on the telephone with Jerry Herman when I heard John's car coming down the drive. I couldn't wait to hang up. It was around the time of one of Sondheim's birthday celebrations and Jerry was complaining that every year someone arranged another tribute concert in his honor. "Sondheim this and Sondheim that . . . He's seventy, let's have a concert! He's seventy-five, that calls for a gala! Now they can take all seventy-six trombones and . . ."

I laughed supportively and begged off. "Jerry my friend, I've got to go."

As soon as he opened the car door John began to rave. "As I was leaving, Steve was opening his mail. He took one look at the size of his electric bill and hollered, 'Six hundred dollars? Who the hell do they think I am—Jerry Herman?'"

It was a real-world "Story of Lucy and Jessie," performed live!

There was another character in *The Catered Affair* that fascinated me: a bachelor uncle. He lives with the family, sleeping on the pullout sofa in the living room, but is somewhat outside the immediate family unit. He reminded me of my own Uncle Paul, but I saw something more that I could make of this character. Here was a man without a family or even a room of his own. He is a guest in his own family's life. It struck me that gays, back then, lived that way. Their families seldom knew or acknowledged the whole story of these bachelor uncles or spinster aunts. They were strangers even to their own flesh and blood. I loved the idea of this character sticking his nose into the family struggles only to realize that he needed to find a life of his own.

With Paddy Chayefsky gone, I called Gore Vidal to bat this idea around. He had a reputation for being argumentative at best and impossible when riled, so I was happily shocked to find him cheery. "How wonderful to hear from you! I love your work," he said.

"You do? Well, thank you. I am more than an admirer of yours, and that's why I want to discuss an idea with you."

He found the whole concept nonsensical. "Sir, I am the one who created that character, not Paddy," he claimed, although that wasn't true: the bachelor uncle appears in the original teleplay. "I can't see how a person who has lived his life in secrecy could suddenly actualize such a revolutionary concept as this. People are simply not that pliable or self-aware."

"You are correct," I answered. "But he doesn't awaken to his own mistake. It's seeing his sister deny herself happiness for twenty years that awakens him."

"Aha," he said, thinking this through.

"None of us sees the error of our own ways, but who amongst us can't list the missteps of everyone we know?"

"True," he laughed.

"So the only question is who among us abandons the comfort of the everyday to venture into the unknown. We both know that answer to be no one, which is why I've motivated this man to take that leap—not for himself, but for the happiness of his niece."

"This is wonderful. Why don't you drive over here and let's wrap our heads around the entire arc?"

"I'd love to, but . . ."

"Come, Michael, and stay for dinner."

Only then did I realize Mr. Vidal thought he'd been speaking to singer/pianist Michael Feinstein this entire last hour. After I explained who I was, he still invited me over for a drink, but, being three thousand miles away, I declined. I was never able to make contact with him again.

Even though I believe that I fully justified the choices this character makes, there were those who saw his leap as a political action ahead of its time. One producer actually said to me, "Gays didn't live together until the sixties."

Which caused me to reply, "Someone better call Gertrude Stein."

Here's the company in the dinner scene on Broadway.

His narrow thinking reminded me of a brilliant Archie Bunker moment from *All in the Family* when he blamed Eleanor Roosevelt for discovering Black Americans, ". . . and we been having trouble ever since."

This gentleman, it seems, only realized that gays existed after hearing about Stonewall. In any case, I thought that with a bit more rewriting, I could clarify that storyline and have it ring true for everyone. If an audience tells you that you're wrong, it doesn't matter how right you think you are. You need to fix it. There is a saying in our business: "No one ever went broke underestimating the intelligence of the audience."

Just for the record: Harry Hay established the Mattachine Society, a pioneering gay rights group, in 1950.

I never did get the tone of that character right either on the page or in my less than stellar performance but I believe the show's death blows were dealt by the production itself. We'd conceived something delicate and intimate, a kind of chamber piece, that was then given an even lower-key mounting.

John wrote beautiful, extraordinary songs, arias of true emotion. We married our work so that dialogue led directly into lyrics and back out again into speech. The songs were organic to the characters. As such, they needed special care to protect them. We took that cue too far, and their delicate beauty was tamped down until their flame went out. Our director had John transpose the tunes into minor keys to muffle their melodies and dress them in a melancholy mood that he felt more befitting this struggling family. A second music arranger was even brought in to further simplify the score. Bucchino was so wonderful about it all, but I began to worry. It's one thing to dress unpretentiously, quite another to drape oneself in shrouds. These were passionate people caught in a whirlwind of life's shifting emotional challenges. Somehow our director equated dour with everyday, and colorlessness for naturalism. As we'd rehearse, he'd cut props out and eliminate costume changes. He cut everything down to the bone while I stood and watched the life bleed out.

Please don't misunderstand. Our director, John Doyle, is a theatrical genius and pioneer. I've loved many of his revolutionary productions. Our entire team was thrilled that he signed on to direct the show. We were all fans. Maybe that's why every one of us stood around watching him deconstruct and strip the production down without objecting. I think we all trusted that he knew where he was going; and if not, certainly one of us would speak up and say, "This is wrong."

None of us did—at least not out loud.

We had an out-of-town tryout in San Diego, where we felt like we were getting good work done. One of the original stars of the movie, Debbie Reynolds, came to our opening night. In fact, many luminaries—Julie Andrews, Jerry Herman—came to cheer us on. But none of them, nor any of our family and friends, told us where we were going wrong. I blamed audiences' lack of enthusiasm on the season-ticket holders, who are notorious for their low energy, and on the New York subject matter, which could not have seemed more out of place than in a theater adjacent to the San Diego Zoo.

We traveled back from the Left Coast thinking we were set for Broadway. We opened at the intimate Walter Kerr Theatre with a show so humble that it practically apologized for taking up the audience's time. Our producers generously allowed us to play through awards season, when we found ourselves nominated for twelve Drama Desk Awards and three Tonys. The only prize we actually took home was the Drama League Award for Outstanding Production of a Musical, which was a welcome and greatly appreciated honor.

Before closing I reminded our director of something he shared with me when he first accepted the assignment. He told me that as a little boy in his small town, if he was feeling blue his grandmother would say, "Let us go see the bride." They'd walk together to the church and wait for the bride to emerge elated in her white gown and veil. He said that the promise held in that joyous sight lifted his whole world and made him happy. I said, "We never put that onstage. The audience came to see the bride and we never showed her to them. Where was the joy?"

A Catered Affair is a show that I would love to see in a new production. I believe there is something great under the mistakes made by me and the director. I'd love to unleash the songs of John Bucchino and let audiences have a chance to hear his original inspiration. I can easily reimagine the show in a contemporary setting. Nothing essential in the story binds it to that period. And how about producing it with an integrated cast? Why not? Ooh, I'm getting excited. Can we get a do-over, please?

45

THE TAVELS

2009–2013

Ronald Tavel died on a flight from Berlin to Bangkok. He'd conquered his agoraphobia and escaped his lightless, airless SoHo tenement apartment to live in Thailand. It wasn't an easy struggle, but he used a rainbow of anger as motivation. While the price of anything else Warhol exploded, lecture fees and an occasional essay assignment seemed to be the frustrating limit of Ron's monetization of the Warhol screenplays he'd written.

The theaters that once sought his plays and the grants that subsidized his expenses now looked for younger writers to produce. There were a few teaching contracts, but he didn't seem as natural a mentor as friends like Maria Irene Fornes and Megan Terry. And while he loved his fellow playwrights, you could not tell him any one of them was fit to touch his robes. Ron suffered from a Jewish mother who'd daily screech, "Who needs a genius? I'd rather have grandchildren."

He never heard the human plea but clung to the first part of her complaint as truth foretold. He believed in his talent and vision, and the lack of recognition he received was beyond his comprehension. He was angry at me for succeeding, angry at his brother, Harvey, for not needing more. Ron made the case to his brother that living in Bangkok would be cheaper than Harvey continuing to support him in Manhattan, so off he flew.

"A library is an act of faith. It's the first thing your relatives dispose of when you die."

That's a line from a radio play Ronnie wrote for me to perform, and how true it is! Buried under the elephantine weight of Ron's collective work, after his death Harvey put it all online—the plays, screenplays, poetry, and two novels, along with essays and photos. He offered it all to the world without fees or royalties. His aim, he said, was to get the work seen and produced as widely as possible. I think the responsibility was simply too much for Harvey to bear. He'd carried Ron their entire lives. Now it was time to put him to rest. How intertwined are grief and relief?

I think about Ron and Harvey's brotherhood and compare their relationship to mine with my own brother Ron. Both Ron Tavel and I were lucky to have brothers who cared deeply for us. There would have been no Ron Tavel without Harvey, and I believe that my brother made my life possible as well. Ron Tavel never minded being a burden to his brother. I do, but I engage my brother in as many business and financial dealings as I can anyway. Someone once asked if I trust him with my money. "Blindly," I replied. "If he does well by me, then his sons inherit a potload. If he bankrupts me, I'm moving in with him."

Another silly brotherly quirk is that we pronounce our surname differently. My father, whose name it was in the first place, pronounced it "*Fire*-steen," and so that's the pronunciation I go by. My mother, for reasons known only to her, pronounced it "*Feer*-stine." She said, "That's how it's spelled."

Okay. Then my brother planted his own flag of independence, calling himself "*Feer*-steen." Now, when the two of us are introduced in meetings, the poor *schlub* stuck with the job has to introduce us as Mr. *Feer*-steen and Mr. *Fire*-steen. I always assumed that my public profile would win the day, but Ron has sired two sons who are following his mispronouncing ways. I'm certain they will multiply, not to mention outlive me, so farewell, *Fire*-steen.

Not long after his brother's death, Harvey Tavel called to tell me that he and his longtime housemate, friend, and lover, Norman Glick, were going to get married. "We want to do it at your house."

"Absolutely. Of course. Do you want to invite friends from the city? Anything?"

"No. Just you and your brother and a justice of the peace."

A dear friend, Ruth, who'd been performing such ceremonies for years, was happy to oblige. Norman and Harvey took their vows in my living room. What a long, strange path they'd traveled together, having first met when Norman was fifteen and Harvey was his French teacher at Lafayette High School in Brooklyn! Fifty years later, they married. Four years after the wedding, Harvey died, and Norman followed two years later.

Without Ron Tavel I never would have dared to write. Without Harvey I would have had no place to grow. My entire life would have been impossible—or at least completely different—without them. That's not a definition of friendship. It's not even a good definition of family. What the Tavels were to my life was so much more.

46

JUGGLING *KINKY BOOTS* AND *NEWSIES* AND *CASA VALENTINA*

2010

My friend Jordan Roth phoned ahead with a warning. His mom, producer Daryl Roth, was looking for me. He had licensed the rights to the British movie *Kinky Boots*, and Daryl was now aiming to turn it into a musical. Jerry Mitchell was already onboard as director and choreographer. They were hoping I'd take on the book duties. I really enjoyed the movie. It had fun musical covers, drag queens, and a wonderfully told true story. What could we possibly add? My instincts told me to turn the project down. Fortunately, guilt is stronger than instinct. I had already said no to Jerry twice in the recent past. I loved him too much to say no three times in a row. And Daryl had been one of the producers of *A Catered Affair*, where she showed such heart and belief that I owed her whatever she asked. There are worse things than agreeing to adapt a movie that you love. So I was in.

Most people think that writing the book of a musical means writing the spoken words. We book writers are in charge of doing that, but that's just the beginning.

First off, we're responsible for the story. Whether it's an adaptation, an original, or even an "inspired by" project, the book writer takes ideas from everyone, at least in the development stage, and pulls them all together into one cohesive story. Structure and style are next. Will this story be told in a linear fashion? Will there be flashbacks? Is this realistic or impressionistic or cinematic? Next, the show needs to be clearly laid out, not only the story but the characters—their personalities as well as their journeys. And then the characters begin to develop both singing and speaking voices. The book writer oversees this as well. And once the writing begins, the composer and lyricist look to the developing script for their song ideas, sometimes even taking the spoken words and musicalizing them. In other words, the book writer is the keeper of the pot in which the stew is brewed. Even when the director or producers have control, it is still the book writer's duty to incorporate them into the whole. Oh, and then we write the jokes!

When I asked about the composing team, the producers told me they wanted to hold auditions. Hal Luftig, Daryl's partner on this, proposed that I mock up three scenes for the show; he'd then invite writing teams to submit a song or two inspired by those scenes. I thought it a perfectly useless way to find a composer, although Jerry Herman told me it's how he got the job writing *Hello, Dolly!* No matter—it still seemed a waste of time. But I was happy to have the producers occupied listening to a mess of audition tapes, freeing me up to figure out what shape the show should take.

Meanwhile, I got another interesting phone call. This time it was actor/director Bob Balaban, along with producers Colin Callender, Fred Zollo, and Bob Cole. They'd just licensed a book of photos called *Casa Susanna* and thought I might be the right person to bring it to life onstage. It seems that two men had discovered a mysterious box of photos at a Manhattan flea market. These were amateur snapshots taken in the late 1950s, the 60s, and the 70s that showed a variety of men rather clumsily, but happily, flouncing about in women's clothing, makeup, and wigs. A cursory inquiry revealed that the photos had been taken at a resort in the Catskill Mountains that specialized in weekends for men who wished to cross-dress. Beyond that, their info was sketchy. As it happened, I knew about this Casa Susanna because of my father's Catskill roots. My brother and I, sitting in the backseat of our car, overheard the adults gossiping about the men who would go food shopping in town wearing dresses and heels. The subject quickly changed as the very next property on that road housed a nudist colony. Little boys, even strange ones like me, are much more intrigued by the promise of naked people than flouncing ones. This phone call already had my mind racing as Mr. Balaban tried to give me an idea of what they were looking for me to write. He wanted a *human* comedy. He saw the absurdity of these men as something very touching and dear, but also rife for a bit of fun if not fodder for all-out farce. With *Kinky Boots* already on my schedule, I wasn't anxious to take on another drag-queen project, but these people . . . the honesty of those photographs intrigued me. There had to be more to their stories than having a good time dressing up. I was ready to dive into research. I said yes and hit the Internet.

Back at Kinky Camp, the audition tapes were beginning to come in. They were, as I expected, a waste of time. A musical requires a marriage of minds. A character can't sing differently than he/she speaks, which means the lyricist and book writer need to be in agreement or at least open to compromise. We want to hear the characters' voices, not the writers'. Writing as an assignment is like drawing from a photograph rather than drawing from life. You can't start fresh from a photograph. The subject has already been interpreted by the photographer's eye. Drawing from life is limited only by the abilities of the observer.

With those auditions behind us, there were more composer ideas I was tasked to oversee. I went through the motions of attending meetings and work sessions with a few of them. I listened and smiled through awful songs that no one would want to hear in a show. Eventually I'd had enough and asked if I might take a whack at finding the right collaborators myself. I called my brother. He reminded me that I'd once spoken to Cyndi Lauper about an idea she wanted to explore. Might she be right for this? *Of course, Cyndi! She knows club music, she's intimately knowledgeable about drag queens, she's emotionally available and has an outra-geous sense of humor. Of course, Cyndi!* Ron had been friends with her manager for years, so I sent him off to find her.

The research into the "girls" of Casa Susanna was fascinating. Far from a sitcom concept of *lawyers in lace,* I began to uncover an entire movement, a society of heterosexual men who believed that they had a female alter ego living inside of them. They published their own magazines and newsletters and harbored political aspi-rations. The more I searched, the more variety I found in this com-munity. Some of these men dressed as an escape while others were acting out their inner realities. Some were satisfied merely looking in the mirror, but some needed the validation of the outside world. Sex seemed to be an aspect of their journeys but not the same for all. Some fetishized the undergarments, others the feel of the fab-rics on their skin, and for others the visual image was the target. There were no simple answers here. Labeling them "transvestites" or "cross-dressers" was as useless as branding all winged insects "flies" and claiming to understand their nature.

When I was a kid, I believed there were straight people and gay people, period. Everyone else was in some sort of denial. As expe-rience opened the world to me, I realized that my views were baby steps from those of bigots who held that there are straight people and sick people. The greater variety of humans I met, the greater variety of humanity I beheld. I came to one dependable and certain conclusion: there is no such thing as normal. There are percentages of male/female attraction/identification, and there are majorities who assign societal limitations, but in actuality no two people feel exactly alike about sexuality or gender. Individuality is the rule. If I was going to write about this society, I needed to pry away and destroy layers of my own prejudice. I studied these people's lives, both real and fantasy. I read clinical opinions and legal cases, police records and psychiatric histories. As the piece I wanted to write began to take form, the first thing I did was to change the name of the hotel from Casa Susanna to Casa Valentina, acknowledging that I could only ever struggle to, but never completely, capture the reality of the life and lives I was learning about. In any case, Casa Susanna was the name of a second, smaller, hotel. The Chateau d'Éon, named for the infamous eighteenth-century cross-dressing spy the Chevalier d'Éon, was where most of the photos were actually shot.

Keeping the story set in 1962 would make it safe for today's audience to view these radical ideas without feeling threatened. I wanted the audience to feel superior to, and more worldly than, the characters presented onstage. I wanted them to judge these men, to watch as they paraded around in cocktail dresses and pearls and think, *These are just homosexuals in denial.* And then, when the play reveals its true conflicts, I wanted the audience to have to rethink all of their old ideas about men who wear dresses just as I was doing.

There is nothing you can do with the petty minded, but for those adventurous enough to listen, I was excited to present this entirely different view of the gender experience. I hoped that the humanity of these characters could reach across the footlights and shake the audience awake. There are no easy answers if you're brave enough to ask the right questions.

We watch people on the news or in magazines, their trials summed up in three-minute bites, and we think we comprehend. We watch celebrities come out as transgender or gay or nonbinary and believe we know what they are going through. Truly, we understand almost nothing about our own thirst for self-acceptance beyond those nagging, ill-feeling internal moments we quash as best we can. The great majority of us are too afraid to know ourselves. Have you ever watched people looking at themselves in the mirror? As soon as they catch their own reflection, they angle their heads, or suck in their cheeks, or widen their eyes to achieve the practiced false image they've convinced themselves the world sees. If we can't face *ourselves* in a mirror, what gall to claim we can understand others!

My producers over at *Kinky Boots* were getting antsy. We'd been at this for months and still had no composer. Beyond her manager's

Working with Cyndi was a blast in so many
ways. We were often on the same wavelength.

promises, I'd heard nothing back from Cyndi, so I decided it was
time to move on. I had been wanting to work with my neighbor,
the incomparable composer of *Beauty and the Beast, The Little
Mermaid,* and *Little Shop of Horrors,* Alan Menken, forever. Drag
queens in a British shoe factory didn't strike me as his obvious
milieu, but this is the guy who gave a singing voice to a man-eating
plant, an evil octopus, and a giant blue genie. Nothing is beyond
his imagination. I brought him a DVD of the movie and waited
for his judgment. Two days later, crazy about the material, he was
ready to meet. I was grabbing my car keys when the phone rang.

"Hey, Haw-vee. Cyn. Whatcha doin'?"

Who could mistake that voice, or more precisely the elongated
vowels of that Queens accent? Even with the sound of water running and plates slapping in the sink I knew who it was saying "Hey,
Haw-vee. Wha's goin' awn dere?"

"Hey, Cyn. What you up to?"

"I'm waw-shin' dishes. So, you lookin' ta do a show, heh?"

"I'd love to do a show. How about you?"

"Yeah, shoo-wah," she said along with the crash of a pot hitting the water. "And Jevvy's doin' it, 'vight? You know I love me some Jevvy."

"That's great. Okay. So, let's do this."

"I'm in."

I hung up the phone and remembered where I was headed. Oops.

I walked into Alan's well-appointed studio to find him waiting with a big grin on his face.

"Stop smiling—it ain't happening," I said.

I apologized, blaming it all on Cyndi taking so long to get back to me. He, too, was sorry. He loved the movie. While telling him how desperate I was to write something with him, I took in the surrounding poster-covered walls. Believe me, it's easier to face one sheets of all of his successes than to stare down the glass-fronted cabinet wherein his eight Oscars, eleven Grammys, seven Golden Globes, and the rest rest.

Something caught my eye. "Hey, what about that?" I asked pointing at a poster for the Disney flop film *Newsies*. "Why don't we do that one?"

He waved me off. "We tried. For two years we tried. We did workshops . . . The whole deal. Could not get it to work."

"But it's something you want to do?"

"Absolutely," he said, wide-eyed.

"Let me give it a try. What have we got to lose?"

I had a real soft spot for that awful movie, because my nephews loved it when they were kids. They watched it over and over.

"I don't know if Disney will let us . . ."

"So, don't ask them. Let me take a whack at it. If I can figure out how to make it work, we'll worry about Disney then. Okay?"

I left Alan's studio on a high. What's more fun than a good challenge?

—

Daryl, Hal, and Jerry were all excited at the prospect of Cyndi writing the score for *Kinky Boots*. It was game on. I knocked out a rough first draft of the entire show so we'd have something to start working from. Jerry, Cyndi, and I met to come up with a strategy of attack. I had a conceit for the opening number where one by one our main characters define their lives in terms of shoes. Mr. Price sees his family history as shoemakers; his son Charlie expresses his disinterest in the damn things; Charlie's fiancée explains the social significance of wearing the right shoe; and Lola, the transvestite performer, extols the life-changing magical powers of high-heeled footwear. Jerry got it right off, but Cyndi seemed overwhelmed. Well, not every show begins at the beginning. We set Cyndi a different task. She'd start with an introductory song for Lola in her drag club. This was a world with which she was familiar. We were on our way.

And it was back to *Casa Valentina*. Reading the letters and articles written by the men about their "girls within," I was struck by how articulate they were. These were not thrill-seeking closeted drag queens. These were professional men who came from strong families and were well educated. Something else grabbed me about the way they expressed themselves. Back before television became the common denominator that dumbed our society down, people read books. They *did*. Reading expanded their vocabulary beyond today's common fillers of "y'know," "sorta," "kinda," "like," "basically,"and the other twenty phrases that pass for intelligent conversating. While most social dramatists struggle to express the verbiage of the common man, I wanted to capture that lost formality of speech. I discovered that the way contestants spoke on old game shows captured what I was after. Before every day's writing session I sat down and watched an hour of 1950s TV: *What's My Line?*, *I've Got a Secret*, *To Tell the Truth*, or *Queen for a Day*. I was constantly amazed at how American vocabulary had diminished in less than a generation. With the more formal sound still in my ears, I'd sit down to write. This approach had

I caught Katherine Cummings and John Cullum
deep in conversation during *Casa* rehearsals.

another advantage. It was a constant reminder of the limitations
these men had in explaining their situations. Sexual diversity is an
almost daily discussion in our world. These men were the Christopher Columbuses of gender. When I'd read back my daily writing output, I was so proud. I was pulling it off. These people were
unlike any characters I could ever have imagined writing. They
were of another age. I felt like a séance medium inhabited by spirits who wanted to have their say. I sent out a mess of inquiries,
hoping to find any survivors. At last, halfway through the writing,
I found someone. Although she'd spent only one weekend there,
she knew almost everyone I was writing about, and she was familiar with their unvarnished stories. Katherine Cummings became
my witness, my truth teller, and my friend. A wonderful woman
who identifies as "the Gender Whisperer," Katherine pointed and
prodded until I felt as if I, too, actually knew these people. Once
married with children and still in love with her wife, Katherine
had returned to her native Australia after university and lived her
life as an activist, author, and librarian. This is where I found her,
halfway across the earth.

Unfortunately, I was struggling. The writer was being swamped
by the researcher. I was uncovering truth, but representing it accu-

rately was destroying the dramatic opportunities. I was taking notes for a play that was still in search of an author. Meanwhile . . .

Damn that Menken—he turned me in! I was suddenly summoned to the principal's office. Tom Schumacher is head of the Disney Theatrical Group and works out of the most magnificent glass offices in the space that was once the New Amsterdam Roof Garden, atop the New Amsterdam Theatre. Tom summoned me in to tell me not to waste my time on *Newsies*. He repeated the story of failure that Alan had relayed. I again said, "What do you care if I work on it? I'm not asking you for anything. If it sucks, nothing lost. If it's good, then we'll have something to talk about."

He shrugged and offered me some young composer to work with, as he didn't want Alan wasting his time.

"The whole reason for doing this is that Alan and I want to work together. Don't worry about it."

This meeting made me want to conquer *Newsies* more than ever. Years earlier, Tom was head of Disney animation development, or something impressive like that, and in a very creative move invited a bunch of playwrights to pick any fairy tale they'd like and create a scenario. The hope was that something might pop and be good enough to develop into a Disney film. I chose "The Snow Queen" and submitted my scenario. I guess they saw some promise, because I was asked to write the first draft of a script, which I did; but I never heard from them again. A few years later, while recording a voice for *Mulan,* I asked about the project. Tom said that *none* of the scenarios led to anything more. I told him that I thought my idea had promise. He agreed but said it had a problem in the second act that they couldn't remedy.

"Well, why didn't you ask me about it?"

"Because it was unfixable."

"How do you know if you never asked me to fix it?"

"Because we tried and couldn't."

"But since it was *my* idea and *my* story, why wouldn't you at least ask me to have a look?"

Alan Menken, lyricist Jack Feldman, and me with
the poster that gave me the idea to adapt *Newsies*

"Believe me, Harvey, if *we* couldn't solve the problem, *you* couldn't solve the problem."

Eventually, as animation history records, "The Snow Queen" turned out to be fabulous source material for Disney. *Frozen*, which I had absolutely *nothing* to do with, opened in theaters and became their highest-grossing film to date.

But that incident with Tom stayed with me and became an itch in an unreachable place. Now, years later, here was Tom again telling me that if *he* couldn't fix the problems with *Newsies,* certainly *I* couldn't. So I had to. I left the meeting with his words ringing in my ears: "It would be a great thing to have a script of *Newsies* for schools to present, but you must understand that there's no way we're producing the show on Broadway."

As if I needed it, I now had even more motivation to crack the project. I sat down with that stupid beloved movie and went to work.

And that, my children, is how I ended up writing three shows at the same time. It wasn't as confusing as you'd think. Cyndi had touring and recording dates that kept her from working with us

full-time. She was absent so much that Daryl and I developed a running gag where she'd call for updates and ask, "Can we fire Cyndi
today?"

It was my job to keep that from happening. I once called Cyndi
and said, "Hal and Daryl are going nuts. You have to send me
something."

She sent back an iPhone recording of her singing a melody while
under a hair dryer. Another time she sent a rock song played on an
autoharp. Thankfully, these were enough to keep the producers at
bay. Still, we brought in the magnificently talented Stephen Oremus
as our orchestrator and musical consultant so Cyndi would have
someone to lean on and the producers could have someone with a
track record they trusted. All in all, it still took us nearly five years
to complete the show.

Newsies, even with all of the corporate steps to climb, was a tiny
bit easier and a year faster. Jack Feldman was the marvelously
exacting lyricist on the movie. A jolly Jewish elf with a brilliant
mind, he was thrilled to take another crack at this material. As for
Alan, he's always game to rewrite. Once, when it was obvious that
a song was not working, I said, "What a shame to throw away such
a gorgeous melody."

To which he replied, "Please. I shit gorgeous melodies."

I had that made into a T-shirt for him.

To prepare for my attack on *Newsies*, I watched the movie
again, cringing as it played. What was this mess? Characters that
served no purpose, no real love interest, no twists or turns—and
an attempted-rape scene for children? There was a musical fantasy
about the Old West, complete with horses and gunslingers, baf-
flingly staged on the streets of the Lower East Side. My job was
to make sense of all this without daring to destroy the inexplicable, magical allure of the original. Knowing that Menken was
classically trained in structure by his genius partner, the late Howard Ashman, not to mention his years with Disney, I looked for

the "I want" song in the score. It was there, but it was that stupid western-fantasy number about going to *Santa Fe*.

All right, I said to myself, *time to squeeze this lemon.*

I devised a prologue to set up Jack Kelly as our hero and leader of the Newsies. I made him an aspiring artist who lives in a rooftop hideout. As the curtain rises he and Crutchie, a physically challenged boy, are just waking up to start their day. The boy worries that he won't be able to keep selling newspapers because his bad leg is getting worse. Jack cheers the boy's spirits with the promise that one day they'll escape the city altogether and make a new life for themselves in the clean open air of Santa Fe. *Cue the song!*

"You want to open with what?" Menken was perplexed to say the least.

" 'Santa Fe,' sung as a lullaby to Crutchie. Yes! It's his promise to make life better for them":

> Don't you know that we's a family?
> Would I let you down? No way!
> Just hold on, kid, till that train makes Santa Fe!

"And then, at the end of Act 1, when the entire world comes crashing in on Jack, the battle is lost, his friends are defeated, he barely escapes with his life, he climbs back to his rooftop hideout and, in desperation, unleashes an emotionally charged reprise of the song, crying out to the skies for salvation!"

> Just be real is all I'm asking,
> Not some painting in my head!
> 'Cause I'm dead if I can't count on you today—
> I got nothing if I ain't got Santa Fe!

Alan listened and nodded. He was sold. Jack was already adjusting the lyrics for both versions, and we were on our way.

For the record—if you think I was happy allowing a physically challenged child to be named Crutchie you still don't know me.

But, as I said, whenever possible, I had to respect the intangible magic that made the original so beloved. Hateful as I found it, I knew there were those who would miss a boy dubbed Crutchie if I renamed him.

When both composing teams were busy working, I hunkered down with *Casa Valentina*. The three projects were so different that I had little trouble keeping them from bleeding into one another, but I found an answer to a *Kinky* quandry in *Casa*. In the original movie of *Kinky*, Lola, the transvestite performer, has no love interest while Charlie, the shoe manufacturer, has two. That was a real sticking point for me. Why do the straight guys always get laid in movies while the gay characters almost never do? Structurally, there wasn't time or opportunity to squeeze a boy/boy relationship into the show without giving it short shrift so, taking a page from *Casa*, I decided that Lola should be a heterosexual transvestite. Not only would this dispense with the gay guy going solo, but it would let me heighten the challenge of the banal definition of masculinity. The look on Cyndi's face was even more puzzled than the one on Alan's had been.

"What kind of girl wants to date a guy who wears dresses?"

"You don't find role-playing sexy?"

"Hell, no," Cyndi trumpeted, leaving no room for negotiation. "I know what a woman wants and that ain't it."

"Okay, so Mick Jagger, David Bowie, Alice Cooper do nothing for you?"

Our discussions eventually led to the sexy tango that opens the second act, "What a Woman Wants," during which Lola brings all of the female factory workers under his alluring spell with his daring sexuality—as a cross-dressing heterosexual male. I couldn't wait to see what Jerry Mitchell would do with a dance such as that.

So there I was doing a basic juggling act, keeping three balls in motion, when the phone rang . . .

47

TEVYE AND I MEET AGAIN
2011

Topol, the Israeli star of the *Fiddler on the Roof* movie, went out on a nationwide tour with the show. After ten months, old injuries acted up and he decided to leave the company. I got the call—yes, that same call and it was Susan again. "Harvey, if you don't step in, the show will close and all of these people will be out of work."

"But I'm writing three projects at once, and I have the London production of *La Cage* opening on Broadway, and—"

"We'll work around your schedule."

"I may not survive my schedule. How are you going to work around it?"

I stood stupified, my brain running computations of how I could do this, what it would be like, did I really want to leave my dogs? I had just finished rebuilding my home. Was this the right time to go away? And Tevye? Did I want to play Tevye again? . . . *But they need me.*

The long and short of it was that my ego won out. Harvey to the rescue!

It's a blessing to be needed, and a curse to believe it's your problem. Producer Randy Buck's office concocted a schedule that allowed me to pop back to New York every six weeks or so to attend readings and rehearsals of my other projects. I packed my bags, and off I went on my first-ever tour of anything.

This production utilized the play's original staging, which is not what I'd performed. Before leaving, I had a week of studio rehearsals with the man who'd been responsible for putting up these *Fiddler* tours for decades. He'd played the Streetsweeper at some point during the original Broadway run. A sweet old geezer, his idea of directing was to point: "Go over there . . . And now go over there and say it like this." He hadn't rethought or reconsidered any part of the show in fifty years. That wasn't his assignment. This original staging was charming but very much of its time. Tevye's house, the main set piece, was built onto a small electric forklift that a stagehand drove around the set. It was fun.

This director encouraged a musical-comedy style that was very natural to me but completely foreign to the way Leveaux had brought me into this material. I tried to fight my clownish nature and stay true to the Tevye I'd first created, but between this director, the challenge of an all new company, and the enormous size of the theaters we were playing, I was not as successful as I would have liked. I often disappointed myself as I tried and struggled. I needed a director and not this stager. But the company? Let me tell you

Dancing "To Life" was always one of my favorite things
to do. Here I am with the touring company.

about the company. I loved them—every one of them. Onstage and backstage, in the pit and in the offices, they were the most terrific people. I adored them all. Touring molds you into a family. You have no one else. It's the theater staff and the company.

I worried that I'd be homesick leaving the new house and my animals behind. I wasn't. I became a different me. A smaller me. A me whose day could be satisfied by applause. This me fit in a suitcase. The performance schedule set the pace of my life. My usual inner monologue was replaced by dialogue. The play did my thinking. The acting did my feeling. It was a life. Not *my* life, but a life. I was busy and fulfilled and even happy.

The cast was not in the best emotional state when I arrived. It might have had something to do with Topol leaving, although I suspected it had more to do with Topol's behavior when he was there. None of my business. My primary job was to keep the curtain up. My second was to assure the cast that I wouldn't crash the show or make them change the performances they'd been giving for the last year. It's a funny thing about actors: We talk about the excitement of creating a new, fresh performance every time, but ask one of us to change the smallest detail and you'll find yourself in a war of wills.

When I was on Broadway, as moods sagged in the depths of winter, I'd started a poker game between Saturday performances. That game grew to include cast members from all over Broadway. Cheering up Broadway in winter was easy. Raising the morale of this company required a full-time camp counselor. In each city of the tour my dresser, Suzayn, and I invented a new game to be played backstage. These were silly, nonsensical activities meant only to distract from the daily repetition of life on the road. In Toronto it was Cheese Bowling, where pins (Diet Coke bottles) had to be knocked over by tossing plastic cheese balls (Tevye was a dairyman, and so we had prop cheese balls). The winner actually got a prize. In Denver, where I was assigned an expansive dressing room, during every intermission the entire company gathered there to play bingo, again complete with prizes. Washington DC had us competing in Mouseketball, which was just mini-basketball using tiny toy mice instead of balls. In Cleveland we had a miniature golf course set up in the long hallways; in San Francisco Suzayn and I gathered all of the crap we'd been lugging around from city to city that actually had no use and we held a Going Out of Business sale. The company's mood improved.

Whenever my schedule sent me back to New York on business I'd be filled with the most annoying guilt. But I knew I was leaving the *Fiddler* company in good hands. My standby for that year was none other than Theodore Bikel. I'd been an admirer of his since I was a child, having seen him play Captain von Trapp in the original production of *The Sound of Music*. Why the hell was I playing Tevye when this legend was waiting in the wings? As I was told, one of the creators of the show never liked Mr. Bikel and banned him from ever playing Tevye on Broadway. Still, he was a natural for the role, and he'd played it on tour and around the world for eons. Hearing that Topol was leaving the tour, Theo jumped at the chance to replace him, but they chose me instead and offered him the standby position. We never met during the tour. He'd arrive as I left and would be gone by the time I returned. Still, the director made sure that I knew how much Theo disliked me and my performance. Sometime after the tour, Sheldon Harnick, *Fiddler*'s lyricist, asked me to sing "Rich Man" at a benefit. When I stepped out onto the stage for my orchestra sound check, there in the first row, dead center in this otherwise deserted concert hall, sat Theo, staring up at me, daggers shooting from his eyes. Halfway through the song I went blank and ran from the stage as soon as I could. I then wrote a note telling him how much his performances and his work as a peace and civil-rights activist meant to me and left it in his dressing room. Not long after, he wrote back, and the two of us were able to find each other. I was so happy about that.

48

STRAPPING MY TITS
BACK ON

2010

I t had barely been five years since *La Cage Aux Folles* was first revived on Broadway, but Terry Johnson's British production had been such a smash that the Weisslers begged for the rights to bring it across the Pond. Mr. Herman had no objection, and since this was "my" production, I was very anxious to see it for myself. Doug Hodge would come over to reprise his Olivier Award–winning performance as Zaza, and TV's Kelsey Grammer was set to play Georges. Obviously, I was not pleased that two straight men had been hired, especially when one of them was well-known for his conservative politics. I soothed myself thinking, *This is how you change the world. If his right-wing buddies see him playing a man happily married to a drag queen, they'll at least have to lower the volume of their rhetoric.* Still, I was haunted by the memory of Gene Barry, who owed the resurgence of his career to *La Cage* but still refused to share a backstage elevator with the drag performers, fearing he'd contract AIDS.

One trip home from the *Fiddler* tour was to give notes to Doug and Kelsey. My fears, for the most part, were blown out the rehearsal hall's windows as I watched. Doug Hodge's take on the character was singularly brilliant. Far from the prissy diva of yore, this Zaza made her first entrance in rubber gloves, a torn bathrobe, and scuffies. Here was a housewife defeated by a chicken dinner. Kelsey's Georges was just the opposite: a preening ham anxious to

always be the matinee idol holding center stage. They were delicious together. By the time Robin De Jesús entered as the maid,
I was entranced. The choreography was inventive and original.
There were giant beach balls tossed about and barefooted ballet
moves thrown in for good measure. The players were all committed to the story, and the set showed the kind of ratty glamour I'd
always hoped for. This was the *La Cage* I'd imagined as I scribbled
on the subway to Jerry Herman's town house. It even had a kiss on
the lips between the two leads at the end of the show! I floated out
of New York and back onto the road.

Sidenote: I later found out that what appeared to be a kiss on
the mouth was actually a kiss on the hand, as Kelsey would slip
his hand between the two of them so their lips wouldn't actually
touch. Why are straight men such cowards?

When May rolled around, I was knocked for a loop to see this *La
Cage* production earn eleven Tony nominations and seven Drama
Desks. *Fiddler* was playing a return engagement in Toronto on
Tony night. I rented the ballroom at my hotel and arranged for a
Sunday-night dinner party with the *Fiddler* cast. I provided food
and a projection-screen TV so we could eat and celebrate together.
Doug won for Best Actor in a Musical, Terry Johnson won for Best
Director of a Musical, and the show won Best Revival of a Musical. It was so freakin' exciting! *La Cage* joined *The King and I* as
the only shows in history to win Best Musical and then Best Revival
of a Musical *twice*. I got Jerry Herman on the telephone, and after
the company sang their congratulations to him, the two of us had
a good happy cry together. A very special memory.

The road makes romantic pairings almost impossible. Ongoing
relationships are strained by the prolonged absences, and new relationships can barely be established before your bags are packed and
you're moving on to the next town. Cleveland was to be our last
stop on the tour. I'd grown very close to our company manager,
DeAnn Boise, and our musical director, DAR—David Andrews
Rogers. We three "adults" spent much of our down time together.

Bemoaning the state of our personal lives, we made a pact that we would each sign up on a dating website when we reached Cleveland and go on at least one date with a new person. Idiot that I am, I was the only one to live up to the challenge. I put a profile on one of those things . . . and whaddaya know? I caught me a man!

Kevin was a doll and a half. Handsome and smart, he was a French-horn player as well as a home-decor entrepreneur. My attraction to him was immediate, which was ridiculous considering that I'd be leaving Cleveland in three days. As it turned out, he was in no state to begin anything. He was in the midst of the very messy dissolution of his last relationship. There were money and pets and a house to separate, not to mention the destructive emotions created by an unfaithful partner. Kevin's journeys, emotional and physical, were long and torturous. They involved career changes, the loss of his precious pooches, and a move to New York. I am happy to say that we've managed our special friendship through the travails of life and remain close. All of this to say that falling in love is so much easier when you're young and your only loyalty is to your libido.

49

ZAZA AND ME

2011

The schedule of performing on the road and slipping home every five or six weeks worked really well. I felt like I was meeting my obligations to all. One week I came home to a workshop of *Newsies*, another for a workshop of *Kinky Boots*. *Casa Valentina* was on the back burner, but I kept up with research material in preparation for the big push on that script. The *Fiddler* tour ended just before July 4th in Cleveland.

It wasn't until I sat down to write this memoir that I realized how many times I'd fallen for the line "If you don't take over the role . . ." There were a bunch of those calls from the Glines that always had me running back to keep *Torch Song Trilogy* afloat. Robert Fox called me from London with the same request when Antony Sher's contract was up. Although I was more than done playing Arnold, I took the bait and ran to the rescue. Years later I returned to *Hairspray* to buoy that box office and remained through the closing of the show. Then there was *Fiddler* on Broadway and again on the road. But of all the calls and requests, the next one offered the most bizarre challenge. The producers of *La Cage* wanted me to take over the role of Zaza when Doug's run was done. It had never occurred to me to tackle that role. I wrote it when I was in my twenties and far too young to play it. And with my particular instrument, I never thought anyone would let me be *in* a musical, let alone play the lead, let alone sing Jerry Herman melodies. This was the man who told me he'd rather have had Caballé sing Dolly than Channing. What the hell would he think of me croaking "A Little More Mascara," "Song on the Sand," "The Best of Times," and that titular ballbuster, "La Cage Aux Folles"?

On one hand, I loved this company, this show, this production, and the idea of jumping in was such a challenge. On the other hand, I may have been too young when I wrote it, but I was now way too old. I was the one who complained whenever they cast older actors in these roles. In my mind both Georges and Albin are in their forties. How could I yell at someone else playing the role if I, who was almost sixty, was going to do it myself? On the other hand (can you tell I'd been playing Tevye too long?) . . . how many roles like this exist in the musical canon? How many such roles would I ever be asked to perform? It was another moment for Jack O'Brien's advice: Do it or spend the rest of your life wondering.

I asked who they were getting for Georges. It was to be Jeffrey Tambor, a comic actor I'd enjoyed from afar but only met once, when I made a guest appearance on *The Larry Sanders Show.* He was a good name to attract business, and I thought the two of us might make a believable couple. But my singing? I had to call Jerry. Well, if I insisted that the writers of *Fiddler* hear me sing, I wasn't doing this without Jerry's express permission. He gasped, he sighed, and let out the most *yiddishe* "Oy!" I'd ever heard. Faced with the alternative of closing the show, he gave me his blessing. I thought to myself, *Well, he'll never complain about Carol Channing's voice again.*

A dress fitting and a photo shoot came before we even began rehearsals. During the six months since *Fiddler,* I had mostly sat at the computer catching up on all three of my shows, squeezing into a corset, I had to admit that I'd filled out a bit. Strapped into a black gown covered in gold spangles I said to the seamstress, "I may not make Jerry Herman happy by *sounding* like Montserrat Caballé, but I'll certainly *look* like her!"

Rehearsals were interesting. Jeffrey had a very informal way of attacking the work. It seemed to me that his goal was to loosen himself up and slide into the role. Not only was my approach a

During the poster photo shoot I stepped
out for a breath of fresh air.

world apart from his, I found myself working through a lot of
ghosts and half-forgotten memories. I tried to recall what my original intentions were for each line and moment. I pushed Arthur's
memory gently aside and restored some lines he'd cut. Mostly I saw
my job as adapting to Terry Johnson's brilliant production while
discovering something new in myself to play. Doug Hodge had
found a place in the title song to impersonate Piaf. It was genius.
I tried to imagine how a performer like Charles Pierce would have
approached that moment, and suddenly my Zaza began to materialize. I think a mistake that many actors have made playing Zaza
is that they let the personality of the mother he will eventually be
called on to impersonate overtake the entire performance. Zaza
should be a naughty, bawdy drag queen for most of the show,
allowing the transformation into "Mother" to be that much more
surprising. In any case, that is the approach I took.

Matthew Wright's outrageously inventive costumes
allowed me to create a Zaza who ruled the
cabaret. The tassles were battery operated!

Considering all of my prejudices and wishes for the role, I knew it would take some time for my performance to gel. But as a replacement, I had no out-of-town tryout or even a preview period. As with *Fiddler*, this faggot was tossed onto the fire and left to either burn brightly or flame out. From the first performance the house was filled with those curious to see what I would do with the role. I clung to Jeffrey and the rest of the cast to keep me afloat. Strangely, Jeffrey, my lighthearted partner from rehearsal, was nowhere to be found. Many of the moments we'd developed were simply gone. Dance moves were skipped and lines were dropped. I put it off to first-night jitters only to find that the more performances we did, the less Jeffrey seemed to remember. I heard him say to the stage manager, "Harvey gets better and better and I get worse and worse."

It was heartbreaking to watch, and I had no idea how to help

With her wild side established, becoming the
subdued Mother was more of a surprise.

him. He placed cue cards and line reminders around the set to no
avail. Panic had set in and was snowballing. "The White Room"
is what I call that place where your mind goes suddenly, inexplica-
bly blank. You're in the middle of your performance and suddenly
you're trapped in a bare place without a clue as to what you are
supposed to be doing or saying. Not a thing to cling to but fear. The
White Room was where Jeffrey Tambor had taken up residence. He
began writing his lines on slips of paper and hiding them around
the stage, under props, stuck to furniture, anywhere he could get
to them when he went blank. I once lifted a piece of toast to take
a bite only to discover lyrics scrawled across it. Our show lost its
pace, its humor, its heart, its reason. The entire company focused
on nothing but getting Jeffrey through the show.

After a bit more than a week Jeffrey called it quits. Whatever
the problem, he was not going to overcome it at this moment and

decided to leave the production instead. Unfortunately, not only did he leave us down a "name" performer, but word had gotten out that the show was in bad shape. Ticket sales went from brisk to nil. The marvelous Chris Hoch was the understudy, and he stepped forward with a truthful and professional performance. Our team powdered down his hair to age him, and we trouped merrily on together while the producers searched for a replacement. Christopher Sieber was about to return to the company of *Chicago* for his hundredth term when the stage manager handed him a ticket to our matinee and ordered him over to the Longacre Theatre. He'd hardly made it through the door of my dressing room when I began to plead, "Will you do it? Huh? Will you?"

As it happened, no one had even mentioned the gig to him. He was simply seeing the show as requested. Happily, this magically talented man leapt into the breach and within days we two were dancing through musical comedy heaven to "The Best of Times." They grayed his hair and gave him a goatee, and I adjusted a few lines to account for our age difference, but other than that we became Broadway's newest devoted married couple. It was another world playing opposite Christopher. He is the total package of voice, looks, humor, humanity, and generosity. It was heaven. Sadly, it was also too late to save the show. We'd lost any momentum that could have seen us through the death days of winter, and now we were competing with the crop of new spring shows for ticket sales. We played, happily, together as long as we could before the closing notice was posted.

One more *La Cage* dream of mine was achieved with Christopher in the role. At the end of the show, when Georges and Zaza reprise "Song on the Sand," we made certain that even the last row could see that our performance ended with us actually kissing! We not only kissed, but we would sometimes erupt into laughter and roll down the flight of stairs in each other's arms as the curtain lowered. At last *La Cage* had the loving married couple I'd longed for nearly thirty years ago.

A little sidebar here: Christopher was game for more *La Cage*. He signed on to tour with the show, only now switching roles to

No one can resist the powers of Christopher Sieber.
Such an angel.

play Zaza opposite the 1960s heartthrob, the King of Tan himself, George Hamilton. Unsure that Mr. Hamilton would be able
to handle the rigors of touring, the producers boxed up all of my
costumes and shipped them to my home. This way, if there was an
emergency, they could send a van to get me and all of my stuff in
one fell swoop. George had no such failure, and the crates of gowns
sat in my basement for years. Slowly I've been auctioning them off
for charity. Oh, how I hate to let them go, but really, pink bugle
beads earn no discounts at The Dollar Tree.

It's a funny thing about theater people—what we do is of the
moment. The curtain comes down and it lives only in the memories
of those in attendance. I think we cling to mementos like posters
and programs and photos because we've nothing else. Several years
ago I tore my house down and built a barn-style home instead.
Fearing that I'd become that old-lady actor in *Stage Door* who
takes any excuse to open her purse to find her newspaper reviews
("I happen to have a few of my notices right on top"), I called
several theatrical institutions and told them, "I am drowning in
scripts, photos, clippings, and the like. I'm going to leave them in
the house along with my collection of wire hangers and lidless
Tupperware for the bulldozers to load into dumpsters. If you have

any interest in this material, I suggest you send a van and a couple of volunteers to rescue it all."

I am happy to say that the majority of the collection is now housed in the libraries of Yale University. The freedom gained by the loss is indescribable. Now, whenever someone calls for an item, I can truthfully tell them that I have none of that stuff and refer them to Yale.

50

BACK TO *KINKY BOOTS* AND *NEWSIES*

2011–2012

Free again, I dove back into wrestling the *Kinky* score out of Cyndi. I'd been torturing my friend so long that she now called me Mommy Dearest and I lovingly called her Christina. One afternoon Jerry Mitchell, Stephen Oremus, Cyndi, and I were together in a rehearsal room for a work session. We were getting close to having a score, but it was time to give Cyndi a big push forward. The end of the first act was a tricky spot. Charlie is gambling his failing family business on manufacturing high-heeled boots for transvestites. It is a totally insane Hail Mary pass. Just as the first pair of these boots is about to come off the production line, his fiancée tells him that he should stop trying, that his father never believed he could run the family business and was in the process of selling off the factory when he died. And as long as she's at it, she lets him know that *she* has no trust in his abilities or judgment, either. Charlie stands alone, center stage, everything he believed in crashing about him. This is how I described the moment in my first draft:

> CHARLIE *almost loses his balance under the weight of what he's heard. He studies* NICOLA *and then turns to face the factory facade. Turning back to his girlfriend, he takes a step towards her but stops himself, deciding to go into the factory, where* LOLA *and the* WORKERS *have been waiting for him.*

LOLA: Ladies, gentlemen, and Charlie Price . . . Long live Kinky Boots!

The WORKERS *step aside, revealing a table holding an outrageous pair of red thigh-high leather stiletto boots.*

The WORKERS *sing* "Long live Kinky Boots!" *They dance and celebrate as* CHARLIE *stands watching, still unsure of his path.*

END OF ACT ONE.

"No," Jerry said.

"What's the problem?" I wondered.

"If we do it that way, then we're writing a show about fixing a factory," he said. "We have to keep the focus on fixing lives. We have to see Charlie make the decision to reject everyone else's opinion of him. We need to see him take hold of his destiny." Jerry was now getting excited. "We need a hero moment."

Thinking on the fly, I offered: "So, Charlie walks back into the factory, where everyone is waiting. They step back and reveal the boots to him. Lola asks, 'So, boss, is this what you had in mind?' And Charlie says . . ."

Jerry jumped into action, pointing at Cyndi excitedly. "'Yeah!' Charlie says. 'Yeah!' And then he goes around the room asking, 'Yeah?' And they answer, 'Yeah!' And Charlie hollers joyously, 'Everybody say yeah!'"

Jerry was on fire. You could see the light bulbs exploding in Cyndi's head while Jerry continued his race around the room screaming and dancing: "Yeah! Yeah! Yeah! Yeah!"

I laughed to myself, thinking of an old show biz phrase: "And that's how the rent gets paid."

Another fun collaboration happened while writing the finale. In the film Charlie, Lola, and the factory workers all return to Lola's club to celebrate the boot triumph in Milan. Charlie and Lola make speeches about what they learned through their trials and the credits roll. The musical would not travel back to England but end on the stage in Milan. I wrote a description of Charlie and Lola coming together as their childhood selves and their fathers appearing to them. The fathers embrace their sons as adult Lola confirms to Charlie, "We're the same, you and me."

I thought this was the spot for some sort of dance of reconciliation between the fathers and sons that we'd then follow with a huge celebratory finale.

"How about the lessons?" Cyndi wondered.

It suddenly struck me as funny if we wrote Lola and Charlie's Twelve Step Program to Happiness.

"Why not?" she asked.

"Twelve Steps?" I flashed back to Sondheim's objection to *A Letter to Three Wives*. "It's the finale. The audience will have their coats on by number seven. But maybe we can get away with six."

"Six Steps, 'cause drag queens do it better!" Cyndi added.

Back in 1992 I wrote and delivered a commencement speech at Bennington College. I had nothing prepared when I drove up there, but after lunching with some students I slipped away for a nap and wrote a speech on a scratch pad. That speech is mostly political bullshit . . . but miraculously, a few quotes from it have lived on to

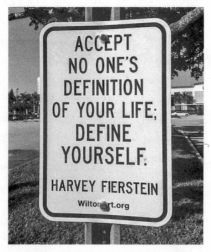

Found this on the Internet

this day. I've even seen the final lines printed on a street sign: "Never be bullied into silence. Never allow yourself to be made a victim. Accept no one's definition of your life, but define yourself."

I've also seen the quote credited to Robert Frost!

Included in that speech was my off-the-cuff Twelve Step Program to Happiness. I was able to find a copy on the Internet and went through it with Cyndi. She picked through my twelve and came up with a brilliant Six Steps to Live By.

1. Pursue the truth.
2. Learn something new.
3. Accept yourself and you'll accept others, too.
4. Let love shine.
5. Let pride be your guide.
6. You change the world when you change your mind.

Over at *Newsies,* we'd done readings and a workshop, all accompanied by Tom Schumacher saying that he'd never put the show on Broadway—but "I'm thinking of producing it at the Paper Mill Playhouse in New Jersey just to test it for school productions."

Watching his belief in the show grow was satisfying, considering where the project began. The first reading he gave of the script was held in his conference room, with office workers and assistants taking on the roles in the little cartoon voices they'd become accustomed to using on Disney projects. Good or awful, I had put actual work into this script. Alan and Jack had composed new material. Certainly it deserved more seriousness than a fifty-year-old man employing a cartoon-mouse voice to play a sixteen-year-old homeless boy. Even listening to that half-assed reading, the magic of *Newsies* was undeniable. *Newsies* had a life all its own. As silly as the original movie was, its fans remained, and still remain, rabid. Once the show was cast, the virus quickly spread through the company, most of whom hadn't been born when the movie opened and flopped, but who were now tasked with bringing these characters to life. The company bonded almost immediately. The spirit I witnessed in every company of *Newsies,* from the Paper Mill production through a suburban high-school performance, displayed the same allegiance. These actors were linked by the work, the message that the future belongs to them, and the chance to show their stuff. The *Newsies* themselves became a life force; they were the stars. You may have bought a ticket to see some big name on the Radio City Music Hall stage, but it's the Rockettes who bring you to your feet. So, too, the Newsies. Embraced by adults and kids alike, the Newsies were contagious. Alan Menken's earworm music, Jack Feldman's inspirational lyrics, and Chris Gattelli's choreography gave these powerhouse performers a launching pad, and they took off like fireworks in the sky over the Paper Mill Playhouse. Tom called the company together to let them know that *Newsies* was headed for Broadway.

The exuberant *Newsies* exploded onstage.

Opening at the Nederlander Theatre in March 2012, *Newsies* had a stellar run, with the young fan base, whom the cast dubbed "the Fansies," gathering to see the show over and over again. It was nominated for eight Tonys; Menken won his first-ever Tony for this score along with Feldman for his lyrics, and Chris Gattelli won for his thrilling choreography. But I walked away with the biggest prize of all—I got to prove the naysayers wrong. By adding a plot twist here, a love interest there, remotivating songs and devising opportunities for Menken and Feldman to create new material, I restructured and reinvented while protecting the magical core that made the underlying story a sacred receptacle for children's aspirations. That work released the show and took it from unproduceable to Broadway hit. *Newsies* is now performed professionally and in schools around the world. Before the touring production closed, Disney brought in the original leads to the Pantages Theater in Hollywood and made a pretty terrific film capture of the show.

Newsies was the last show that my mother would see. Undiagnosed at the time, Jackie was growing frail as cancer spread through her body. Ron got her to the theater as usual and even up a flight of stairs into the opening-night party at a restaurant next to the New Amsterdam Theatre. She enjoyed the show, no doubt, but she wasn't totally present. There was a surrender in her eyes that I'd never seen before. Usually, on such occasions, she was anxious to see everyone and have everyone see her. She wore her pride in my recognition like a uniform encrusted with war medals. That night her smile was vacant, almost apologetic, her stance unsteady, her speech halting. I'm sorry this was her last opening night, as it just was not her show. Despite her career as a teacher and her love of children's literature, she preferred more adult entertainment. *Newsies* had nothing to say that she didn't already know. The unyielding beating of drums that accompanied so much of that score was exactly the opposite of the healing harmonies she could have used. No, this was not her show.

The following week she was at my brother's house preparing for a family seder celebrating the start of Passover. Jackie excused herself to use the ladies' room, where she produced a puddle of blood. Ron rushed her to the hospital, and the diagnosis of colon cancer was swift. Unsure how much to share with her, as her mind was becoming more and more addled, we decided to keep her as comfortable, as worry- and pain-free as possible. Obviously, she knew she was ill, but we weren't going to tell her she was dying. She would stay in her Sheepshead Bay home with around-the-clock care, surrounded by her loyal friends, where she could sit outside on her terrace and watch her beloved fishing boats sail on. Ron and I took turns visiting. On my first stop-in she told me the story of how she bled on the floor, sheepishly asking, "Do you think it's possible that I got my period?"

My heart broke to see her so diminished and frightened as she silently negotiated her beliefs. She'd never speak the words, but I knew she was thinking about my father and her own father, whom she adored, and whether a reunion with them waited just beyond surrender.

I spoke to her about a lot of shit, most meaningless, some heart-felt. She smiled and nodded and bit her tongue to keep herself from crying. I ached to batter down her wall of bravery and let her emotions run free, but who was I to take that dignity from her? Instead, I smiled and nodded and bit my tongue to keep from crying myself.

When I called her on the phone she'd never say "Come and visit." Her greeting was always "Come shopping."

She wanted us to take her precious treasures from the apartment. She didn't need them anymore and wanted to be sure they were safely dispersed among the family.

A few weeks after the *Newsies* opening night, the Tony nominations were announced, and among them were eight nods for us. I received one for writing the book. Following the Midtown luncheon where nominees were presented with their documents, I drove out to Sheepshead Bay to bring the Tony pin and framed certificate to Jackie, as had become our tradition. I didn't have to drive out there that Wednesday, since she was scheduled to spend the weekend with me at my house, but I did, and we had a quiet sit-down and chat. Our last.

Mom passed two nights later.

I still wish she'd seen *Kinky Boots*. With its theme of healing between a son and a parent, that was a show she would have loved.

51

KINKY BOOTS

2013

I thought *Kinky Boots* was in pretty great shape when we packed up the New York rehearsal rooms and headed to Chicago for our out-of-town tryout. On our final day in the rehearsal studio we ran through the show twice for the producers, friends, and a few members of the press. Everyone went nuts. I kept thinking, *If they are this wild about it now, wait until they see it with costumes and lighting and sets!*

I went home to pack, absolutely certain we were on the cusp of a five-year run.

I arrived in Chicago a few days after everyone else. No one needs the book writer getting in the way during tech. Besides, I wanted to experience the full effect of the physical production and orchestra with an audience. I hung back for that first preview. I entered a very buzzy theater with butterflies fluttering all through me. Cyndi's name ensured strong ticket sales, and that first preview was packed. The lights went down, the music began, and halfway through the opening number my heart began sinking. Not only my heart, but the performance itself was going down as well. Something was terribly wrong. Our show was not projecting across the footlights. Here were our music and story and performances, but somehow muted, foggy, meaningless. Where the audience in the rehearsal room was bouncing in their seats, the audience in Chicago sat uninvolved. We all looked at one another. By intermission Hal and

Daryl were absolutely panicked. We clustered together down by the offices. What was happening? Someone blamed the lights. Someone else claimed too many costumes. Could it be the sound? Was it just nerves? Was the theater too big? Was the show too intimate?

We all looked to our fearless leader, Jerry Mitchell, who you could see was pulling his own thoughts together and formulating a plan. He called DB and Rusty, his assistants, to his side and whispered something about an early start for the next day's rehearsals. What we witnessed that following week was theater craft at its best. Jerry began with the opening moments of the show and, with the precision and trained eye of a diamond cutter, methodically chipped away the excess, scene by scene, cue by cue, costume by costume, until the hidden jewel emerged. A film director points his lens and frames exactly what he wants the viewer to see. So, too, Jerry. He highlighted every detail, eliminated every distraction, magnified every emotion until our story rose up to meet the audience. It was beyond impressive—but not totally unexpected, as I'd witnessed him do similar work on *Hairspray*. I was onstage during that transformation, so I couldn't see exactly what he was doing. Now I could, and I bowed with respect.

We got a lot of work done in Chicago, even adding a new song on our final day there, but the show had one more seemingly unsolvable moment that we couldn't crack. Realizing that the factory is going under, Charlie has to give notice to the workers. It's an important scene, but how much fun can be had watching people get fired? I came up with what I thought was an ingenious idea. I'm sure you've seen that old magic act where a person is put into a large box and then the magician sticks swords through it, yes? Well, how about if Lola was performing that act on one side of the stage, and for every sword she stuck through her victim, Charlie fired a factory worker on the other side of the stage? Fun, right? The juxtaposition would elevate the entire sequence. So Cyndi wrote a great song and Jerry staged it beautifully . . . and it totally died in front of an audience. Well, the problem had to be the song. So Cyndi wrote another one and Jerry restaged it, and it still fell flat. By now I was feeling so guilty for having the idea and no solution as to why it wasn't working. Jerry still believed in my concept and went at it with gusto, but to no avail. Clever as it was, it was bad storytelling. Ultimately, he cut the new song, had Lola sing a reprise of the number she'd just finished, and *voilà*, without the magic act distraction the audience was able to concentrate on Charlie firing the workers, which was, after all, what the scene was about. Finally the entire sequence made sense. It was a good reminder that we're here to tell a story, not to show off how clever we are. We were ready for New York.

Our Broadway fans were rabid. From first previews we heard that audience members were snatching up tickets to see the show multiple times. That's the kind of response usually conferred by teens and tweens, but our fans were adults—not just adults, heterosexual men. *Kinky Boots* spoke to the relationships between

Cyndi, Jerry's back, me, and producer
Daryl Roth onstage at *Kinky Boots*

grown men and their fathers, the expectations, disappointments, and regrets. The drag identity made the discussion absurdly safe. The emotional truth of the show made it vital. *Kinky Boots* is not about cross-dressing or making boots or saving a factory. *Kinky Boots* is about finally making peace with who you grew up to be.

52

CASA VALENTINA

2014

J oe Mantello accepted the assignment of directing *Casa Valentina,* and we decided to premiere it at Manhattan Theater Club's Broadway house, the Samuel J. Friedman, where I knew that Lynne Meadow and her team would be marvelously supportive of the work we had ahead. Knowing it could be a challenging piece, our first thought was to protect it by playing to a subscription audience of dedicated theatergoers. I'm not sure we made the right decision. Although their patrons are theater devotees, they tend to be older. As Nathan Lane once quipped, "I love MTC. It sleeps six hundred comfortably." And since they are buying seats for an entire season, they are seeing shows that they wouldn't ordinarily buy a ticket to see. On the other hand, thanks to the subscribers, the cast never played to anything but full houses, which is not always the case when introducing a new play to the world. Once we ran through the subscription ticket holders, the regular theater audiences arrived, delivering wildly enthusiastic reactions to the very appreciative cast.

In preparation we'd done a few readings with some magnificent actors. Although I wrote Bessie for myself and was dying to play her, I wanted as heterosexual a cast as we could interest. An actor's sexuality shouldn't be important but in this case it seemed to matter. I had meant the gay lead in my play *Spookhouse* to be the antagonist, but because it was a play of mine, critics and audiences assumed any gay character that I wrote had to be the hero, thus misconstruing the entire story and missing the tragedy of the play. Although I adored Billy Porter's portrayal of Lola in *Kinky Boots,* and we never could have developed the show without his singular talent and showmanship, it wasn't until Wayne Brady took over the role that audiences finally listened to the character say that he preferred women and accepted him as a cross-dressing heterosexual. Some in the audience saw a drag queen and so never questioned that they were watching a homosexual. I was afraid that the same thing would happen if I played Bessie. They'd be missing so much if they thought Bessie was a closeted gay.

Prejudice is art's greatest enemy. If you walk into a gallery thinking you already know what a Picasso looks like, you will never really see a Picasso. How you look circumscribes what you see.

To avoid any confusion I sought the most heterosexual men I could find. In early readings Brian Dennehy played the Judge, Adam Driver played the innocent Miranda, and Bertie Carville was the first to read Valentina. Testosterone ruled. The play was fascinating, much too long, and it lost its way two-thirds through, but there was a lot of uncharted territory being explored. There were aspects of gender and sexuality that I had never heard spoken of before. This was a worthy effort—but not a finished one. Back to the computer I went.

I'd never had a play produced that needed as much work as this one, and I couldn't figure out why. I had been true to the actual people, their stories were authentic, there was nothing you could ask about any one of these characters that I could not answer; and yet it was not adding up. Poor Joe Mantello tried to get through to me, and I begged my brain to open up to others' questions and suggestions. But the pieces simply refused to fall into place, because no matter what the suggestion, I was always armed with the nonproductive reply "But that's not what happened."

The weight of representing these people's truth imprisoned me. I began to understand why movies about historical events are never factually accurate. This wasn't Pearl Harbor I was writing about, so what the fuck was I blocking?

We were well into previews before Joe opened me up enough to seek the question that would satisfy the play. It was the most difficult question of all. We've spent two hours listening to these men say that they have a female personality living within them. Some claim it to be psychological, some sexual, and some social, but they were all driven to manifest this persona physically. With Katherine Cummings sitting in front of me, this woman who despite every obstacle had fashioned her own destiny, it finally dawned on me that I hadn't asked any of my characters for their ultimate truth: *Who are you really? Are you male or female? If you had the choice to live as one or the other, which would you choose?*

The answer to that question was most likely different for each of the characters in the play. I'd been very careful to let them express their individual needs to cross-dress. But drama demanded an answer for at least the play's lead, George/Valentina. This is his resort. Everyone has come at his request. He's been the presumptive leader who's brought them all together. And now it's his confusion or unwillingness to speak the truth that is threatening them all with destruction. What secret could he be hiding? His wife, who has supported his every whim, deserves to know. His friends who've lived by his rules and under his auspices deserve to know. And the audiences who have been invited into this world deserve answers as well.

I captured the girls as boys in rehearsal.

And here are the boys as girls in performance.

At last the right final scene came into focus. George/Valentina's wife, after years of blind acceptance, muses, "Is today the day that George goes upstairs to change and I never see him again?" She finally focuses everything that's come before and asks the most difficult question of all: "Are you George or Valentina? If you had the choice to be one or the other, who would you be?"

The play, after all of that, simply wants each of us to ask "Who am I?" and then have the courage to live up to that truth.

The play was finally solved for me. I was able to breathe and enjoy the rest of the run. Thank you, Joe Mantello.

Mantello thinks the play was a few years ahead of its time, and he's probably right. If *Casa* was produced with today's open discussions of nonbinary, transgender, and other life experiences, the audience would have broader reference with which to view these characters. Okay . . . let's add this to the list as another work worthy of revival. My only fear is we'd never top some of the performances from that first company. Reed Birney killed in the role of the manipulative Charlotte, outwardly calm but as ready to strike as a venomous snake.. John Cullum was absolutely heartbreaking as the elder matriarch speaking of her glory days in petticoats. Every one gave marvelous, brave, loving performances that brought this world to life. This was an ensemble of which to be proud.

53

DID SOMEONE CALL
FOR A PLUMBER?

2015

After nearly twenty years I was settled into boozelessness. Never missed the stuff. Lauren, Patty, some others, and I built a strong circle of supportive friendship in Connecticut. We have few secrets among us and always a shoulder when needed. I have another group of intimates led by Richie and Susan and Stephen whom I love to see in New York. The two energies of my friend circles seem to fulfill my need of intimacy. My personal life is no longer potential fodder for romance novels, and I like it that way. I've had enough drama, more than enough heartache, and ample proof that I am not the marrying kind. My personality is simply too addictive. I don't love, I obsess. I don't share, I possess. I don't partner, I control. What more proof do you need than my confession to mourning the loss of Sam for ten years? I wonder if I have the capacity to heal. I think I just scab over. My youthful goal was marriage and children. I still want the nest, but I'm fine filling it with furry offspring. As for marriage, I seem to be happier alone than I ever was partnered. I'm so much more myself. As for sex—I've found a balance that's right for me. My desire for physical contact has not waned, but satisfying it seems best when kept casual, nonromantic, and in most cases entre nous. I am happily too old to drag my ass to the Trucks or leaf through bridal magazines on the toilet. Instead, I dabble in dalliance. There's been a power lifter, a transit cop, an airline pilot, a porn star, and a couple of Broadway's finest ensemble members among my most cherished trysts. Keeping to these new parameters has resulted in nothing but happy memories jotted down in my diary. Is there a human price for remaining single? Probably. They say that couples live longer. I'd rather live happier.

As for my career, just during the previous few years I had *Newsies, Kinky,* and *Casa* produced on Broadway, performed *Hairspray* at the Hollywood Bowl, and provided a bunch of TV-cartoon voices. I was ready for relaxation. The last thing I was seeking was a new project; so, naturally, the phone rang with an offer. It was Kenny Leon asking me to rewrite *The Wiz* for a live NBC television production he'd be directing. He asked to discuss it over dinner. Have you ever seen Kenny Leon? That man is so fine, not a chance in hell I was passing up dinner with him! Chitchatting away over a chopped salad at Joe Allen, I finally said, "Kenny, I'm too white to write *The Wiz*."

"That's not true."

"No? Even the original writer's name is Brown!"

"And Mr. Brown is white."

After a good laugh I promised to look the piece over. I had loved the challenge of working on *Newsies*. *The Wiz* offered some of the same problems. It's a piece that is greatly beloved and badly dated. Fans don't want it changed, but it *had* to be changed. The assignment was to update, leaving as few fingerprints as possible. Oh, there were two more minor requests. Cirque du Soleil was one of the producing entities, so I had to develop a few spots in the show for them to display their specific acrobatic skills. Secondly, recording stars would most likely be involved, so I needed to identify opportunities for songs to be created by one or more of these artists. Kenny got the dinner bill and I got busy writing.

Meanwhile, back in my regular life, Jerry Mitchell phoned. Broadway Cares/Equity Fights AIDS is a nonprofit group that supports AIDS-related causes. Every June since 1992 Jerry and a team of choreographers put together a charity extravaganza for them like no other. *Broadway Bares* is a huge burlesque show where dancers and featured players perform elaborate striptease routines in front of sellout crowds. I hadn't performed in it for a few years, so when Jerry asked, I couldn't say no. All in good fun, I pulled together an outrageous outfit from *La Cage* leftovers. Arriving at the venue, I dragged my suitcase up three flights of stairs to find that I'd be sharing a dressing room with comedian Bianca Del Rio. It was love at first fight, and we've been sisters ever since. We did the show, raised a billion dollars, and went on with our lives.

A few days later I was at my doctor's office for my annual checkup. My health, despite my ever yo-yoing weight, has always been terrific. No high blood pressure, no sugar problems or severe allergies.

I should have mentioned that I'd given up my two-pack-a-day smoking habit years earlier. It was by accident. I was about six months into sobriety when my friend Barbara went through a cancer scare. I said, "Why don't we ditch real life for a few days?" We checked into Canyon Ranch Spa. The package deal included rooms, meals, endless exercise classes, and your choice of two introductory specialties from a long list. I chose hypnosis and acupuncture. I had no agenda scheduling them but somehow came away a nonsmoker.

The acupuncture session was supposed to be about deep relaxation. I took my place on the massage table and listened to the New Age soundtrack as the purveyor of needles gently screwed them into my body, head to toe. I don't know how long I was lying there when suddenly I was struck with a jolt of energy that practically blew me off the table. The acupuncturist called out for me not to move, as I was still covered in needles. She pulled them out as quickly as she could, and off I went with this new, unexplained energy level. I guess I had relaxed enough.

When the hypnotist asked if there was anything specific I'd like to achieve through the session, I said, "Well, I can always use a suggestion to give up ice cream."

She asked if I smoked and I nodded, but it had been hours and hours between butts. There was nowhere to light up in this place other than an atrium, where I did escape to have a cigarette before bedtime. The yucky part of it was that every staircase faced that atrium, so anyone traveling anywhere saw this poor addicted schmuck sucking nicotine in the midst of this temple of well-being. Anyway, the hypnotist turned her New Age soundtrack on and led me on a journey down a stream to freedom, self-acceptance, and happiness. I didn't jump off her table when she was done. I actually felt relaxed and ready to enjoy the rest of my day.

Meanwhile, the woman I hired to watch my dogs and my house while Babs and I were off to the spa had asked me to please put away any ashtrays, lighters, cigarettes, and smoking paraphernalia of any sort. She was going to use these few days to attempt to break her own smoking habit. Her strategy was to pretend that mine was a nonsmoking house and see if that worked for her.

At the end of our weekend, I paid the bill and sat out in the car waiting for Barbara, who was having a final massage. Free at last to do as I pleased, I smoked a cigarette, I think, while I waited. Having abstained for so long, it made me dizzy and slightly nauseated. Arriving home, I immediately noticed the absence of ashtrays, lighters, cigarettes, and other smoking paraphernalia and remembered my deal with the house sitter. Realizing that I'd smoked, at most, two cigarettes in the last few days, I wondered if I dared to test myself. Could I really go from two packs a day to nothing? When I was writing, I would sometimes have a cigarette in my mouth, another in my hand, and a third burning away in the ashtray. Smoking was part of my thinking process. Could I write without it? There was only one way to find out. I remembered hearing from others that nicotine withdrawal was actually painful. Hey, between losing booze and Sam I was already in so much withdrawal discomfort that the added hardship of losing cigarettes might be negligible. I dumped my stash of butts into the garbage and soaked them with water. This was only a test, but it worked. I never smoked another cigarette from that day until this. The house sitter, on the other hand, lit up as soon as she reached her car and, as far as I know, never did quit.

Ooh! Another fun fact about that getaway. They had you wait for your evening massage in a romantically lit hot-tub room. One evening another gentleman joined me in the warm waters. It was none other than singer/scribe James Taylor. Obviously, I didn't want to bother him, but I'm such a fan, so as I was called away for my massage I quickly said, "Not meaning to disturb you, but I have to say that the mere sound of your voice gives me goosebumps, and as long as I'm doling out compliments, that's a really nice penis you've got there." I think he was on his honeymoon.

So . . . I was at my general practitioner's office for my annual checkup when he heard something he didn't like.

"Something wrong with my heart?"

"It could be nothing, but it sounds like a leaky valve."

"Excuse me?"

"What are you doing after this?" he asked.

"Going home."

"Humor me," he said, and the next thing I knew I was getting an echocardiogram.

Several days later I was scheduled for surgery to replace a large part of my aorta. It seems I had a congenital condition where my aorta was enlarged and leaking. The doctor said that it could rupture at any moment. "Until you have this surgically repaired, you should not lift anything heavier than ten pounds or climb stairs quickly."

"But Doctor," I said, "last week I did a show where I carried a fifty-pound suitcase up three flights of stairs to my dressing room."

"Well, don't do that again," was his sage advice.

My big bro, as usual, came to the rescue. He called a doctor friend from his premed days and they hooked me up with a top-notch surgeon. I can't say I was scared. I really wasn't. We humans are no more mysterious to surgeons than toilets are to plumbers. The cardiologist said that the valve replacement was routine, and I believed him. He gave me a choice between pig, cow, and manufactured. How serious could this be if it involved shopping? And if they ever needed to replace this new valve, they wouldn't even have to crack my chest open again—they'd insert it through a vein in my groin. Whoopee!

I arrived at the hospital bright and early the morning of the operation. I don't remember much beyond undressing, signing papers, and then being led down a long hallway into a rather chilly, sterile-feeling, all-white operating theater. There were a mess of folks, gowned, gloved, and occupied. No one so much as glanced my way, which relaxed me. If they weren't nervous why should I be? I was told to lie down on the operating table, lights above, sheets thrown over me, and goodnight, nurse.

The next thing I knew I was breaking through the fog of drugs to find myself lying on a bed in the recovery room. My bro was there at my feet, looking exhausted and relieved. I remember saying some stuff, but not being really sure I was making any sense. I saw the jumble of tubes coming out of me and realized that a bunch of people went to a lot of trouble to work on me. The least I could do was be cheery. I tried to smile gratefully, even flirting with a male nurse, but another emotion was rising up within me. It was anger. I was pissed. I was seething. Here's the deal: I felt as if I were conscious of being dead. I knew that I had been dead, and I was just fine with it. So why the fuck was I now lying on this bed with all of these tubes and machines attached to me? Who was the genius that thought I needed to be dragged back here? I was dead. I'd achieved the ultimate goal of living and been rewarded with eternal peace. WTF? Where I'd been was nowhere. There were no clouds or angels, no rainbow bridge with relatives running to greet me. It was black and quiet and peaceful, over and done. Take a bow and turn the lights out when you leave. There was no more struggle or pain or restraint. No one was cutting me open and cracking my ribs and pulling the heart out of my chest. All of that was going on, but I was out of there. And now, suddenly, for some reason, I was forced back, shoved back where it was cold and I was hurt and bleeding and frightened and my own life was out of my control. Why the fuck couldn't they have left well enough alone?

I knew that I needed to keep those thoughts to myself. If I wanted out of that hospital, and I wanted out of that hospital, I needed to smile and wave, have no pain and no complaints. I needed to rise from that bed just as soon as they'd allow and show that I was fully recovered. The anger that had taken up residence in my gut had to be packed in my overnight bag and shoved under the bed for now. If anyone were to find out how I was feeling, they would never set me free. I had to do whatever it took to get free. Meanwhile, my room was a hotbox. It was summer and the sun baked my windows, making it almost impossible to rest. As soon as I was allowed, I dragged my ass and my intravenous pole to the waiting area and sat, making believe I was reading or writing on my laptop, or gossiping with relatives of other patients who came by. My plan worked as well as it could, and I was released a few days earlier than scheduled.

Back home, I began to realize that my anger might have been masking something bigger. Speaking to other people who'd survived this kind of major surgery, I came to realize that I was not alone. Depression, anger, and fear were common after-effects for all of us. How could you not have desperate thoughts? Parts of your brain may have been disarmed, but it was still alive and recording. Somewhere inside your head was the knowledge of everything they did to you. You heard the conversations. You were aware of saws ripping you open, hands invading the most private recesses of your body. If the surgeons ever expressed worry, you heard them. If they talked about your prognosis, somewhere in your unconscious that conversation is logged. Who wouldn't awaken in anger? You've been violated. But here's the thing—these doctors all know the score, so why not warn us? What's the big secret? Wouldn't we be better off knowing and being prepared?

Now, whenever I hear of a friend or acquaintance who's having that kind of operation, I do my best to arm them with knowledge. The procedures are real. The feelings are only feelings. Knowing you might experience them, knowing you are normal, might soften their effect.

The result of my adventure is that I am more certain than ever that there is no afterlife. Some reporter questioned my atheism: "What would you do if you died and found yourself standing before God at the Pearly Gates? What would you say?"

I thought a moment and said, "Oops. Wrong again."

There's something else they don't prepare you for. After they crack you open and fix everything, they shove it all back in and sew you up. Well, I'm here to tell you that not everything goes back precisely the way it came from the manufacturer. The pieces don't fit back in the box the way they used to.

My friend Lauren brought dinner over for us to share a few days after I got home. We were sitting at the dining table when I realized that the front of my T-shirt was wet. Was I dribbling my soup down my chest? No. One of the still unhealed holes in my chest had liquid pouring out of it. I panicked and called the surgeon's office.

"Nothing to worry about. It's extra saline from the operation still draining off. It's to be expected."

To be expected? I could have filled a juice glass with what was pouring out. Okay. Some extra fluid still needed to drain: I'll buy that. But what about all the rest of the stuff that's sloshing around in there? A bit of intestine has wandered a little this way, my diaphragm has shifted a bit that way, some rib bones didn't knit back as they were. To this day my body emits gurgles, cracks, snaps, and pops as if there's a sound-effects machine run amok in my chest. I pity the poor recording engineers who have to block this crap when I'm dubbing a movie or cartoon. I try to warn them, but I've seen engineers tear up rooms looking for the source of the noises while I sit calmly on a stool, waiting for them to accept the fact that it's just me. There's a beat box playing where my heart used to be.

54

THE WIZ LIVE! AND HAIRSPRAY LIVE!

2015–2016

The Wiz was waiting.

Since childhood I've always hated how, at the end of *The Wizard of Oz*, Dorothy accidentally misses her ride home in the balloon, leaving her to be rescued by magic. The Lion, the Scarecrow, and the Tin Man come to realize that what they sought was inside of them all along. Dorothy, on the other hand, has to hitch a ride with a broken-down huckster? No! Not in my world. To me, Dorothy has earned the biggest breakthrough of all.

Furthermore, everyone is on a journey to find something they've been missing (heart, brain, courage) except for Dorothy. The MGM version had her seeking a place with no troubles. What kind of bull is that compared to those other goals? And so, besides restructuring the show for commercial breaks, adding opportunities for the Cirque performers to show their stuff, and updating social references and jokes, I took the liberty to adjust a few plot points. Hey, if anyone didn't like my interpretation, Judy Garland's wasn't going anywhere.

So here's my big twist: In this *Wiz* Dorothy was born in Omaha, but when she lost her parents, she was sent to live on her Aunt Em's farm in Kansas. Feeling like an outsider at school, hating this new life, Dorothy wants to return to Omaha. Home is the prize she is seeking. The tornado is then the death of her parents. I think that makes a lot more sense and puts her more firmly on her personal Yellow Brick Road. When she meets the Wiz and discovers that he, too, is from Omaha, hitching a ride back seems to be the answer to her quest. It's only at the last moment that she realizes what she really wants is to be with Aunt Em and the people who love her in Kansas.

When Glinda arrives, Dorothy has already learned her lesson; all she needs now is directions to get home. Glinda's gorgeous eleven o'clock number, "Believe in Yourself," is now more fully motivated as she hands Dorothy the power of her own destiny. With her victory firmly in sight, Dorothy claims the stage and sings the triumphant anthem "Home."

It was amazing to have this opportunity to redefine Dorothy's journey. Kenny was on board the moment he read the pages, but it took our producers, Bob Greenblatt, Neil Meron, and Craig Zadan, a moment longer to agree. I am so grateful that they did. Of course, I bawled my eyes out watching it live on television, but I may have been the only one. The day after the broadcast I checked reviews and articles to see what people thought of the new ending. I found no mention, positive or negative, of the changes, which only goes to prove once again that *prejudice* is the greatest enemy of art. Everyone assumed they heard the ending they already knew and never saw the new one right in front of their eyes. The flip side is that children growing up with my version will now expect Dorothy to be stronger and more empowered. That's a good thing.

Working on *The Wiz Live!* was a perfect project while my body was healing from surgery. I attended a few rehearsals but didn't hang out daily, since William Brown, the original book writer, was there much of the time and I thought my presence might be uncomfortable for him. Rewriting a living author is a touchy proposition. If I live long enough, I am sure to find myself in the same position. Gotta watch that karma tote board.

The show made for a wonderful broadcast. The all-star company turned out great performances with nary a hitch. Cirque du Soleil was supposed to move the production to Broadway the following year. Sadly soon after, Cirque was forced to reorganize their finances and refocus their goals, so the production never materialized. A real shame. It's a great show ready for reviving.

It wasn't too long after New Year's that the NBC Live! team of Bob, Neil, Craig, and Kenny called again. The next musical they'd be producing would be *Hairspray* and they wanted me to do the adaptation. "With pleasure," I said.

Besides the original, I'd already created the version we did in Las Vegas, another we performed at the Hollywood Bowl, and a third to be produced on Royal Caribbean cruise ships. Writing it for television, getting to work with Kenny and the gang again, would be fun.

I'd already handed in my first draft of the script when I got a call from Neil and Craig asking me to play Edna. For months the grapevine had been buzzing about the bold-faced names who'd been offered and turned down the role before me. I've been in this racket way too long to wonder why they went to others first or to hold a grudge about them coming to me as a last resort, although the mental image of someone like Alec Baldwin sporting my bra and girdle gave me the giggles. The only question was whether or not I wanted to strap those boobs on again. I seriously thought I'd kissed Edna goodbye after we performed the show at the seventeen-thousand-seat Hollywood Bowl. Truthfully, I only performed at the Bowl because I thought it would be fun, having skipped playing Los Angeles with the tour. Although I'd been contracted to play LA, Bruce Vilanch, who'd been performing Edna on the tour, asked me to let him play that leg, too. Bruce lived there, his friends were all there, he said it would mean a lot to him. Playing the Pantages Theatre with my old costars Marissa and Matthew Morrison might have been fun, but this was important to Bruce, so I let him take the booking. Mr. Vilanch possesses one of the drollest minds in show business, which he proved again when he returned from his year-long tour with *Hairspray* and reported, "When I die my epitaph will read: 'Here lies Bruce Vilanch. He was no Harvey Fierstein.'"

This *Hairspray Live!* was beginning to look like fun. After hiring Jerry Mitchell to choreograph, they began assembling a cast

There were true jewels among the star-studded
cast. Ariana Grande, her mother, her brother,
her entire entourage were adorable.

of powerhouse performers—Ariana Grande, Jennifer Hudson, Kristin Chenoweth, Rosie O'Donnell, Ephraim Sykes, and Martin Short as my husband. The concept was to spread the sets all across the backlot of Universal and shoot as much outside as we could. Audiences would be placed in strategic locations where they'd be able to watch and react live. It was an exciting idea to mix the live responses with the live performances. We rehearsed and drilled the scenes, the costume changes, the moves around the backlot, and the musical numbers over and over. I was absolutely sure this was going to be terrific. But then something changed. Almost at the last moment, a decision came down from on high that the audiences would still be in attendance but not allowed to react to the show. No laughter, no applause, no response until the final scene, where they were obviously part of the setting as the studio audience for the show's TV broadcast within the TV broadcast. Only then could they react. To this day I don't know why that decision was made. Pulling the audience reaction out at the last minute didn't destroy anything, but it sucked a certain energy from the ether and robbed the show of this explosive element that could have launched the entire endeavor to the skies.

As it was, I will never forget the rush of it all. Having more than a thousand performances of Edna under my belt kept me from being nervous. She and I were old friends. I handed her the reins and wished her luck. Still, knowing that you are performing live for ten million people—more than could see the show in a sold-out twenty-year theatrical run—was mind blowing. The cast all pulled together. We locked eyes and hearts and breathed as one. It was a once-in-a-lifetime event that I will always treasure.

55

GENTLY DOWN THE STREAM

2017

The great producer Robert Fox brought Martin Sherman's new play to me, a gorgeous piece of writing about a senior expat living in London, trying to leave his ghosts at rest. Into his life comes a young man obsessed with the past. They fall in love, or a negotiable facsimile of what follows when you grow comfortable with lust. The play is split between scenes of the men navigating their relationship and monologues, performed for the younger man's benefit, in which the older gentleman reveals the details of his historically significant past.

As I said, it's a gorgeous piece of writing, and it immediately blew me away. Spanning the late sixties until the legalization of same-sex marriage, I had more than a little in common with this man's experiences. I jumped when Robert offered it to me. But it wasn't familiarity alone that bonded me to the piece. Martin's words and the way this character experienced life are unique; given the same assignment, I'd never have come up with the viewpoint he took. That's what makes acting another author's work so vital to me. Acting demands that you get out of your own head and instead reason and experience through someone else's eyes and heart.

The struggle for actors is not to make a character's thoughts their own, but to ditch themselves and allow the character to inhabit their body and voice. When faced with an actor abusing that old cliché "My character wouldn't say that," my stock answer is, "Then you're playing the wrong character, because this one does!"

Escaping yourself is the best way to grow. A favorite quote of mine has always been "I never learned from a man who agreed with me" (Robert A. Heinlein).

Sherman's monologues were so heartfelt, so true and so real that I could not read them aloud without breaking down in tears. We put together a few readings of the play, one of them with Martin's friends Sting and Trudie Styler in attendance. Imagine being an overly emotional dyslexic giving a cold reading of a play in front of the two of them! One monologue involved experiencing the fire at New Orleans's gay club the UpStairs Lounge, which left thirty-two men, including his lover, incinerated. I had to take breathing breaks several times in order to make it through that one.

Unsure of its commercial viability, Robert gave the play to the Public Theater to produce. For all of my years in downtown theater, other than performing in their cabaret, I had never been offered work there. I think we were at the Obie Awards one year when I asked its founder, Joe Papp, if he'd ever do a play of mine. He said, "I do theater for everyone." Again I asked if he'd do a play of mine. He looked at me with the practiced impatience of a father shutting down a request from a troublesome child: "I do theater for everyone." He never did one of my plays; nor was I ever offered a role in anyone else's. There was not a lot of openly gay work done there during his reign.

Oskar Eustis, who now ran the joint, actually did produce theater for everyone and jumped at the chance to put this on. "Grateful" is an understatement for how I felt. To be in this building where *Angels in America* and *Hamilton* and *Hair* were born and where the name Judith Peabody, an angel spoken of in this play, is painted on a pillar, felt like the right home for Martin Sherman's *Gently Down the Stream*. Gabriel Ebert, an actor with whom I am passionately in love, had appeared in *Casa Valentina*. I'd never met anyone so nuts about acting with a British accent, and the character of the younger man was British, so I guessed that Gabe would love to take it on. Somehow I thought that his statuesque stature and

Romanesque profile would make a fascinating visual contrast to my own comfortably worn-in physique. I thought we'd look like a matched pair—an overstuffed chair aside a reading lamp. I brought the idea to Sean Mathias, our director, and he agreed. Come to think of it, "comfortable" is not only the right word for my frame but for the entire production. Perhaps a bit *too* comfortable. Beautiful as it was to look at, and true as the histories it presented, in one detail Martin shied away from the very thing the audience had been promised. From the opening moment we are presented with a love story. We are ready for one: two misfits finding love, challenging as it may be; one has paid love's price too dearly and the other is too young to know what's truly at stake. In my opinion, Martin wrote a play that should have built to a battle for love. Instead, when faced with difficulty, one man deserts the battlefield while the other waves a white flag of surrender, accepting loss as the inevitable ending of everything. I begged Martin to rethink this ending, but he, like the character he wrote, lacked the appetite or passion

Gabe Ebert and I were doing all the
rehearsing. Why are Martin Sherman and
director Sean Mathias the sleepy ones?

for war. His truth won out. But I believe rethinking would have made the play a much more challenging and ultimately satisfying experience.

After our very warmly received production in New York, Robert asked if I'd be willing to play the show in a fringe theater in London. Again I pleaded with Martin to rethink the play. "Give the audience the love story you promised and that these characters deserve. Please."

He did, in his way, rewrite. He retooled some lines in the final scene, but nothing substantial enough to warrant the continental crossing, and certainly not enough of a change to justify the investment for a commercial run in the States. They produced the play in London and, again, received respectful responses. It really is a shame that this is the end of this story. Martin is a great writer, and this is a laudable play right on the edge of being so much more. I salute his steadfastness while wanting to throttle him. Every day I come closer to the correct age of the character, so I am going to hold out hope that Martin decides to take on the challenge, if only for a lark. But the older I get, the harder those monologues will be to learn—and believe me, they were no easy task first time around. So he'd better get to typing now.

In a play filled with tender moments,
this was one of my faves.

56

TORCH SONG REVIVED

2017

Reviving *Torch Song Trilogy* was all about Richie Jackson. If plays are hard to produce, they are even harder to revive. There has to be a really great reason—an unexposed audience, a revolutionary new concept, or the attachment of a big star—to justify the amount of work and money required to remount a play. As much as I would have loved to see and hear *Torch Song* again, I couldn't think of an unselfish reason to bring it back. I had no unfulfilled dreams of what I longed to see in a production. I had no trampled visions to avenge. *Torch Song Trilogy* had always been presented as I wished, with only the most minor compromises. Why revive it now? I once allowed an experimental production at a London fringe theater, which begat a less-than-stellar event. A New York theater arranged an exploratory reading of the plays not long before. The actors were so obviously miscast that I wanted to abandon the effort less than halfway through. I knew then that the play and I could live happily without a new production.

Not so for my Richie. At seventeen, when his mother took him to see the show, she let him know that she would accept him if he was gay. Richie walked away from that experience not only with gratitude for his mother's love but with a new belief in his own life goals. In Arnold's struggles Richie found a spiritual brother. He, like Arnold, aimed to find true love with someone and together they'd create a family of their own. This life vision had rooted deep in his heart, and now here it was, enacted onstage, bigger than life. The character of Arnold became a role model for his struggle against society's status quo. And thanks to Lawrence Lane taking him under his wing and bringing him into the fold, Richie found a friend and colleague in me. Through his many career changes, as I noted earlier, he's been my assistant, agent, manager, and even my producer when I appeared on *Nurse Jackie*, a TV series he was coproducing. When he asked for permission to revive *Torch Song*, I hardly hesitated. Richie had a personal journey that this effort was somehow vital to complete. I gave him the plays and stepped back. I would, of course, be there for him, but I knew that this endeavor involved me letting go and allowing him to fulfill his mission. I had written a speech for Teddy Roosevelt to deliver at the end of *Newsies* and it came to mind as I gave my blessing for this new production: "Each generation, at the height of its power, must step aside and invite the young to share the day."

There's nothing magical about coincidences, but sometimes they feel *bashert* (Yiddish for "meant to be"). Richie had the idea to star Michael Urie as Arnold in a production directed by Moises Kaufman. Meanwhile, Moises had already spoken to Michael about the play and was bringing that idea to Richie. They all came together happily to create this gorgeous new production.

I still wanted to help by giving this effort a reason for being. I'd chopped and reshaped the plays so many times; what more could I do without rewriting? And I was *not* rewriting. *Torch Song Trilogy* had poured forth from a me that no longer existed. If I changed the words it would be with an old man's distorted judgment of what a young heart feels. That was not going to happen. So what could? Two possibilities: The first would involve restoring most of the trimmed material, adding back the live musicians into *Fugue* and presenting the plays as originally conceived. Forget that idea—it would cost a fortune, and we'd be selling multiple tickets requiring multiple viewings. That production would be unfeasible outside of a well-funded regional theater. (Note to all well-funded regional theaters: I'm ready when you are.) The second possibility challenged me to cut as deeply as I could, creating a version of the plays that could be presented with only one intermission. In our current world where theatergoers ask what time a show lets out before they even buy tickets, I decided this was the way to go. I'd also drop the word "trilogy" and dub it *Torch Song*, marking it as something new. This rebranding could make the evening a curiosity for those already familiar with the material and a less challenging effort for the what-time-does-it-let-out? crowd.

Addressing the material again was akin to visiting the school you attended as a child. It was all familiar and yet changed. This was no longer me, which, I guess, was cause for mourning as well as celebration. When I put down the red pencil, the text hadn't lost much more than it had in the Broadway version; a joke here, a jab there. *Stud* lost its torch singer; *Fugue*, as always, was attacked most brutally; but Mrs. Beckoff, with her bunny slippers and Sweet'n Low stolen from the airplane, still reigned over the final act. I also thought of how those who'd only known the movie version would surely miss the most, even if what they missed only existed in the movie and never onstage.

I was determined to allow Moises and Richie freedom to create the experience they envisioned. The plays were vital and life affirming to both of them, and I wanted their urgency realized. I stayed away from auditions until they were down to final choices. After voicing an opinion or two, they assembled a marvelous cast to support and surround Michael Urie. Mercedes Ruehl, a piss and a half in life, on screen, or on stage, was their ace in the hole. I believed, no matter what else, she'd light the play afire. I'll confess to wishing that the actor playing the son, terrific as he was, had been younger. Unless the audience is judging the character of David as too innocent to be living with sexually active gay men, there is an aspect of their experience that's diminished. They need to feel concern for this child's well-being, living among adults, until they realize that he can more than take care of himself.

I can't underline enough how important it was to me that this be Richie and Moises's production. They chose marvelous designers for the set, lights, costumes, and sound, all of whom brought unique visions—a truly solid team. I visited rehearsals often enough not to freak the cast out when I appeared in the room, but not enough for them to lean on me instead of Moises.

Michael was finding his unique voice for Arnold, and that was exciting. But I shook my head watching him take on the back-room episode in *Stud*. This is the scene where Arnold gets fucked up the bum (mimed) in the crowded back room of a bar. Moises and I met with him in a private rehearsal. Michael flipped the curly bangs from his forehead defensively. "I'm still working on it. I know I have farther to go, but—"

I cut him off. "I'm guessing you're a top."

He guffawed. "Why, sir, I don't know what you mean!"

"'Cause you get fucked like you ain't never been fucked! Or at least not fucked right. So, you are either trying to impress someone or you need to go home and get that gorgeous boyfriend of yours to give you bottoming lessons."

Well, acting is sense memory, albeit with little sense.

Second Stage, in association with Richie, was producing the show at their Tony Kiser Theater, a wonderful space built in a converted bank on Forty-Third Street and Eighth Avenue. The production looked great in that auditorium, and I was anxious to see how it would play more than thirty years after its Broadway closing. Ticket sales were lively, and the audiences seemed excited as they arrived and took their seats. Back in the day, our audiences were generally heterosexual with a sprinkling of gays. Times had changed. My people turned out. The house was generally gay with a sprinkling of straight folks. Something else was different. The gays were relaxed, social, and festive. That was quite a difference from the pensive, guilty, insular, and cautious feel of the gays we played to in the 1970s and '80s. This bunch felt as if they were comfortably visiting an old friend. Yes, there was a familiarity, almost an ownership, in their attitude. This was *their* show, *their* history, *their* lives that they'd come to see. Even the younger members took their seats with almost impudent anticipation.

Once the curtain rose, the mood was maintained. They laughed at all of the jokes, they listened studiously and applauded with zealous appreciation. They were into it, loving it, and somehow to me it felt wrong. Not wrong exactly, but foreign. I felt something was missing from the reaction. And then it struck me: there was no tension left. No danger. The fear was gone. Back in the day, the moment the lights came up on a drag queen the audience, straight or gay, tensed: "What the hell is that?" Only when she turned and addressed them directly, making jokes and speaking offhand, could you sense them begin to breathe easily again. It took the entire first monologue, brimming with Arnold's humor and humanity, to relax them enough to let him guide them into his world—a world that was unfamiliar. But today's bunch was already at home. They'd seen drag queens on TV for years. They knew all the letters that made up the LGBTQLMNOP community better than I. This crowd had come to enjoy and celebrate, which is exactly what they did. For whatever sting *Torch Song* lost, it had now gained familiarity.

As for the performers, I found correlating behavior. The actors were speaking their truth, giving it their all, but they were performing from a safe place. No one was going to break down the door and arrest them for crimes against nature. I'm not sure how to describe this without making it sound like they should be hiding out in an attic, but the risk, unconscious as it might be, the in-your-face daring, was absent. No one on that stage was going to lose their career for playing a homosexual. None of them would be accused of hiding their sexuality because they were in the play. I don't know how else to express it but to repeat: the danger was gone. The actors were not spouting heresy in the public square. They were not frightened that police were waiting in the wings to handcuff them. The audience was not ashamed to be seen in this place. Well, not until the mother arrived onstage—and then it was 1979 all over again. I guess none of us ever outlive the fear of a disapproving parent. It's built into our DNA and every lesson since birth. It was with that knowledge that I gave her a line that would define her entire role in the play: "How do you do? I'm the mother."

The concept of Arnold wanting exactly the life of his parents was revolutionary when I wrote the play. Actually, that's wrong. It would have been considered reactionary by much of my community. Going out and fucking anything you wanted without consequence was the revolutionary position. Same-sex marriage was so far from possible that it seemed a throwback to prefeminist and preliberation days. The first time I noticed an organized group of marriage-equality protesters at the Gay Day Parade I thought, *Really? With lesbian and gay equality in the workplace and housing and the military eluding us, you want to fight to have a wedding?* But then I noticed how young most of them were and I thought, *This is your world, your future. If this is where you want your front line to be, then I'm right there with you.*

Damn if they weren't right. Marriage equality was something that heterosexuals could understand and identify with. It has led to opening discussions on the rest of our road to equality.

When I wrote *Torch Song Trilogy*, gay adoption was such a dangerous idea that Rosie O'Donnell went ahead and risked her entire career by coming out so that she could make her case for having a family. I had to wonder what *Torch Song* was now in this age of same-sex marriage and legal adoptions and gays in the military and LGBTQ elected officials. Had the play outlived its usefulness? Were we performing an oddity, a period piece? Were we listening to cassettes found in a box at the back of the closet?

I sat and watched a few previews. I did my best to eavesdrop on the audience's conversations during the intermission and as they left the theater. Pride held the performance aloft. *Torch Song* was no longer something to look at from a safe distance and wonder if it could ever come to be. It *has* come to be. It's no longer something you wish for; it's something you live with. The play's become a history, a personal diary, a testament to point to when you want someone to understand your life. It's proof of our struggle and a road map for how we got here. Richie's dream of one day falling in love, marrying, and raising children had come true. Now his efforts to celebrate our existence were paying off. Our community embraced the show with new purpose.

57

COMING OUT:
A TRUE STORY

Previews of *Torch Song* were coming to an end. The critics had been in to see the show and all that was left to be nervous about was our official opening-night party and the publication of reviews. The premiere conflicted with my brother's taking a wine tour of Spain or some equally lovely adventure. In any case, knowing he'd miss the official opening, he wanted to watch a preview, so I got us seats toward the rear of the theater for a performance. At intermission he was quite upbeat. He thought eliminating the intermission between the first two plays worked well, and he was anxious to see *Widows* again. There was the usual genuine anticipation in the room as the lights came down and the music for the final play kicked in. The cast had been giving a good, solid performance and the audience repaid them with strong reactions. Now, into the meat of *Widows*, there were audible gasps each time Ma let fly a stinging comment about her son's homosexuality, and there were visible tears on the faces around us when she told her son, "What do you think? You think you walk into a room and say, 'Hi, Dad, I'm queer,' and that's that? Believe me, if I had known I wouldn't have bothered."

I looked over toward my brother at some point during that scene and he seemed engrossed. Nothing here was new to him. He'd heard these words dozens of times over the forty years since I wrote them. I wasn't expecting a huge reaction from him, but he did seem unusually restrained.

The audience greeted the curtain call with a boisterous standing ovation before filing out of the theater. Ron didn't move from his seat, and when we were finally alone, his eyes still glued to the now darkened stage, he blankly said, "That really happened, didn't it? What the mother said to Arnold . . . Mom really said that."

Caught completely off guard, I could do no more than whisper, "Yes."

He sat silently a few more moments and then moved on. We never discussed it again.

I don't know what gave it away that evening. As wonderful as Michael Urie and Mercedes Ruehl were, that scene, those lines, the intentions hadn't changed. But I guess that after years of inventing stories—"No, that's not our mother. That's how our grandmother was, but not our mother"—I guess at last he heard the absurdity of the lie. So, now he knew the truth, but I wonder how much he really remembered of the actual incident.

One of my favorite political cartoons appeared in *The Advocate* decades ago. It pictured two chickens running for their lives from an egg that was cracking open. One of them was screaming, "Oh, no! Not another coming-out story!" We've all got them. They are deeply personal—perhaps the most intimate moment of our lives. Even when they go well, they can be painful and embarrassing and frightening. They can also be joyous and freeing and affirming, but never simple. Mine, sadly, falls into the first category.

I've never related this to another person. Only the principals knew all of the pieces. And now they are all gone, dead, and only I know. I suppose I could carry this story with me to my grave and no one would ever find out what a stupid, thoughtless kid I was, but the important word of this sentence is "carry": "I could actually *carry* this story . . ." And that's the problem. In all of these years of silence, I've never found a way to put it down, to let it go, to give it up, to have it over and done. Maybe writing it . . . ? *Look back, but don't stare.* Here I go staring.

So . . . second year of high school. I'm around fourteen and, as you may remember from many pages ago, I was very involved with the Gallery Players and with my best friend, Michael. My brother was away at college, Stony Brook out on Long Island, and my parents were taking a very infrequent vacation on their own—a cruise, I think. My parents asked if I'd like to have a friend stay over to keep me company and I said sure.

Michael was dating an older man named Marvin. This was his second serious lover. The first, Rick, was a very attractive man who had a great studio apartment in the West Village with a bright red lacquered wooden floor and a staggering record collection. It was where we hung out, smoked dope, and listened to Nina Simone sing "Pirate Jenny" while cutting school. Rick had been arrested several times for pedophilia and had spent time away in prison, so he was, to say the least, an unreliable boyfriend. Michael replaced him with Marvin, who had a posh apartment on the Upper East Side where we'd hang out, smoke dope. and listen to him talk about how rich and important he was.

On the Friday that my parents left, Michael and I took the train home after a performance at the Gallery Players and were excited to have a house all to ourselves. We smoked a little, warmed up the dinner my mother had left wrapped in tinfoil, and settled in to watch TV. Then the front doorbell rang. I was puzzled. I wasn't expecting anyone, and even so, no one came to the front door except Jehovah's Witnesses. I looked at Michael and he grinned. "Go and see who it is."

It was Marvin. He stood on the front steps, smiling, looking behind me to find Michael. "Can I come in?" he asked.

My mind flashed to some vampire story I'd read that said they could not enter a house unless invited. "Sure. I guess. Michael didn't tell me."

"I wanted it to be a surprise," Michael said, reaching out and pulling his guest inside.

They kissed hello and Marvin turned back to me with his offerings. "I brought chocolate-covered strawberries and sweet liquor. You'll like it. It's like candy."

I was already ill at ease. I've told you that I kept my worlds as far from one another as I could. The Gallery Players were one world, school was another, and my home was a completely separate entity that belonged to my parents. It was not one that I controlled or was free within or had ownership of. The Harvey that Michael knew from school was not the Harvey who lived in this house. The fact that Michael was staying over was excitingly dangerous but innocent. I had my parents' permission. Marvin's appearance changed everything. I became frightened.

I studied the amber liquid in the tall, elegant bottle while we all moved into the warm house.

We ate the strawberries and drank the liquor and I had quite a buzz when suddenly my stomach turned, and I bolted for the bathroom. I tossed up those lovely chocolate strawberries along with my mother's dinner. It was all swimming in a puddle of sickly yellow liquor. My company knocked on the bathroom door to be sure that I was all right.

"Fine. I'll be right out."

I could barely stand the taste of the mouthwash; it was so much like that booze. But I pulled myself together and rejoined the party.

Michael suggested it was time for bed. *Great,* I thought. *We'll all go lie down and it will soon be morning.* I needed to lie down. We went upstairs, where I offered them my room; but Michael, always the one with new ideas, said, "Can't we have your parents' room? It has that nice big bed, and there are two of us."

I immediately calculated that I had the whole weekend to do the laundry, wash the sheets, and get everything back as it should be in plenty of time before my parents returned on Sunday evening.

So I said, "Sure."

They went immediately to my parents' bed and off I went to mine. I just wanted it all to be over. It wasn't long before Michael appeared next to me with his camera in hand. "How are you feeling?"

"I'm good."

"I brought my camera. It would be so great if you took some shots of me and Marvin. Then you could develop them in your darkroom and no one has to know."

"You mean now?"

"It'll be fun."

I followed Michael back to the other room. My stomach and head were reeling. It wasn't just the booze and the smoke and the sweets but the wrongness of it all that weakened my knees almost to the point of collapse on the red shag rug my mother had proudly installed the year before.

I shot some photos of them naked together on the bed. Nothing more than posing. I have little memory of the details, although I am positive that I did not get involved with the pair. As soon as I could I went back to my bed and watched the night sky, willing it to brighten.

Marvin disappeared before dawn. Michael left soon after. I did my utmost to erase any signs of anything untoward or unwelcome. I washed dishes, double-bagged the garbage, scrubbed the bathroom, did the laundry, vacuumed the red shag carpet and even combed it with the special shag-carpet rake that came with the installation. As I walked from room to room, I examined the house and began to breathe again. Then I remembered the the roll of film I'd shot the night before. I wrestled with myself, *Should I develop and print them? Should I just give the film to Michael? Haven't I done enough already?* But the simplest answer seemed to be to print the stupid things, give them to Michael, and be done with it all. So that's what I did. I went down to my little darkroom in the basement and developed the film. I printed a selection of the photos, dried them as quickly as I could using my mother's industrial mangle, placed them in a plain manila envelope, and put them on the side with my things. Done with this whole mess.

My parents arrived home late Sunday afternoon. They had a great time and were anxious to tell me all about it, but as it happened, I had a performance of *Dark of the Moon* at the Players, so I had to go. I was glad to go. Michael would be there and I'd be able to hand him the envelope and never have to think about any of this again.

I gathered my things into my shoulder bag and headed out. The moment I saw Michael I tore open my bag and reached for the envelope and . . . it was gone. The manila envelope was not there. I panicked.

"If you dropped them on the subway and someone finds them, I will kill you!" Michael fumed.

I went into a blind panic. *Did I drop them on the way? Did I forget them? Could I have dropped them in the house?* Somehow I made it through the performance and headed home, praying that everyone would be asleep when I got there and I'd find the envelope left behind in my bedroom. I've never prayed so hard . . .

My parents were waiting for me in the kitchen. The manila envelope was on the table. I froze.

"Is that our bedroom?" was my father's first question.

"I'm sorry," I breathed out.

"You took these?" he asked. "You know we could have that man arrested."

"Daddy, don't . . ."

"Don't what?" my mother injected. "We trusted you and this is how we're repaid? I've never been so ashamed in my life."

I ran from the back door through the house to the living room. I don't know why I didn't run away. I was confused and frightened and ashamed . . .

My mother followed me. She sat down on a wing chair and just stared.

"So, you're a queer? I raised a queer? Nice for your father. I gave him a queer."

I wanted to lie but I couldn't think of one. I tried to imagine a way to blame Michael for everything, but I knew that wouldn't get me anywhere.

"In my own bed. How am I ever going to get into that bed again?"

"I did the sheets."

She glared at me.

Truthfully, I remember very little else of the incident other than locking myself in my room. where I hid until it was time to leave for school on Monday morning. I'd heard my father leave at his usual time, so I knew that I only had to face my mother.

She met me with silence until I reached the back door and was almost out. "We've decided not to pursue this man. If this is who you are, it's not his doing, and getting the law involved would only complicate things for you later. This is killing your father. I want you to know that. How could you . . . ? You broke my heart. Just so you know. You broke my heart. I'll never trust you again. How could I? I don't even know who you are. You're not my son."

She turned away and I left.

During the night I composed a note to my parents and left it for them to find in the morning. I apologized for lying and used Joni Mitchell's "Both Sides Now" to explain my explorations:

But now old friends are acting strange
They shake their heads, they say I've changed
Well something's lost, but something's gained
In living every day.
I've looked at life from both sides now
From win and lose and still somehow
It's life's illusions I recall
I really don't know life at all.

I didn't think it was ever discussed; but many years later, when I went backstage after seeing Ms. Mitchell perform somewhere, she said, "Your brother told me that you used my song to come out. I think that's lovely."

So I guess it was discussed after all.

Jackie didn't bring up the subject again until my high-school graduation. My mother and brother witnessed my proud walk across the Carnegie Hall stage to get my diploma. I was so happy that they got to hear the applause and cat whistles from my class. I was pretty popular in school, and now they knew it. My mother asked if I'd like to do anything special afterwards.

"Dustin Hoffman's new movie is playing right around the corner. Maybe we can go see it?"

I knew she'd want to go for Hoffman. She loved *The Graduate*. I wanted to see it because I heard that there was a party scene with a bunch of Warhol superstars in it, so I was thrilled when she agreed. That's all I knew about *Midnight Cowboy*.

Halfway through the film Jon Voight is desperate for money and pimps himself out to men on the street. A young man takes him to a public bathroom, gives him a blowjob, which makes him nauseous, and then tells Voight that he has no money to pay. I was pretty much dying through this entire scenario. Voight checks the young man's pockets to see that he isn't lying and then spots his watch.

"Give me your watch."

"I can't," the boy pleads. "My mother gave it to me. She'd kill me."

Jackie pointedly spoke under her breath: "She should!"

Writing *Widows and Children First!* allowed me to pour my mother's vitriol out of my stomach and onto the page, but I've held the blame for the incident within all of these years. It's retained just enough acid to continuously burn my insides. Will this telling heal? I can barely read it over to myself.

Thrust into the limelight by the play, Jackie became a beacon of love and acceptance to the community. She was an extraordinary woman in so many ways, but I don't think the issue between us was ever completely settled. A resentful or angry edge remained a constant in our relationship. Maybe "angry" is too strong a word. A curtain of denial dropped between us. Silence was our answer to issues too sensitive to discuss. On more than one occasion she blamed my grandmother's fighting with my father for his early death. I wondered what percentage of that blame she placed on me. My cousin Sheldon recently told me that he and she never once discussed his sexuality. Jackie had numerous dinners, luncheons, and theater dates with Sheldon and his partners over decades, but the words were never spoken—not about him, not about me. I guess it wasn't a curtain that fell; it was a wall. Jackie was always an intimate part of my life. She stayed at my home quite often. She knew and was friends with my lovers over the years. I kept no secrets from her. Sometimes the expression of her feelings took a wry turn. When *Torch Song Trilogy* opened on Broadway, her gift to me was a small Beatrix Potter figure of a mother mouse pointing her finger at her son and saying, "Are you a man or a mouse?"

As for my father, I mostly avoided him during that period. I probably avoided him most of the time. But that next Saturday after the photography incident, my dog, Coco, had an appointment to get shots at the vet. Our vet was the brother of a friend of my father's whose office was out in New Jersey. There were veterinarians right around the corner, but this is the way our lives were organized. If a friend's father was a dentist, you went to him. If a friend's uncle was a pickle man, that's who you used to spice your jars at pickling time. So, Sam Oliver had a brother who was our internist in Brooklyn. His other brother was a vet in Jersey City, and that's where my father and I were headed with Coco that morning.

"You know we love you," is how my father began.

"I know"

"We had fags in the Navy. The fellas would go see them when we were out to sea too long . . ."

He suddenly stopped speaking. Perhaps the image of his son doing what those fags did was not something he wanted to imagine.

After a while he picked up the conversation. "You can talk to me. You know that, right? I had an idea . . . Whaddaya say, if you want, I take you to a whorehouse? Just to see. If you want. You never know, you might like it."

I had no answer for him. My heart was so filled with love for this man at that moment. My friend Richie actually wrote a book about how happy he was that his son was gay. But that's Richie and this was Irving, and Irving was being forced to rethink his entire vision for my life. There'd be no grandchildren. His friends would ask questions he wouldn't want to answer. He could imagine me being beaten and abused as he probably saw those queer sailors treated. I might never be happy or successful or . . . What would become of his son?

I watched him stare straight ahead at the road as he drove to New Jersey. I guess I'd always been a mama's boy. Now I realized I'd been wasting my time on the wrong parent.

Irving lit up a cigarette and I almost asked to bum one off him, but then I realized I was still keeping that secret. I bet it would have been a great bonding moment: a boy and his dog, he and his dad smoking together.

Ten years later, four in the morning, I was at the desk in my basement apartment writing the third play of *Torch Song Trilogy*. I reached the moment when the mother attacks Arnold for being gay and, with tears streaming down my face, I didn't allow Arnold to just sit there and absorb the attack as I had. Finally, a decade later, in the middle of the night, I found my voice. The words poured out of me as quickly as I could type them: "I have taught myself to sew, cook, fix plumbing, build furniture, all so I don't have to ask anyone for anything. There is nothing I need from anyone except for love and respect. And anyone who can't give me those two things has no place in my life. You're my mother. I love you. But if you can't respect me, then you've got no business being here."

58

BELLA BELLA

2019

Artists return to paint the same landscape over and again, but they do so looking forward. The goal isn't to copy what they've already done, but to try to capture it all anew. The question isn't "What did I see?"—it's "What *do* I see?"

Richie, Moises, Michael, and the rest were busily exploring the landscape of *Torch Song*. Embracing that last chapter, I knew there was nothing more for me there. Not right then. I needed to find a new challenge. Life is not endlessly fascinating, but living is.

Shirley MacLaine brought her pal Congresswoman Bella Abzug backstage to meet me after a performance of something; I don't remember what. Bella was great. So real and down to earth that you couldn't help but love her. We met a mess of times after that, although we never became friends. After her death, Liz and Eve, her daughters, approached me about writing a show based on their parents' lives. Liz thought it should be a musical. I had my doubts but spent some time researching Bella. Fascinating as her life had been, I didn't find the makings of a musical. I passed on the project. But then Hillary Clinton ran for president and my ears began to catch criticisms that sounded oddly familiar: Hillary was anti-Israel, she had a hidden agenda, she's owned by foreign interests, and my favorite—a woman is not strong enough to be president. If her hormones were off, she could start a nuclear war. I recognized this as the same playbook aimed against Bella Abzug's run for the Senate. Maybe there was something to write about, after all.

I returned to the Bella research and a play began to form in my mind. Not a sweeping narrative, and certainly not a musical, but a play that focused on a single moment that summed up her war against the status quo.

How about this lineup? Jesse Jackson, Patti LaBelle, Bella Abzug, and me at the Human Rights Campaign dinner.

Bella was a groundbreaking congresswoman from New York who'd already had a storied career as an attorney when, in 1976, against the advice of everyone, she abandoned her secure seat in Congress to run for the Senate. Bella was a smart cookie. She knew that she could count on her popularity and perseverance to muster the support of voters and win that seat. What she didn't count on was the Democratic establishment fearing her radical antiwar positions. They changed rules, ran five challengers against her, employed lies, conspiracies, and dirty tricks to deny her the chance to become the only woman in that Senate term.

I envisioned a play set in a Midtown hotel room in the middle of the night, where Bella and her supporters are awaiting the final vote count of that Senate primary. Liz hooked me up with a bunch of Bella's beloved, bold-faced-named friends and colleagues, most of whom were wonderfully helpful creating the piece. Marlo Thomas, Renée Taylor, Lily Tomlin, Jane Wagner, and Bella's press secretary, Harold Holzer. It was Mr. Holzer to whom I first told the idea.

"I'm writing about the night of the Senate primary when you were all in the hotel room waiting for the election results."

"That's wonderful," he said. "So you'll have people playing Shirley and Liz and Martin and me?"

"No. I'm thinking it's a monologue. Overwhelmed with the excitement, Bella goes off to the bedroom to change outfits and, alone at last, her brain rushes through the events that brought her to that moment."

"What bedroom? There was no bedroom. We had a hotel room."

"Right. The bedroom of the hotel room."

"We had a hotel room."

"No bedroom?"

"We had a hotel room. A room. One room that we were all shoved into. Though I guess there was a toilet."

That got me laughing. Could I actually write an entire play where the character told her life story while sitting on the toilet? Well, that's what I did, and when Harold came to watch a rehearsal, I showed him John Lee Beatty's exacting design for the set.

"Does this or does this not look like that 1970s bathroom?" I asked with pride.

"How should I know?" was his retort. "You think Bella let any of us use it?"

I offered the role of Bella to every actress I thought could carry it off, but owing to some cosmic coincidence, several of them were already booked to play her in other projects. It's true. Bette Midler, Kathy Bates, and Margo Martindale were among those names, and every one of them was playing Bella elsewhere that year. Patti LuPone was kind enough to come into the city to read the play aloud for us. I had to hear whether it was going to work or not. Patti was terrific, and she would have made a great Bella if she weren't already booked to open in a revival of *Company*.

So there I was, with a promising play that had no director, no producer, and no actor. Chris Till, my agent, thought we might be able to jumpstart some interest in the project if I did a reading of the play myself. We gathered in Creative Artists Agency's gorgeous Chrysler Building offices and I performed two readings. The joint was packed with theater types for both, and we came away with several offers. Audible, the books-on-tape company, was in for a recording and would be happy to partner with someone for the stage version. A pair of commercial producers said they'd do it in a minute if we could find a female star. A couple of theater festivals and regionals displayed interest as well. But the most important thing to come from those readings was the revolutionary concept that I could perform the play myself. I had written a feminist piece using the words and thoughts of a woman. Still, I was a male writer digesting and reinterpreting those very words and thoughts. What kind of feminist statement would it be if I, a male playwright, now used a female actor to speak those words? Wouldn't I, in the purest sense, be turning her into my puppet? Wasn't it more honest for me to go out on the stage, in men's clothing, inhabiting Bella's spirit as best I could, and speak her truth? I wouldn't imitate or mimic her. Instead, I would channel her strength and resolve, allowing her words to be the star. After a career of wearing dresses, this proposed a fascinating new challenge for me.

This was the summer of 2019, leading up to the election. The plan was to premiere the play in the fall and then release the script to any theater or actress wanting to perform it as a benefit in support of a woman running for political office. It could be done in full production or in a simple concert version or even an informal reading. I hoped that Bella's friends would be the first to jump at the opportunity to raise funds for women candidates.

Most theaters were already booked until spring of 2020. Waiting would mean we'd be too late to influence the upcoming elections. Again Lynne Meadow and the Manhattan Theatre Club came to the rescue offering us one of their intimate theaters under City Center. Stage I's womblike atmosphere was the perfect venue to birth this effort. *Bella Bella* was coming together.

Since I'd be playing the role, I wanted the rehearsal room to contain the least amount of testosterone possible. Chris introduced me to director Kimberly Senior, and we were in sync from our first discussion. We then assembled a group of three women stage managers. The rehearsal room became a creative space for discussion and the exchange of ideas. We invited anyone from the MTC offices to sit in on rehearsals and then talk about what they saw and felt. We wanted young people to tell us what they arrived knowing and what was new information for them. Older folks helped us focus on what was important to retell and what could be skipped over. Harold Holzer, Lily Tomlin, and Bella's daughters were among those who came to watch the preparations, but it was Gloria Steinem who proved to be our most inspiring witness.

I was running a section of the play where Bella predicts which factions would vote for which primary candidate. "The Irish will back O'Dwyer and Moynihan, while the progressives will split between Clark and me. I should get the Hispanic vote, and I can't see Moynihan getting Black support after complaining about welfare and the intransigence of poverty. Which leaves women. Women who far too often vote the way their husbands tell them to."

Ms. Steinem called out. "No! No, no, no!" She stood, waving her hand. "*White* women. The problem is *white* women."

We were now about to be enlightened by a person who didn't merely live these events but shaped them. We leaned in to learn.

"You say it earlier in the play that women make up the majority of voters. But women don't vote as a bloc. Black women voted for Hillary. White women voted to protect the interests of their husbands who pay the bills."

Ms. Steinem went on, mapping out the field of this struggle for us. I looked at the glow of wonder on the face of our nineteen-year-old African American script supervisor and could not help tearing up. She knew that, like in one of those sci-fi fantasies, she was in the room with living history.

On the fly I rewrote the line in the play. "Which brings us to women—or more accurately, *white* women, who if they joined their minority sisters could elect anyone they want. But who, history predicts, will vote the interests of the men who support them."

Performing the play was more of a challenge than I had expected.

I'd thought, *How hard could this be? It's only ninety minutes. It all takes place in a bathroom, so I don't have to run around the stage or anything. And it's conversational. There's no screaming or wailing. This'll be a breeze.*

How wrong I was! What I wrote takes Bella back through her entire career. She relives losing her parents, being attacked by the Klan, taking on Nixon, McCarthy, and the Supreme Court of Mississippi. Bella wasn't Medea, but neither was she June Cleaver. The play demanded an emotional price be paid at each performance. Easy it was not.

It's funny to look back at it now, but this production offered more than its share of challenges. Most one-person shows are self-contained. The actor is speaking to an unseen character or sometimes to themselves, but the actor exists in their own bubble. I constructed *Bella Bella* as a play where the theater audience is the other character and so requires a connection of actor to audience in order to reach the truth under the guise. The actor speaks to the audience honestly, directly. Stage I provided the perfect space for that communication. I was close to the audience, and no seat was blocked from view of my every gesture. MTC, however, as I mentioned when discussing *Casa Valentina*, has an older subscription base, some of whom can require wheelchairs, crutches, braces, and canes while others employ oxygen masks and even ventilators. Because of safety concerns these patrons are always seated in the first row, inches from the stage. I would never deny my audience oxygen, but the mechanical rhythms of such accoutrement during a very quiet play can be distracting. My concentration was tested. Many of the audience, even in a small space, availed themselves of the theater's headsets, but very few availed themselves of the instructions on how to use them. The result of which was often a chorus of piercing whistles, like dozens of angry teapots going off at irregular intervals. Delightful to listen to while orating.

These are all distractions that we theater artists willingly accommodate, because we love the patrons who love live theater and would never want to lose them. So we laugh about a person snoring, or we take an elongated pause while someone adjusts a hearing aid. All understandable. But there are other audience members who seem to think that the lights going down in the auditorium suddenly makes them invisible. And it's not just the ringing of phones and the beeping of pagers and the flashes of light from texts and emails and cameras that have become legend in theater stories. I cannot tell you how many people brought along snacks or even a boxed dinner to enjoy while watching the play. One such woman, as soon as the lights dimmed, opened a shopping bag and started passing sandwiches down the row to her friends: "Marlene? Did you have tuna or chicken?" Others decide to dig in their purses for that roll of Life Savers they were sure they took along. At one performance our audience contained a man who could not contain himself. Having to pee, but not wanting to miss the play, he went out the side door of the auditorium, relieved himself on the corridor wall within earshot of the entire audience, and, when the faucet ran dry, reappeared in the doorway to scurry back to his seat. I guess I should be grateful that he didn't climb onstage to use the toilet that was part of our set. That incident actually made the newspaper.

New York audiences are notoriously bold and will actually talk back to the stage. There was a woman who decided I was mispronouncing the Yiddish word for coin box. I called it a *pishke* and she hollered back at me, "*Pushke!*"

Again I said, "*Pishke.*"

Only to have her repeat, "*Pushke.*"

I finally asked, "Where do you live?"

"The West Side," she answered.

"That's the problem," I said. "On the West Side it's a *pushke* but here on the East Side it's a *pishke*! Now can I go on with the story?"

There is nothing like live theater!

For all of the quirks and silliness, the production was a joyful success. MTC's subscription audience was the right age to remember Bella, and younger audiences were fascinated by this political period, which doesn't get nearly enough attention.

It was thrilling to have the Clintons attend opening night. Hillary followed the visit by sending an autographed copy of *The Book*

Carrying a bright red Bella hat, I walked
you through her remarkable life.

of Gutsy Women, written with her daughter, Chelsea, which con-
tains a chapter on Bella.

As life would have it, the pandemic hit suddenly, which shut
down all of theater for well over a year. The plan for producing
benefit performances simply melted away. We managed to record
the show for Audible before Covid restrictions shut down the studios. Now Bella waits.

Her story, like her legacy, will not diminish with time. *Bella Bella*
will rise onstage again.

59

THERE'S A BRIGHT GOLDEN HAYES . . .

2018–2022

ack in the world of, *Torch Song*, the reviews for the revival were glowing. They loved the production, the actors, the direction and treated the script with affectionate respect. Richie had gotten what he needed to move forward and transfer the play to Broadway. He chose, of all places, the very same theater that we'd played almost four decades earlier—the Hayes Theater, which had been the Helen Hayes Theatre, which had been the Little Theatre, where I first sat and watched Dick Briggs stage-manage *The David Frost Show* in 1972. The Little Theatre was also where I saw Albert Innaurato's play *Gemini,* which allowed me to imagine that I could one day play Broadway. Five years to get your marbles. Fifty years to come full circle?

As always, our press agent, Rick Miramontez, devised a cute photo op to announce the show's transfer. I'd carry the *Torch Song* neon sign from the Tony Kiser Theater around the corner and down the block to be installed at the Hayes.

The press arrived, the press shot photos, the press departed. Everyone gone, I snuck back to stand across the street alone, to look at the marquee and have a think. There was my name . . . *my* name. My mind flashed back to a conversation I overheard as a child. It was Yom Kippur and the adults were hanging out on our front stoop, taking a break from temple, while trying not to think about how hungry they were as they fasted, atoning for their sins.

Almost four decades between photos.
What the hell? I'm still smiling.

Roz Portnoy was raving about a girl she'd seen in a Broadway show. "Mark my words. A star is born," she repeated. "This girl is going to be huge. Huge!"

Naomi Barson, who lived around the corner, had an unassailable opinion about everything. She waved Roz off. "I don't care how talented she is. No one is going to put a name that long on a marquee. They'll tell her there's not enough room, but you and I will know the real reason why."

Needless to say, they were talking about Streisand and her much-too-Jewish name. Standing on Forty-Fourth Street, fifty years later, I couldn't help wondering what Naomi and Roz thought the first time they looked up and saw "Fierstein." I laughed, and in my best *yenta* accent I said to myself, "Look at you, Mr. Big Shot, on a Broadway marquee! You got your name in lights, a star on the Hollywood Walk of Fame, and your bunny slippers in the Smithsonian goddamn Institution. Not bad for a fat cocksucking drag queen from Bensonhurst!"

When I sat down to write this book, I asked Shirley MacLaine for guidance. Who better than a woman who's written a dozen books about her life and lives? She advised me, "Just tell the truth as you remember it. Time has a way of editing out what isn't important anymore."

"My crap is pretty easy," I said. "But I feel a need to tell the stories of the people we lost."

"Yes," she answered. "But primarily the truth of their effect on you. Your writing belongs to your life."

I've tried.

From Bensonhurst to Hollywood. What a ride!

Sitting at my desk, preparing this manuscript, I now understand the warning to not look back and stare. Once you dig up a grave it's almost impossible to fill back in again. Much like my innards after heart surgery, now displaced, the pieces don't nestle together as before. The ghosts churn and groan. Regrets shove and prod their way forward, demanding attention.

I'm not sorry I took this look back. I may find use for these unearthed memories someday, even after this thing's put to bed. A painter can never have too many colors. A writer can't know too many words. An actor can't access too many emotions. And there's no such thing as having lived too much.

ACKNOWLEDGMENTS

Most folks responsible for keeping me alive will find their names within this text but here are a few who may have thought they escaped blame:

Molly Barnett, Paul Bauer, Ray Benkoczy, DB Bonds, Charlie Cantonese, Stephen Jew-Boy Cohen, R. A. Dow, Jack Drescher, Stuart Dummit, Richard Eagan, Susan Edwards, Perrin Ferris, Brad Fierstein, Matthew Fierstein, Sally Fisher, Gary Gersh, Juliet Green, Stephen Gruse, Keith Hallworth, Duke Heimelreich, Dale Hemsley, Hope Hollander, Nina Holmgren, Lauren Hughes, Jay Kallman, Bonnie Klein, Dr. Barry Kohn, Lisa Kuller, Joan Lader, Priscilla Lightcap, Reed Livingston, Aaron Lustbader, Joe Machota, Terry Marler, Billie McBride, John McCarthy, Jeanne McComsey, Patty McQueen, Aaron Meier, Billy Mocko, Wendy Modic, Rusty Mowery, Chelsea Nachman, James Nederlander Jr., Adam Norris, Sue Packard, Karin Peers, Warren Platz, Anna Portnoy, Kathy Powers, Mikki Rallo, Anne Ramov, Danis Regal, Dorothea W. Regal, Jordan Roth, Stacey & Siggy Scolnik, Arthur Shanfeld, Keith Shaw, Scott Sparks, Cheri Steinkellner, Larry Tarzy, Karen Thorman, Chris Till, Aliza Wassner, Barry Weissler, MA Whiteside, Steve Zemo.

As for the book you are holding I need to thank Chris Till for suggesting I try to write this along with my agent, Cait Hoyt, who brought me to my benevolent editor, Peter Gethers, and his assistants, Morgan Hamilton and Tatiana Dubin. While Chip Kidd designed this outstanding cover, it was Kevin Bourke who verified every detail of the text. Rounding out the Knopf team were Kathy Zuckerman, Amy Hagedorn, Rose Cronin-Jackman, and marketing maven Julianne Clancy.

And to those most intimate with whom I've shared more than my bed: Penny, Coco, Georges, Bubbie, Buster, Maggie, Butchie, Zach, Elvis, Little Shit, Lola, Big Boy, Samson, and Good Time Charlie Brown.

INDEX

Page numbers in *italics* refer to illustrations.

East Village (Greenwich Village), 82
Ebbets Field, 11
Ebert, Gabriel, 334–5, *335, 336*
Edinburgh Festival, 218
Edmee (Pratt teaching intern), 42
82 Club, 48
Elmo Saves Christmas (TV show), 227
Ely, Ron, 21
Emmerich, Roland, 214–15
Emmy Awards, 160, 210
Empty Nest (TV show), 211
Epstein, Rob, 180
Equity card, 98
Etheridge, Melissa, 228
Eustis, Oskar, 334
"Everything's Coming Up Noses"
   (song), 227, 261
Eyen, Tom, 107, 230

Factory (Warhol's studio), 51, 54, 57,
   125
family court, 139
Feiffer, Jules, 159
Feingold, Michael, 94
Feinstein, Michael, 268
Feldman, Jack, *285, 286,* 307–9
female impersonators, 154, 162, 187
feminism, 356
Ferrer, Miguel, 217
Fiddler on the Roof (film), 289
Fiddler on the Roof (musical), 251–8,
   253, 255, 257, 259, 289–92, *290,*
   293, 294, 296
Field, Crystal, 106
Fierstein, Harry (HF's grandfather), 12
Fierstein, Harvey:
   as actor, 21, 98, 117, 210, 235,
      244–5, 256, 290–1, 330, 333–4, 356,
      358–9
   alcohol use by, 89, 100, 102–3, 104,
      145, 174, 188, 199–202, 205, 210,
      213, 216–17, 220–2
   anonymous sex and, 66, 105
   art talent of, 18–19, 23, 42–3
   awards won by, 161–2, 228, 244–5,
      256
   bar mitzvah of, 19–20, 27
   Bella Bella and, 353–60

Broadway and, 144–6, 148–9, 157–63,
   167–9, 178, 207, 241–2, 291, 321,
   361–2
La Cage Aux Folles and, 147–56,
   160–1, 164–9, 226, 248–50, 264–5,
   289, 293–4, 296–302
Canada trip taken by, 81–2, 118
in car accident, 127–8
Casa Valentina and, 278, 282–4, 288,
   296, 316–19, 321
in *A Catered Affair,* 269
causes supported by, 130, 219, 227,
   321–2, 354
childhood of, 7–10, 13–16
children's television and, 227–9
clothing of, 25–6, 82, 205–6
coming-out of, 344–52
drag performing and, 52, 68, 81, 109,
   154, 187, 243, 244, 256, 298, 362
drug use by, 33, 43–5
dyslexia of, 13, 98, 231
early acting roles, 3, 4, 36–7, 46–8,
   52–7, 60–3, 70–1, 80, 84, 93–4
education of, 3, 4, 13, 14, 19, 23–6,
   41–5, 54–5, 57, 68, 81
family background of, 9, 11–12
father's death and, 99–102
in *Fiddler on the Roof,* 251–8, 259,
   289–92, 293, 294, 296
as film fan, 10, 15, 204
film roles of, 76–7, 181–2, 184–91,
   194, 214–15, 217, 223–4
finances of, 83, 88, 98, 226, 273
first sexual encounter of, 33–4
friendships of, 14–15, 24, 26, 114, 126,
   160, 162, 172–3, 182–3, 188, 199,
   223, 228, 274, 320
in *Garbo Talks,* 179–80
gender identity of, 4–6, 20–1, 80–1
in *Gently Down the Stream,* 333–6
in *Hairspray,* 231–47, 251, 252, 257,
   258, 296, 321
Hairspray Live! and, 238, 330–2
health of, 81, 88–9, 99, 210, 213, 220,
   224, 246, 322–7, 329
homosexuality of, 26–7, 37–40, 68,
   91–2, 108, 115, 125, 139, 155–6,
   200–1, 203–8, 213, 344

Index

ILLUSTRATION CREDITS

page